AZ-700 Practice Tests: 500 Questions and Answers for Designing and Implementing Microsoft Azure Networking Solutions

Q1: Contoso Ltd. is a global e-commerce platform that uses Azure to host its web applications. The company has been experiencing frequent DDoS attacks, which has led to outages and loss of revenue. As part of their solution, they want to implement Azure DDoS Protection to ensure that their services remain available even under attack. They have multiple virtual networks spread across different Azure regions and they want to ensure that all resources are protected under a single DDoS Protection Plan. However, their budget is constrained, so they also need to monitor the cost closely. Given these requirements, what is the best approach to configure DDoS Protection for Contoso Ltd.? ---

A) Enable DDoS Protection Standard on each virtual network individually.

B) Create a single DDoS Protection Plan in one region and link all virtual networks to it.

C) Create separate DDoS Protection Plans for each region and link the respective virtual networks.

D) Use Azure Traffic Manager to distribute traffic and mitigate DDoS attacks.

E) Implement Network Security Groups (NSGs) with advanced security rules to block attack vectors.

F) Configure Azure Application Gateway with Web Application Firewall (WAF) to handle DDoS attacks.

Answer: B

Explanation: Azure DDoS Protection Standard is designed to protect resources within a virtual network. By creating a single DDoS Protection Plan and linking all virtual networks to it, Contoso Ltd. can ensure comprehensive protection across multiple regions without incurring the cost of multiple plans. This approach is cost-effective and simplifies management. Azure DDoS Protection Standard provides always-on traffic monitoring and real-time mitigation of common network-level attacks. By centralizing the DDoS protection under one plan, Contoso Ltd. can also benefit from unified logging and reporting, making it easier to monitor both the protection status and associated costs.

Q2: When Azure DDoS Protection Standard is activated, it provides logging information that can be integrated with Azure Monitor for advanced analytics.

A) True

B) False

Answer: A

Explanation: Azure DDoS Protection Standard offers detailed logging that can be integrated with Azure Monitor. This integration allows users to analyze the logs for insights into potential attack vectors, traffic patterns, and mitigation actions taken by Azure. The logs provide valuable data that can be used to enhance security measures, understand the effectiveness of the DDoS protection, and ensure compliance with organizational security policies. The integration with Azure Monitor also enables setting up alerts and visualizing data using Azure dashboards, making it a powerful tool for network administrators to keep track of the system's security posture.

Q3: Which of the following statements is true about configuring DDoS Protection Standard in Azure for a virtual network? ---

A) DDoS Protection Standard requires a public IP address to be associated with each resource in the virtual network.

B) DDoS Protection Standard is automatically enabled for all Azure subscriptions.

C) DDoS Protection Standard can be enabled at the individual resource level rather than the virtual network level.

D) You can configure DDoS Protection Standard through the Azure CLI by using the command az network vnet ddos-protection enable.

E) DDoS Protection Standard provides a guarantee of zero downtime during an attack.

F) DDoS Protection Standard can be applied to both IPv4 and IPv6 traffic.

Answer: F

Explanation: Azure DDoS Protection Standard is designed to protect both IPv4 and IPv6 traffic. It is important to note that it operates at the virtual network level rather than the individual resource level, meaning it protects all resources within a virtual network that have a public-facing IP address. While the service offers enhanced security and mitigation capabilities, it does not guarantee zero downtime as the severity and nature of attacks can vary. The service requires a DDoS Protection Plan to be created and associated with the virtual network, and it is not automatically enabled for all subscriptions. Commands to configure DDoS Protection typically involve associating a DDoS Protection Plan with a virtual network through the Azure portal, PowerShell, or Azure CLI, but not through the mentioned command.

Q4: A company has noticed an increase in their Azure DDoS Protection Standard charges and wants to optimize their configuration to minimize costs while maintaining protection. Which of the following actions should they take? ---

A) Reduce the number of public IP addresses associated with protected resources.

B) Switch from DDoS Protection Standard to DDoS Protection Basic.

C) Disable DDoS Protection Standard during periods of low traffic.

D) Limit the number of virtual networks using the DDoS Protection Plan.

E) Implement Azure Bastion to reduce exposure.

F) Use Azure Cost Management to track and limit spending.

Answer: A

Explanation: Azure DDoS Protection Standard charges are based on the number of public IP addresses protected by the service. By reducing the number of public IP addresses associated with resources in a protected virtual network, a company can effectively lower its DDoS Protection costs while maintaining coverage for critical assets. It is not recommended to switch to DDoS Protection Basic or disable the service during low traffic periods, as this would reduce the level of protection and expose resources to potential attacks. Limiting the number of virtual networks using the plan without strategic consideration may not yield significant cost savings if the same number of IP addresses are still associated. Implementing Azure Bastion and using Azure Cost Management are useful for other security and financial management purposes, but they do not directly reduce DDoS Protection costs.

Q5: An organization has implemented DDoS Protection Standard for their Azure resources, and they want to ensure they receive immediate alerts for any DDoS activity detected. What is the most efficient way for them to set up alerts?

A) Configure email alerts directly in the DDoS Protection Plan.

B) Set up Azure Monitor alerts based on DDoS metrics.

C) Use Azure Security Center to monitor for DDoS attacks.

D) Implement a third-party solution to monitor Azure resources.

E) Create a custom script to query Azure DDoS logs for anomalies.

F) Rely on Azure Service Health for notifications.

Answer: B

Explanation: Azure Monitor provides a robust platform for setting up alerts based on metrics and logs from Azure services, including DDoS Protection Standard. By configuring Azure Monitor alerts, the organization can receive immediate notifications when specific DDoS-related metrics surpass predefined thresholds. This allows for timely response to potential threats. Azure Monitor integrates seamlessly with DDoS Protection, offering a centralized view of alerts and enabling automated actions such as sending email notifications or triggering Azure Functions. While Azure Security Center provides security recommendations, it does not directly alert on DDoS events. Third-party solutions and custom scripts could add complexity and may not provide the same level of integration and reliability as Azure Monitor. Azure Service Health is more focused on Azure-wide service issues rather than specific security events like DDoS attacks.

Q6: Your company, Tech Innovators Inc., is migrating its on-premises data center to Azure. As part of the network design, you are tasked with setting up a hub-and-spoke architecture. The hub virtual network (VNet) will host shared services like an on-premises network gateway and a firewall. The spokes will contain various application tiers. You need to ensure that all traffic from the spoke VNets to the internet goes through the firewall in the hub VNet. Which configuration step must you perform to achieve this?

A) Associate the route table with a default route to the firewall with each spoke subnet.

B) Associate the route table with a default route to the internet gateway with each spoke subnet.

C) Enable DDoS protection on the hub VNet.

D) Set up a VPN gateway in each spoke VNet.

E) Configure a Network Security Group (NSG) on each spoke subnet.

F) Enable Azure Bastion for secure remote access to the VNets.

Answer: A

Explanation: In a hub-and-spoke configuration, to ensure that the spoke VNets route internet-bound traffic through the firewall in the hub VNet, you need to associate a route table with each spoke subnet. This route table should contain a default route with a next hop pointing to the firewall's private IP address in the hub VNet. This configuration directs all outbound traffic from the spoke VNets to the firewall before it exits to the internet, effectively centralizing security and monitoring at the firewall. The other options do not address this requirement correctly. Enabling DDoS protection, setting up VPN gateways, configuring NSGs, or enabling Azure Bastion are distinct tasks unrelated to routing traffic through a firewall.

Q7: When associating a route table with a subnet in Azure, is it possible to have multiple route tables associated with a single subnet?

A) True

B) False

Answer: B

Explanation: It is not possible to associate multiple route tables with a single subnet in Azure. Each subnet can be associated with only one route table. The route table contains routing rules that dictate how traffic should be directed, and associating multiple route tables would lead to conflicting rules. Therefore, Azure maintains a one-to-one relationship between route tables and subnets, ensuring clear and enforceable routing policies.

Q8: You have a VNet with three subnets: SubnetA, SubnetB, and SubnetC. You create a route table with a rule to route traffic destined for a specific IP address range to a virtual appliance. How would you apply this route table?

A) Associate the route table with SubnetA only.

B) Associate the route table with all three subnets.

C) Associate the route table with SubnetB only.

D) Associate the route table with the VNet, which will automatically apply it to all subnets.

E) Associate the route table with SubnetC and SubnetA only.

F) Route tables cannot be associated with subnets.

Answer: B

Explanation: When you create a route table with specific rules, you must associate it with each subnet that requires those rules to take effect. In this scenario, if you want the routing rule to apply to all three subnets, you need to associate the route table with each one individually. Azure does not support associating a route table with the entire VNet; instead, you must associate it with subnets. This allows for more granular control over routing policies within the VNet. Associating the route table with all subnets ensures that the specified traffic routing is uniformly applied across the entire VNet.

Q9: You are designing a secure and efficient network for a multinational corporation using Azure. The network includes several regions, each with its own VNet. Your goal is to minimize latency and improve network performance by using Azure's advanced networking capabilities. Which feature should you consider to facilitate direct and fast connectivity between the VNets across different regions without using the internet?

A) Azure ExpressRoute

B) VNet Peering

C) Virtual Network Gateway

D) Azure Front Door

E) Azure Traffic Manager

F) Azure Load Balancer

Answer: B

Explanation: VNet Peering is the feature that allows direct, low-latency connectivity between VNets within the same region or across different regions. It provides a high-bandwidth, private connection between VNets without using the public internet, thus improving performance and security. VNet peering effectively creates a mesh network topology within Azure, allowing resources in different VNets to communicate with each other as if they were in the same network. ExpressRoute, while a powerful tool for connecting on-premises networks to Azure, is not used for connecting VNets directly. Other options like Azure Front Door, Traffic Manager, and Load Balancer serve different purposes related to traffic distribution and management.

Q10: In a complex Azure setup, you have multiple VNets configured with peering and individual route tables. An issue arises where traffic between two specific subnets is not taking the expected path through a network virtual appliance (NVA). What troubleshooting step should you take to resolve the routing issue?

A) Update the peering settings to allow gateway transit.

B) Check and update the route table associated with the source subnet.

C) Enable forced tunneling on the peered VNets.

D) Enable BGP on all VNets.

E) Increase the SKU of the NVA.

F) Use Azure Traffic Analytics to identify the issue.

Answer: B

Explanation: When there is a routing issue where traffic is not taking the expected path, especially through an NVA, it is crucial to verify the route table associated with the source subnet. The route table should have the appropriate routes to direct traffic to the NVA as the next hop for the desired traffic. If the route is missing or incorrectly configured, traffic will not be directed through the NVA as intended. Updating the peering settings, enabling BGP, or increasing the NVA SKU are unrelated to the specific problem of misconfigured routing rules. Using Azure Traffic Analytics can help identify issues but won't directly resolve routing path problems without correcting the route table configurations.

Q11: A company, Contoso Ltd., is expanding its operations globally and needs to establish secure and reliable connections between its on-premises datacenters in Europe and Asia and its Azure resources. They have critical workloads hosted in Azure that require high availability and low latency. The company is considering using Azure VPN Gateway to establish these connections. As the cloud architect, you need to decide on the appropriate scale unit for the VPN Gateway to ensure optimal performance and availability. The company has a bandwidth requirement of 1.25 Gbps and requires redundancy. What is the most appropriate gateway scale unit for Contoso Ltd.?

A) VpnGw1

B) VpnGw2

C) VpnGw3

D) VpnGw4

E) Basic

F) HighPerformance

Answer: C

Explanation: The choice of the VPN Gateway scale unit is crucial for meeting the bandwidth and redundancy requirements. VpnGw1 and VpnGw2 do not meet the 1.25 Gbps bandwidth requirement, as they offer maximum bandwidths of 650 Mbps and 1 Gbps, respectively. The VpnGw3 SKU provides up to 1.25 Gbps, making it suitable for the stated bandwidth needs. The Basic SKU is not recommended for production workloads due to its lower performance and features. VpnGw4 would exceed the requirements, potentially leading to unnecessary costs. HighPerformance is a legacy SKU not aligned with current offerings, and VpnGw3 provides the best balance of performance and cost for Contoso Ltd.'s needs.

Q12: To support a new application deployment, your team needs to choose a gateway scale unit that can handle multiple point-to-site connections for remote users, with a maximum of 1000 simultaneous connections. Which scale unit would be most appropriate?

A) VpnGw1

B) VpnGw2

C) VpnGw3

D) VpnGw4

E) Basic

F) VpnGw5

Answer: C

Explanation: The selection of a VPN Gateway for point-to-site connections depends on the number of simultaneous connections it can handle. VpnGw1 supports up to 250 connections, and VpnGw2 supports up to 500 connections. VpnGw3 supports up to 1000 connections, making it appropriate for handling the required number of simultaneous connections. The Basic SKU supports only up to 128 connections, which is insufficient for the needs. VpnGw4 and VpnGw5 are more powerful but unnecessary for the specified requirement, leading to higher costs without additional benefits.

Q13: Your organization is planning a hybrid cloud strategy by connecting multiple on-premises locations to Azure. The requirement is for a connection that supports up to 10 Gbps and provides the highest availability possible. Which Azure gateway type and scale unit should you choose to fulfill this requirement?

A) ExpressRoute Standard

B) ExpressRoute Premium

C) VpnGw3

D) VpnGw4

E) UltraPerformance

F) VpnGw5

Answer: B

Explanation: For a high bandwidth requirement of up to 10 Gbps and the need for high availability, ExpressRoute is the preferred solution as it provides private, dedicated, and high-throughput connections. The ExpressRoute Standard SKU does not support this level of bandwidth across all peering locations. ExpressRoute Premium enhances the capabilities of the Standard by providing higher bandwidth limits and global reach, making it suitable for connecting multiple on-premises sites to Azure with high availability. VpnGw SKUs, including VpnGw3, VpnGw4, and VpnGw5, do not support such high bandwidth when compared to ExpressRoute Premium, and UltraPerformance is not a recognized SKU for this scenario.

Q14: A company has multiple Azure Virtual Networks (VNets) in different regions and needs to connect them using Azure VPN Gateway. They also need to ensure that the connections can support high throughput and latency-sensitive applications. Which VPN Gateway SKU should they use to optimize their performance?

A) Basic

B) VpnGw1

C) VpnGw2

D) VpnGw3

E) VpnGw4

F) VpnGw5

Answer: F

Explanation: For connecting multiple VNets across different regions that require high throughput and are sensitive to latency, VpnGw5 is the optimal choice. This SKU supports the highest bandwidth and offers the best performance characteristics among the available VPN Gateway SKUs. The Basic SKU is inadequate for production-grade, high-throughput applications. VpnGw1, VpnGw2, VpnGw3, and VpnGw4 offer progressively higher performance, but only VpnGw5 provides the maximum throughput capability, making it ideal for latency-sensitive and high-throughput requirements in a cross-region VNet peering scenario.

Q15: True or False: The Basic SKU of Azure VPN Gateway supports BGP (Border Gateway Protocol) for dynamic routing.

A) True

B) False

Answer: B

Explanation: The Basic SKU for Azure VPN Gateway does not support BGP, which is used for dynamic routing. BGP is crucial for scenarios where route exchange between on-premises networks and Azure is needed. The feature is available only in higher tiers such as VpnGw1 and above. This limitation makes the Basic SKU less suitable for complex networking scenarios where dynamic routing and BGP are required, as it only supports static routing.

Q16: Contoso Ltd., a global e-commerce company, is planning to migrate its on-premises data center to Azure. The company has e-commerce applications that experience significant load variations, especially during holiday seasons. These applications require high availability and disaster recovery capabilities. Contoso also anticipates rapid growth in user demand, which necessitates scalable performance. The company is considering Azure Virtual Network services to ensure optimal performance and cost management. Which Azure Virtual Network tier should Contoso choose to meet its requirements for high availability, scalability, and cost-effectiveness?

A) Basic

B) Standard

C) Premium

D) Enterprise

E) Advanced

F) Pro

Answer: B

Explanation: The Standard tier is designed to provide enhanced performance, scalability, and high availability, making it suitable for applications that experience variable loads and require disaster recovery options. It supports features such as Azure Load Balancer for distributing traffic, allowing for rapid scaling and high availability across regions. The Basic tier offers limited features and is not suitable for high-demand applications, while the Premium and Enterprise tiers do not exist for Azure Virtual Network specifically. The Advanced and Pro options are not valid tiers in the context of Azure networking services.

Q17: Your company is planning to deploy a series of microservices in Azure that need to communicate securely with low latency across different regions. You need to choose a tier that allows for optimal network performance and security while considering cost efficiency. Which Azure Application Gateway tier should you select?

A) Basic

B) Standard

C) WAF (Web Application Firewall)

D) Premium

E) Enterprise

F) High Performance

Answer: C

Explanation: The WAF tier of Azure Application Gateway provides enhanced security features, including protection against web vulnerabilities and DDoS attacks, which is crucial for microservices needing secure and low-latency communication. It also supports autoscaling and zone redundancy, ensuring high performance and availability across multiple regions. The Basic and Standard tiers do not offer the same level of security features. Premium and Enterprise are not valid tiers for Azure Application Gateway, and High Performance is not a recognized tier name in this context.

Q18: True/False: The Azure ExpressRoute Premium tier is required if you need to connect to Microsoft's global network at higher speeds and with increased limits on the number of routes supported.

A) True

B) False

Answer: A

Explanation: The Azure ExpressRoute Premium tier is specifically designed for scenarios that require higher bandwidth and increased route limits compared to the standard tier. It allows for connectivity to Microsoft's global network, enabling connections across multiple regions and supporting more routes, which is essential for enterprises with extensive networking requirements. This makes the Premium tier necessary for accessing these advanced features.

Q19: You are tasked with selecting an Azure DNS tier for a multinational corporation that requires advanced traffic management with geo-redundancy and the ability to handle millions of queries per second. Which tier should be chosen to meet these requirements?

A) Basic

B) Standard

C) Advanced

D) Premium

E) Large Scale

F) Azure DNS Private Zones

Answer: D

Explanation: The Premium tier is designed to provide advanced features such as geo-redundancy and enhanced traffic management capabilities, which are essential for handling high query volumes and ensuring reliability across multiple regions. While Basic and Standard tiers may handle typical workloads, they lack the advanced capabilities needed for such a large-scale operation. Advanced and Large Scale are not recognized Azure DNS tiers, and Private Zones pertain to managing DNS zones within a private virtual network, not public-facing DNS needs.

Q20: A retail chain with multiple branch offices across the globe is moving its infrastructure to Azure. They need a VPN gateway solution that supports point-to-site and site-to-site VPNs, offering high availability and the ability to scale bandwidth as needed. Which VPN Gateway tier should they deploy?

A) Basic

B) Standard

C) High Performance

D) Ultra

E) VpnGw1

F) VpnGw3

Answer: F

Explanation: The VpnGw3 tier is part of the Azure VPN Gateway offerings that supports both point-to-site and site-to-site connections, providing higher bandwidth and the ability to scale as required. It is suited for organizations with global operations needing robust and scalable connectivity solutions. Basic and Standard tiers offer limited scalability and performance compared to VpnGw tiers. High Performance and Ultra are not official names for VPN Gateway tiers, making VpnGw3 the optimal choice for the retail chain's needs.

Q21: A multinational corporation is designing a new application architecture in Azure that must handle high traffic volumes across multiple regions. The application must provide low-latency access to users worldwide and comply with local data residency requirements. The company is considering using Azure Load Balancer for distributing traffic. They need a solution that supports cross-region load balancing and provides disaster recovery capabilities. Additionally, they need a solution that offers a single public IP address to serve their global audience. Which Azure Load Balancer SKU and tier should the company choose to meet these requirements?

A) Basic SKU, Regional Tier

B) Basic SKU, Global Tier

C) Standard SKU, Regional Tier

D) Standard SKU, Global Tier

E) Premium SKU, Regional Tier

F) Premium SKU, Global Tier

Answer: D

Explanation: The Standard SKU of Azure Load Balancer offers the functionality required for cross-region load balancing, which is crucial for handling global traffic across multiple regions. The Global Tier provides a single public IP address that can be used to serve users worldwide, ensuring low-latency access and compliance with data residency requirements. The Basic SKU does not support cross-region load balancing, and the Premium SKU is not an option in Azure Load Balancer, as it is not a recognized SKU for Azure Load Balancer. Standard SKU provides advanced features such as higher availability and more robust performance metrics essential for high-traffic applications.

Q22: You are tasked with designing a high-availability solution for an e-commerce platform hosted on Azure. The platform requires an Azure Load Balancer that supports inbound and outbound traffic, offers zone redundancy, and needs to be integrated with Azure Virtual Network. Which load balancer configuration will best meet these needs?

A) Basic Load Balancer with Availability Zones

B) Standard Load Balancer with Zone Redundancy

C) Global Load Balancer with Zone Redundancy

D) Basic Load Balancer with Zone Redundancy

E) Standard Load Balancer with Availability Zones

F) Premium Load Balancer with Availability Zones

Answer: B

Explanation: The Standard Load Balancer with Zone Redundancy option is designed to handle both inbound and outbound traffic and supports integration with Azure Virtual Networks. Zone redundancy in the Standard SKU ensures high availability by distributing resources across availability zones, providing resilience against zone failures. The Basic Load Balancer does not support zone redundancy, and the Global Load Balancer is not a recognized SKU in Azure's Load Balancer offerings. The Premium Load Balancer is not applicable as it is not a SKU for Azure Load Balancer.

Q23: An organization plans to deploy a web application across two Azure regions to ensure global availability and redundancy. The application requires a load balancer that can direct user traffic to the closest region based on latency. Additionally, the load balancer should provide a failover mechanism if one of the regions becomes unavailable. What is the most appropriate Azure Load Balancer configuration to accomplish this?

A) Basic Load Balancer with Geo-Proximity Routing

B) Standard Load Balancer with Geo-Proximity Routing

C) Basic Load Balancer with Cross-Region Failover

D) Standard Load Balancer with Cross-Region Failover

E) Traffic Manager with Performance Routing

F) Traffic Manager with Priority Routing

Answer: E

Explanation: Azure Traffic Manager with Performance Routing is the correct choice for directing user traffic to the closest region based on latency. Traffic Manager uses DNS to direct client requests to the best endpoint based on a performance-based routing method, effectively providing a failover mechanism if one region becomes unavailable. Azure Load Balancers do not inherently provide geo-proximity or cross-region failover capabilities; these are features typically handled by Traffic Manager. Priority Routing could be used but does not optimize for latency.

Q24: True or False: The Basic SKU of Azure Load Balancer supports zone redundancy and can be used in production environments requiring high availability across multiple regions.

A) True

B) False

Answer: B

Explanation: The Basic SKU of Azure Load Balancer does not support zone redundancy. It is primarily designed for scenarios that do not require the advanced features provided by the Standard SKU, such as higher availability, zone redundancy, and cross-region capabilities. The Standard SKU, on the other hand, supports these advanced features, making it suitable for production environments requiring high availability across multiple regions.

Q25: You are an Azure Solutions Architect for a company that needs a load balancing solution with advanced traffic management features, such as SSL offloading, URL-based routing, and web application firewall capabilities. The solution must also be cost-effective and suitable for both internal and external applications. Which Azure service should you recommend?

A) Basic Load Balancer

B) Standard Load Balancer

C) Application Gateway

D) Traffic Manager

E) Front Door

F) Network Security Group

Answer: C

Explanation: Azure Application Gateway is the ideal choice for scenarios requiring advanced traffic management features like SSL offloading, URL-based routing, and a web application firewall (WAF). It provides Layer 7 load balancing, which is necessary for managing HTTP/HTTPS traffic with the specified requirements. While Traffic Manager and Front Door offer some routing capabilities, they do not provide SSL offloading or URL-based routing at the same level as Application Gateway. Load Balancers and Network Security Groups do not offer these advanced Layer 7 functionalities.

Q26: A multinational corporation, Contoso Ltd., is planning to expand its services across different regions using Azure. They have on-premises data centers in the United States and Europe and want to connect these data centers to Azure to leverage cloud computing capabilities. They have a significant amount of internal data traffic between their on-premises locations and their Azure VMs, and they also need to access Microsoft SaaS services like Office 365 and Dynamics 365. Contoso Ltd. is concerned about security and wants to minimize latency and data transfer costs. Considering these requirements, which peering option should they choose?

A) Azure private peering only

B) Microsoft peering only

C) Both Azure private peering and Microsoft peering

D) Public peering only

E) ExpressRoute Direct

F) VPN Gateway with Microsoft peering

Answer: C

Explanation: For Contoso Ltd., both Azure private peering and Microsoft peering are necessary. Azure private peering is suitable for connecting their on-premises data centers to their Azure VMs, allowing them to move internal data securely over a private connection, which minimizes latency and enhances security. Microsoft peering is needed for accessing Microsoft's SaaS services like Office 365 and Dynamics 365 since these services are accessed over the public internet. By using both peering options, Contoso can ensure secure, low-latency, and cost-effective connectivity for both internal data transfer and access to Microsoft services, optimizing their overall network architecture.

Q27: A company has decided to utilize Azure ExpressRoute for connecting its on-premises network to Azure. Which of the following configurations is suitable if the company's requirement is to exclusively access Azure PaaS and IaaS services?

A) Microsoft peering only

B) Public peering only

C) Azure private peering only

D) VPN over ExpressRoute

E) ExpressRoute Global Reach

F) Microsoft and Public peering

Answer: C

Explanation: If the company's objective is to exclusively access Azure Platform as a Service (PaaS) and Infrastructure as a Service (IaaS) services, Azure private peering is the appropriate choice. This configuration allows for a direct, private connection to Azure services without traversing the public internet, ensuring enhanced security, reliability, and reduced latency compared to public peering. Azure private peering allows seamless integration with virtual networks and other Azure resources, making it ideal for accessing Azure PaaS and IaaS services.

Q28: A startup company uses multiple Microsoft services, including Azure, Office 365, and Dynamics 365. They plan to establish a secure and efficient connection to Microsoft services through ExpressRoute. True or False: Microsoft peering is the best peering type for accessing both Azure resources and Microsoft SaaS services.

A) True

B) False

Answer: B

Explanation: While Microsoft peering is indeed the best option for accessing Microsoft SaaS services like Office 365 and Dynamics 365, it is not suitable for accessing Azure resources directly. Azure resources are accessed through Azure private peering. Therefore, to access both Azure resources and Microsoft SaaS services efficiently, the startup company would need to use both Azure private peering and Microsoft peering.

Q29: A large enterprise is evaluating its networking strategy in Azure. They need to connect multiple on-premises sites to Azure with high availability and redundancy. Additionally, they want to ensure seamless access to Microsoft 365 services. Which configuration should they implement?

A) Azure private peering with ExpressRoute failover

B) Microsoft peering with VPN backup

C) ExpressRoute with Global Reach and both Azure private and Microsoft peering

D) Hybrid Connection with Microsoft peering

E) Direct Internet Access with Microsoft peering

F) Azure private peering with Public peering

Answer: C

Explanation: For a large enterprise requiring high availability, redundancy, and seamless access to Microsoft 365 services, using ExpressRoute with Global Reach, along with both Azure private and Microsoft peering, is optimal. ExpressRoute with Global Reach allows for connecting multiple on-premises sites, providing a reliable and redundant connection. Azure private peering facilitates secure access to Azure resources, while Microsoft peering ensures efficient access to Microsoft SaaS services like Microsoft 365. This configuration offers comprehensive coverage and connectivity for various enterprise needs in Azure.

Q30: A company is planning to migrate its workloads to Azure and wants to ensure secure, high-performance connectivity to its on-premises network with the ability to access Azure services and Microsoft SaaS applications. They have a limited budget and want to avoid unnecessary costs. What is the best peering configuration for this scenario?

A) Azure private peering only

B) Microsoft peering only

C) Both Azure private peering and Microsoft peering

D) Public peering only

E) ExpressRoute with Azure private peering and Microsoft peering

F) VPN Gateway with Azure private peering

Answer: E

Explanation: The best configuration for the company is to use ExpressRoute with both Azure private peering and Microsoft peering. This setup provides a secure, high-performance, and reliable connection to Azure resources and Microsoft SaaS applications. Although ExpressRoute involves some cost, it offers significant benefits in terms of security, performance, and availability, which are critical for a successful cloud migration and operation. By using both peering types, the company ensures seamless access to Azure services and Microsoft SaaS applications, optimizing their network strategy while adhering to their performance and connectivity requirements.

Q31: You are working as a cloud solutions architect for a global e-commerce company that hosts its website on Microsoft Azure. The company's traffic is highly variable, with peak loads during sales events and holidays. Recently, they've noticed that the current manual scaling strategy for their Azure virtual machine scale sets is inefficient, leading to either over-provisioning or under-provisioning resources. They are considering implementing an autoscale solution to optimize resources and costs. Which of the following Azure features would be the most appropriate to implement for handling automatic scaling based on CPU usage and HTTP queue length?

A) Azure Logic Apps

B) Azure Monitor Autoscale

C) Azure Traffic Manager

D) Azure Virtual Network Manager

E) Azure Load Balancer

F) Azure Advisor

Answer: B

Explanation: Azure Monitor Autoscale is designed to automatically scale your resources based on specific metrics and predefined rules. It's highly suitable for scenarios where workloads have variable traffic patterns, like the e-commerce company in this scenario. By using Azure Monitor Autoscale, the company can define rules to scale out or in based on CPU usage and HTTP queue length, which are common performance indicators for web applications. This leads to optimized resource allocation and cost savings by ensuring that resources are only added when necessary and deallocated when demand decreases. Azure Logic Apps and Traffic Manager do not offer direct autoscaling capabilities, while Azure Virtual Network Manager, Load Balancer, and Advisor serve different purposes.

Q32: Consider the following statement: "Azure's autoscaling feature allows applications to automatically scale up or down based on predefined schedules or metrics, which can result in cost savings and improved application performance." Is this statement true or false?

A) True

B) False

Answer: A

Explanation: The statement is true. Azure's autoscaling feature is designed to dynamically adjust the number of resources allocated to an application based on predefined metrics such as CPU usage, memory usage, or custom-defined schedules. This ability to automatically scale up or down helps ensure that applications have the necessary resources during peak demand periods while reducing costs during low-demand periods by deallocating unnecessary resources. This approach not only optimizes performance by providing sufficient resources but also helps manage costs effectively.

Q33: An IT consulting firm is tasked with optimizing the resource usage of an Azure-hosted web application. The current deployment uses a manual scaling strategy, leading to frequent performance issues and unnecessary costs during non-peak hours. The firm is evaluating different options for implementing autoscale. Which Azure service would provide the most comprehensive solution for configuring and managing autoscale settings based on custom application metrics?

A) Azure Application Insights

B) Azure Automation

C) Azure Monitor

D) Azure Resource Manager

E) Azure Cost Management

F) Azure Policy

Answer: C

Explanation: Azure Monitor offers comprehensive tools for configuring and managing autoscale settings based on custom application metrics. It integrates with Azure Application Insights to provide detailed telemetry data that can be used to create autoscale rules tailored to specific application needs. Azure Monitor allows for the creation of autoscale profiles that can scale resources up or down based on metrics like CPU usage, HTTP response times, or any custom metrics emitted by the application. Azure Automation, Resource Manager, Cost Management, and Policy serve different functions and do not directly manage autoscale settings.

Q34: A tech startup is experiencing rapid growth, and its customer-facing application hosted on Azure is under constant load fluctuation. The company wants to ensure that the application remains responsive without incurring unnecessary costs from over-provisioning resources. They are debating between manual scaling and autoscaling. Which of the following is a key advantage of choosing autoscaling over manual scaling in this context?

A) Increased control over resource allocation

B) Simplified billing and invoicing

C) Improved application security

D) Reduced need for monitoring and alerts

E) Automatic adjustment to workload changes

F) Better integration with on-premises systems

Answer: E

Explanation: The key advantage of autoscaling in this context is its ability to automatically adjust to workload changes. Autoscaling allows the application to dynamically scale resources up or down in response to real-time demand, ensuring that the application remains responsive under varying loads without incurring unnecessary costs. This is particularly beneficial for a tech startup experiencing rapid growth and fluctuating demand, as it reduces the risk of over-provisioning or under-provisioning resources. While manual scaling provides more direct control, it requires constant monitoring and can lead to inefficiencies. Autoscaling automates this process, optimizing resource usage and cost.

Q35: A financial services company has deployed a critical application on Azure VMs, which experiences predictable spikes in usage at certain times of the day. The IT team wants to implement an autoscale strategy that minimizes costs and ensures the application is always responsive. They are considering using a schedule-based scaling approach. Which Azure feature allows them to define scaling profiles that automatically adjust the number of VMs based on specific times and dates?

A) Azure Scheduler

B) Azure DevTest Labs

C) Azure Scale Sets with Scheduled Autoscale

D) Azure Functions

E) Azure Event Grid

F) Azure Virtual Machines Reserved Instances

Answer: C

Explanation: Azure Scale Sets with Scheduled Autoscale allows the IT team to define scaling profiles based on specific times and dates. This feature is particularly useful for applications with predictable usage patterns, such as those experiencing spikes at certain times of the day. By configuring scheduled autoscale rules, the company can ensure that additional VMs are automatically brought online during peak periods and deallocated during off-peak times, optimizing performance and cost. Azure Scheduler, DevTest Labs, Functions, Event Grid, and Reserved Instances do not provide this specific capability for managing VM scaling based on schedules.

Q36: In a multinational company, the IT department is tasked with designing a network solution on Azure that supports both customer-facing web applications and Internal services for employees. The web applications need to be accessible globally, while the internal services should only be accessible within the company's virtual network. The company wants to ensure high availability and fault tolerance for both the web applications and the internal services. Considering these requirements, which Azure load balancing solution should be implemented for the internal services? ---

A) Azure Application Gateway with WAF

B) Azure Traffic Manager

C) Azure Front Door

D) Azure Public Load Balancer

E) Azure Internal Load Balancer

F) Azure DNS with traffic routing

Answer: E

Explanation: An Azure Internal Load Balancer (ILB) is specifically designed to handle network traffic that must remain internal to an Azure virtual network. It is ideal for balancing load between internal services that do not need to be accessed from the internet. By using an ILB, traffic is distributed across a set of virtual machines within a region without exposing the services to the internet, thus enhancing security. This solution aligns with the company's need to keep internal services accessible only within their virtual network while ensuring high availability and fault tolerance.

Q37: You are designing a high-availability solution for a web application hosted in Azure. The application must be accessible to users across multiple regions with minimal latency. Which service should you choose to direct traffic based on the lowest network latency to the user? ---

A) Azure Public Load Balancer

B) Azure Internal Load Balancer

C) Azure Traffic Manager

D) Azure Front Door

E) Azure CDN

F) Azure Application Gateway

Answer: D

Explanation: Azure Front Door is a global, scalable entry point that uses a split TCP-based anycast protocol to direct user traffic to the backend with the lowest latency. It provides fast global failover and high availability for your applications. Front Door is particularly effective for applications that require low latency and high availability across multiple regions, as it routes users to the nearest available backend using its own global point of presence.

Q38: A company is looking to optimize its cloud expenses while maintaining a robust load balancing solution for its web applications that are subject to fluctuating traffic volumes. Which Azure service can dynamically adjust to changes in traffic load to ensure efficient resource utilization? ---

A) Azure Public Load Balancer

B) Azure Traffic Manager

C) Azure Front Door

D) Azure Application Gateway

E) Azure Virtual WAN

F) Azure Internal Load Balancer

Answer: D

Explanation: Azure Application Gateway provides application-level routing and load balancing services that include auto-scaling, which dynamically adjusts the number of gateway instances based on your traffic load. This auto-scaling feature helps optimize costs by ensuring that you only use the resources necessary to handle current traffic volumes, thus preventing over-provisioning and underutilization of resources.

Q39: You need to ensure secure and efficient load balancing for a set of RESTful APIs hosted in Azure, which are only accessible from within a corporate network. The solution must support URL-based routing and SSL termination. Which Azure service is best suited for this requirement? ---

A) Azure Public Load Balancer

B) Azure Traffic Manager

C) Azure Front Door

D) Azure Application Gateway

E) Azure Virtual Network

F) Azure CDN

Answer: D

Explanation: Azure Application Gateway is designed to handle advanced application-level routing and load balancing, which includes URL-based routing and SSL termination. It is well-suited for RESTful APIs that require secure, efficient load balancing and is capable of functioning within a virtual network, making it a suitable choice for services that need to remain internal to a corporate network. This ensures that all traffic is efficiently managed and secure, meeting the specified requirements.

Q40: True or False: Azure Traffic Manager can be used to distribute incoming traffic to multiple Azure regions based on geographic location, ensuring that users are directed to the closest region.

A) True

B) False

Answer: A

Explanation: Azure Traffic Manager is a DNS-based traffic load balancer that enables you to distribute traffic optimally to services across global Azure regions. It supports geographic routing methods that direct users to the nearest geographic location, helping to reduce latency and improve user experience by routing them to the closest region. This capability makes it an excellent choice for applications that require efficient global traffic distribution based on the user's location.

Q41: A multinational organization operates its primary data center in the United States but has regional offices across Europe and Asia. They are deploying a new customer-facing application hosted on Azure, which needs to be highly available and responsive to users worldwide. The application is expected to handle significant traffic from all geographical regions, and latency is a critical factor for user experience. The organization wants to ensure that user requests are directed to the closest available backend pool to minimize latency while maintaining a centralized control plane for ease of management. Given these requirements, which Azure load balancing solution should the organization implement?

A) Azure Traffic Manager with weighted routing

B) Azure Front Door with dynamic site acceleration

C) Azure Load Balancer with geographic distribution

D) Azure Application Gateway with URL-based routing

E) Azure Traffic Manager with performance routing

F) Azure Front Door with session affinity

Answer: B

Explanation: Azure Front Door is the most suitable solution for this scenario because it is a global load balancer that provides low latency and high availability by routing user requests to the nearest backend pool. It supports features such as SSL termination, URL-based routing, and dynamic site acceleration, which are essential for optimizing the performance of global applications. Azure Traffic Manager, while capable of routing based on performance, does not provide the same level of acceleration and features as Front Door. An Application Gateway is region-specific and does not offer global load balancing capabilities.

Q42: An organization is planning to deploy an Azure-based solution that will serve both regional and global audiences. They need a load balancing strategy that minimizes latency for regional users while ensuring global reach and scalability. Which of the following statements is true regarding the choice between Azure Load Balancer and Azure Front Door?

A) Azure Load Balancer is designed for global load balancing across multiple regions.

B) Azure Front Door provides regional load balancing with low latency.

Answer: A

Explanation: The statement is false. Azure Load Balancer is primarily a regional service and is intended to distribute traffic within a specific Azure region. It is not designed for global load balancing across multiple regions. Conversely, Azure Front Door is a global service that routes traffic across regions, providing features like latency-based routing to direct user requests to the nearest available backend, thereby minimizing latency on a global scale.

Q43: Which Azure service should you choose to implement a global load-balancing solution that also provides SSL offloading and web application firewall (WAF) capabilities?

A) Azure Load Balancer

B) Azure Traffic Manager

C) Azure Front Door

D) Azure Application Gateway

E) Azure CDN

F) Azure VPN Gateway

Answer: C

Explanation: Azure Front Door is a global load balancer that offers SSL offloading and integrates with Azure Web Application Firewall (WAF) to provide enhanced security for web applications. It enables global routing, ensuring that user requests are directed to the nearest available backend, reducing latency and improving application performance. Azure Load Balancer and Azure Application Gateway are regional solutions, and while Application Gateway supports WAF, it does not provide global load balancing. Azure Traffic Manager is a DNS-based global load balancer but lacks integrated SSL offloading or WAF features.

Q44: A company is deploying a multi-region architecture in Azure to support disaster recovery and high availability for its web applications. They require a load balancing solution that can dynamically route user traffic to the healthiest endpoint across different regions, with automatic failover capabilities in case of a regional outage. Which Azure service best meets these requirements?

A) Azure Load Balancer

B) Azure Traffic Manager with priority routing

C) Azure Front Door with geo-filtering

D) Azure Application Gateway with URL-based routing

E) Azure Traffic Manager with performance routing

F) Azure Load Balancer with failover groups

Answer: E

Explanation: Azure Traffic Manager with performance routing is the ideal solution for routing traffic based on the performance of different endpoints, ensuring that user requests are directed to the healthiest and most responsive endpoint across regions. It provides automatic failover capabilities by continuously monitoring endpoint health, redirecting traffic to alternative endpoints during outages. Unlike Azure Load Balancer, which is regional, Traffic Manager operates at the DNS level and can manage traffic globally, making it suitable for multi-region architectures.

Q45: An e-commerce platform hosted on Azure needs to optimize its load balancing configuration to ensure both high availability and low latency for users accessing from various continents. The platform's backend services require session persistence, and the company also seeks to benefit from Azure's global presence to enhance user experience. Which Azure load balancing service should the platform use?

A) Azure Load Balancer with session persistence

B) Azure Front Door with session affinity

C) Azure Traffic Manager with geographic routing

D) Azure Application Gateway with path-based routing

E) Azure CDN with caching rules

F) Azure VPN Gateway with routing policies

Answer: B

Explanation: Azure Front Door with session affinity is well-suited for this requirement as it is a global load balancing service that ensures low latency by routing traffic to the nearest backend and allows for session persistence, which is crucial for maintaining user sessions across multiple requests. Additionally, Azure Front Door takes advantage of Microsoft's global network to optimize the user experience. Unlike Azure Load Balancer and Application Gateway, which are region-specific, Front Door provides a global reach and integrates features like SSL offloading and WAF, which are beneficial for e-commerce platforms.

Q46: A multinational company, Contoso Ltd., is expanding its operations to multiple regions and needs to deploy several Azure web applications across these regions. The network team is tasked with ensuring that each application has a unique public IP address for direct access. The team also needs to manage costs and simplify the IP management process. Given these requirements, the team is considering the use of a public IP address prefix. What should be their primary consideration when deciding to use a public IP address prefix for their Azure resources?

A) Ability to assign static IP addresses for all applications.

B) Simplifying DNS management by using a single domain name.

C) Ensuring all IP addresses are within a single region's availability zone.

D) Reserving a range of IP addresses upfront to avoid future conflicts.

E) Reducing latency by using a geographically closest IP address.

F) Enforcing network security policies through IP filtering.

Answer: D

Explanation: When a company needs to deploy multiple applications across different regions, using a public IP address prefix can be advantageous. The primary consideration should be the ability to reserve a range of IP addresses upfront. This ensures that all IP addresses are unique and reduces the risk of IP address conflicts in the future. By reserving the IP address range, Contoso Ltd. can manage their resources more effectively and predictably, without having to worry about future allocations and potential changes that could disrupt service continuity. Additionally, using a public IP address prefix can simplify management and provide a streamlined approach to handling network configurations across multiple regions.

Q47: You are planning a deployment strategy for a new set of Azure virtual machines that will host a public-facing web service. The service must scale out to accommodate increased traffic, and each instance should have a consistent public IP address configuration. In this context, when would it be most appropriate to use a public IP address prefix?

A) When the service requires dynamic IP addresses for each instance.

B) When the service instances are distributed across multiple regions.

C) When the service requires a single IP address for all instances.

D) When the service instances require consistent IP addresses within a single region.

E) When the service needs to minimize DNS propagation delays.

F) When the service demands high availability and load balancing.

Answer: D

Explanation: A public IP address prefix is most appropriate when the service instances require consistent IP addresses within a single region. This is because a public IP address prefix allows you to reserve a contiguous block of IP addresses, which can be used to provide a consistent and predictable IP address configuration for each service instance. This setup is beneficial for services that scale out, as it allows new instances to be assigned an IP address from the reserved range, ensuring consistency. While the prefix does not span multiple regions, it facilitates efficient IP management and helps in maintaining a stable network configuration.

Q48: For a company planning to expand its Azure infrastructure, selecting between using individual public IP addresses or a public IP address prefix is crucial. What is a key advantage of using a public IP address prefix over assigning individual public IP addresses?

A) Enhanced data encryption across the network.

B) Simplified access control configuration.

C) Improved performance through load balancing.

D) Cost savings by reducing the number of IP configurations.

E) Easier integration with on-premises resources.

F) Better compliance with regional network regulations.

Answer: D

Explanation: A key advantage of using a public IP address prefix is cost savings by reducing the number of individual IP configurations. When using a public IP address prefix, multiple IP addresses are managed as a single entity, which simplifies configuration and management processes. This makes it easier to maintain and update network configurations, reducing the administrative overhead and potential costs associated with managing multiple individual IP addresses. By having a contiguous range of IP addresses, organizations can ensure a more efficient allocation and management of their networking resources within Azure.

Q49: A large e-commerce platform plans to deploy their application across multiple Azure regions to ensure availability and lower latency for their global users. They are evaluating the use of public IP address prefixes in their architecture. Which of the following is a limitation that they should consider when deciding to use a public IP address prefix?

A) Inability to use the prefix for private endpoint connections.

B) Limited support for prefix management across multiple subscriptions.

C) Restricted to a maximum of 10 IP addresses in a prefix.

D) Unavailability of prefix support in certain Azure regions.

E) Complexity in integrating with Azure CDN services.

F) Difficulty in associating prefixes with application gateway.

Answer: D

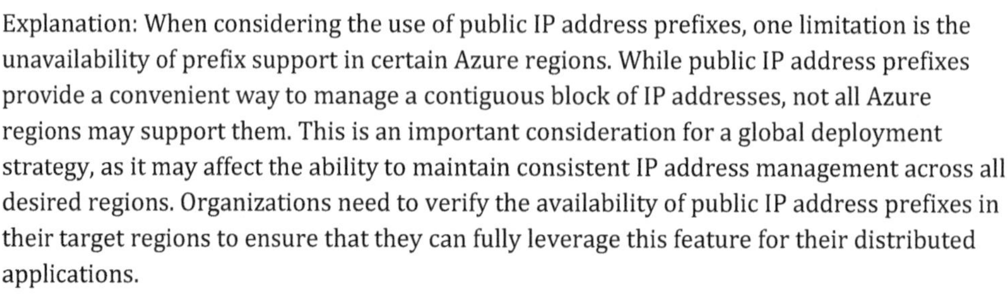

Explanation: When considering the use of public IP address prefixes, one limitation is the unavailability of prefix support in certain Azure regions. While public IP address prefixes provide a convenient way to manage a contiguous block of IP addresses, not all Azure regions may support them. This is an important consideration for a global deployment strategy, as it may affect the ability to maintain consistent IP address management across all desired regions. Organizations need to verify the availability of public IP address prefixes in their target regions to ensure that they can fully leverage this feature for their distributed applications.

Q50: Public IP address prefixes can be used to simplify network management in Azure. True or False: Public IP address prefixes automatically provide redundancy and failover capabilities for critical applications.

A) True

B) False

Answer: B

Explanation: Public IP address prefixes do not automatically provide redundancy and failover capabilities. While they simplify the management of IP addresses by allowing the reservation of a contiguous block of addresses, redundancy and failover are determined by other components of the network architecture, such as load balancers and high-availability configurations. Public IP address prefixes primarily aid in the management and organization of IP addresses, but additional configurations and services are needed to establish redundancy and failover for critical applications in Azure.

Q51: A financial services company is in the process of migrating its on-premises applications to Azure. They have several Azure resources, including Azure Storage and Azure SQL Database, that need to connect securely to their on-premises network. They are concerned about data leakage over the internet and want to ensure that their data remains secure while being accessible only from their network. The company is considering using service endpoints to secure their data. Which of the following scenarios justifies the use of service endpoints in this context?

A) The company wants to encrypt data in transit using Azure Key Vault.

B) The company needs to provide internet access to the Azure services for external clients.

C) The company wants to ensure that traffic to Azure services remains within the Azure backbone network.

D) The company wants to achieve high availability by deploying resources in multiple regions.

E) The company needs to apply network security group (NSG) rules to control traffic to Azure resources.

F) The company is looking to enhance disaster recovery by using geo-replication.

Answer: C

Explanation: Service endpoints in Azure allow you to extend your virtual network's private address space and its identity to Azure services over a direct connection. This means that traffic between your virtual network and the Azure services remains within the Azure backbone network, providing improved security by not exposing the data to the public internet. This is particularly important for a financial services company that is concerned about data leakage. By using service endpoints, the company can ensure that their data remains secure and accessible only from their network, without the need for public IP addresses. This solution is ideal for scenarios where secure, private access to Azure resources is needed without the overhead of setting up a VPN or ExpressRoute.

Q52: You are managing a cloud infrastructure for an e-commerce platform hosted on Azure. The platform relies heavily on Azure SQL Database and Azure Blob Storage for its operations. Due to compliance requirements, all data traffic to these services must be restricted to certain trusted subnets. How can service endpoints be leveraged in this scenario?

A) Service endpoints can be used to enable VNet peering across multiple regions.

B) Service endpoints allow you to restrict access to Azure resources based on IP addresses.

C) Service endpoints enable the use of Azure Traffic Manager for global distribution.

D) Service endpoints allow for the integration of Azure AD for user authentication.

E) Service endpoints can be used to connect on-premises data centers directly to Azure services.

F) Service endpoints allow you to define network security rules that restrict access to trusted subnets.

Answer: F

Explanation: Service endpoints provide secure and direct connectivity to Azure services from within your Azure virtual network by extending the VNet identity to the service. In this case, by using service endpoints, you can define network security rules that restrict access to Azure SQL Database and Azure Blob Storage to only those requests coming from specified trusted subnets. This ensures compliance with security and regulatory requirements by isolating traffic within a controlled environment and prevents unauthorized access from outside these subnets, while still leveraging the Azure backbone network for communication.

Q53: A retail company is planning to improve its disaster recovery strategy for its Azure-hosted applications. They are considering whether to implement service endpoints to support this strategy. True or False: Service endpoints are primarily designed to enhance disaster recovery capabilities by replicating data across multiple regions.

A) True

B) False

Answer: B

Explanation: Service endpoints are not primarily designed for enhancing disaster recovery capabilities. Their main purpose is to provide secure and direct connectivity to Azure services from within a virtual network by extending the VNet's identity to the Azure service. This involves securing traffic within the Azure backbone network and does not inherently provide data replication or recovery features across regions. Disaster recovery strategies generally involve using features like geo-replication, Azure Site Recovery, and backups, which are separate from the functionality provided by service endpoints.

Q54: An organization runs a healthcare application on Azure that needs to communicate securely with an Azure Key Vault instance to store sensitive patient data. The application resides in a designated subnet within an Azure VNet. What is the best use case for implementing service endpoints in this scenario?

A) To enable faster data processing by using Azure CDN.

B) To allow the application to connect to Azure Key Vault without public internet exposure.

C) To reduce costs by using Azure Reserved Instances.

D) To increase the virtual network's bandwidth capacity.

E) To enable the application to use Azure Monitor for performance tracking.

F) To integrate Azure DevOps for continuous deployment.

Answer: B

Explanation: In this scenario, the primary concern is securely communicating with Azure Key Vault without exposing the application to the public internet. By implementing service endpoints, you can extend your virtual network's private address space to Azure Key Vault, effectively making access to it a part of your virtual network. This allows the application to connect directly to Azure Key Vault over the Azure backbone network, eliminating the need for public IP addresses and enhancing security by ensuring that data traffic does not traverse the public internet. This is especially critical in healthcare applications where patient data must be protected according to strict compliance standards.

Q55: A multinational corporation has deployed multiple Azure services across different regions to support their global operations. They have a requirement to ensure that all traffic between their Azure Virtual Network and Azure services like Azure SQL Database remains secure and within the Microsoft network. In which situation would service endpoints not be appropriate?

A) To ensure high performance and low latency for Azure services.

B) To secure data in transit between Azure services across different regions.

C) To eliminate the need for public IP addresses for Azure services.

D) To control access to Azure services based on VNet configuration.

E) To enable connectivity between Azure services and on-premises networks.

F) To apply NSG rules to filter traffic to Azure services.

Answer: B

Explanation: Service endpoints are designed to secure data in transit within the same Azure region by allowing traffic to flow through the Microsoft backbone network, without exiting to the public internet. While service endpoints ensure that traffic remains secure within Azure's network, they do not inherently address cross-region security concerns. For cross-region scenarios, other solutions such as VPNs, ExpressRoute, or using Azure's native encryption features would be more appropriate to ensure secure data transit. Service endpoints are primarily used to provide secure connectivity within the same region and not across different regions.

Q56: Your company, Contoso Ltd., is migrating a critical application to Azure. This application consists of multiple Azure services that need to interact securely without exposing data over the internet. The architecture includes Azure SQL Database, Azure Storage, and Azure Web Apps. The application must comply with strict data privacy regulations, and you are tasked with ensuring that these services communicate over a private network. You also need to ensure that developers can access the logs and metrics of each service without compromising security. Which configuration should you implement to meet these requirements?

A) Deploy all resources in a single virtual network and use service endpoints.

B) Configure private endpoints for each service and use Azure Bastion for developer access.

C) Use Azure VPN Gateway to connect services securely.

D) Set up a private link service for the Azure SQL Database only.

E) Use a combination of Azure Firewall and Network Security Groups (NSGs).

F) Implement Virtual Network Peering between the services.

Answer: B

Explanation: Configuring private endpoints for each service ensures that Azure SQL Database, Azure Storage, and Azure Web Apps communicate over a private IP address within the Azure virtual network, thereby keeping the data private and secure. This setup complies with data privacy regulations by preventing exposure over the internet. Azure Bastion provides secure RDP and SSH connectivity to the virtual machines directly from the Azure portal over SSL, allowing developers to access logs and metrics securely without needing public IP addresses on the VMs. This solution balances security and accessibility while adhering to compliance requirements.

Q57: Which component is essential for enabling connectivity between a virtual network and private endpoints in the same region within Microsoft Azure?

A) Virtual Network Gateway

B) Azure Front Door

C) Network Security Group

D) Azure DNS Private Zones

E) Application Gateway

F) Azure Traffic Manager

Answer: D

Explanation: Azure DNS Private Zones is crucial for enabling connectivity between a virtual network and private endpoints within the same region. By using Azure DNS private zones, you can manage and resolve domain names in a private network, ensuring that traffic intended for private endpoints remains within the Azure network. This setup is vital for accessing services through private endpoints, as it allows for the resolution of the private endpoint's IP address without exposing it to the public internet.

Q58: When configuring access to a private endpoint in Azure, which of the following actions is necessary to ensure that the DNS resolution is correctly set up for on-premises systems connecting to resources in Azure via a private endpoint?

A) Configure a custom DNS server in Azure to forward queries to Azure DNS.

B) Enable public DNS forwarding from on-premises to Azure DNS.

C) Use Azure Policy to enforce DNS settings.

D) Set up an Azure ExpressRoute to handle DNS queries.

E) Create a conditional forwarder in the on-premises DNS server pointing to Azure DNS.

F) Use a VPN Gateway to redirect DNS traffic.

Answer: E

Explanation: To ensure that on-premises systems can resolve the DNS names of Azure resources configured with private endpoints, you need to create a conditional forwarder in the on-premises DNS server that points to Azure DNS. This allows DNS queries for the specific Azure private domain to be forwarded to Azure, where the private endpoint's IP address can be correctly resolved. This setup is essential for maintaining seamless name resolution when extending your network to Azure and using private endpoints.

Q59: True or False: Configuring private endpoints in Azure automatically disables public access to the associated Azure service.

A) True

B) False

Answer: B

Explanation: Configuring private endpoints in Azure does not automatically disable public access to the associated Azure service. While a private endpoint allows traffic to flow over a private IP address within a virtual network, the service may still be accessible publicly unless explicitly configured otherwise. To disable public access, additional configurations such as firewall rules or service-specific settings need to be implemented to restrict or block public traffic.

Q60: An organization has deployed multiple Azure services using private endpoints to ensure secure communication within their virtual network. They want to monitor and analyze traffic patterns to and from these endpoints. Which Azure service should they use to achieve detailed traffic analysis?

A) Azure Monitor

B) Azure Traffic Analytics

C) Network Watcher with Traffic Analytics

D) Azure Log Analytics

E) Azure Sentinel

F) Azure Security Center

Answer: C

Explanation: Network Watcher with Traffic Analytics is the appropriate service for detailed traffic analysis of Azure resources using private endpoints. Network Watcher provides tools to monitor and diagnose conditions at a network level, and Traffic Analytics offers insights into traffic flow patterns, network anomalies, and security threats. This combination allows the organization to gain deep visibility into traffic to and from their private endpoints, making it ideal for security and performance monitoring within a virtual network.

Q61: Contoso Ltd, a multinational corporation, has multiple Azure virtual networks (VNets) deployed across different regions to support its global operations. The company needs to ensure secure access to Azure Storage accounts from these VNets without exposing the storage accounts to the public internet. The network team at Contoso wants to leverage Azure service endpoints for this purpose. They have a specific requirement for configuring service endpoints to connect a VNet in the East US region to a storage account in the same region. The network team is considering different configuration steps to achieve this, but they also want to ensure that the service endpoints are limited to specific subnets within the VNet. Which configuration step should the team focus on to ensure secure access while adhering to their requirements?

A) Enable service endpoints for the storage service on the entire VNet.

B) Create a service endpoint policy to allow access from specific VMs.

C) Enable service endpoints for the storage service on the required subnet.

D) Configure a network security group (NSG) to allow traffic to the storage account.

E) Use a virtual network peering to connect the VNet to the storage account.

F) Configure a private link to the storage account.

Answer: C

Explanation: To ensure secure access to Azure Storage accounts while keeping the storage resources off the public internet, service endpoints should be configured. Service endpoints allow you to secure the critical Azure service resources to only your virtual networks by extending the VNet identity to the service. In this scenario, enabling service endpoints for the storage service on a specific subnet within the VNet ensures that only the resources within that subnet are granted access to the Azure Storage account. This approach adheres to the principle of least privilege by not exposing the entire VNet, thereby enhancing security. Enabling service endpoints on a subnet level also allows for more granular control and management of network traffic.

Q62: Contoso Ltd wants to optimize its network traffic costs while using Azure service endpoints for its various services. They plan to connect multiple VNets located in different regions to a central storage account using service endpoints. What should Contoso consider to minimize costs associated with this configuration?

A) Service endpoints are cost-free; focus only on bandwidth charges.

B) Use regional service endpoints to avoid cross-region data transfer charges.

C) Implement a traffic manager to balance loads across regions.

D) Utilize ExpressRoute to eliminate internet-based data transfer costs.

E) Use Azure Firewall to manage and minimize network costs.

F) Implement Azure Front Door to optimize traffic routing costs.

Answer: B

Explanation: When configuring service endpoints across multiple regions, it is important to consider the data transfer costs associated with cross-region traffic. Azure service endpoints themselves do not incur additional charges, but the data transferred between regions can incur significant costs. By using regional service endpoints, Contoso can ensure that data transfer remains within the same region, thus avoiding cross-region data transfer charges. This approach helps in optimizing the overall network traffic costs while maintaining secure access to Azure services.

Q63: True or False: Service endpoints provide a mechanism for extending a virtual network's identity to Azure services, allowing resources within the virtual network to securely access these services over the Microsoft backbone network.

A) True

B) False

Answer: A

Explanation: Service endpoints in Azure extend the identity of a virtual network to Azure services over the Microsoft backbone network. This extension enables resources within the virtual network to securely access Azure services such as Azure Storage, SQL Database, and others, without the need for a public IP address. The traffic between the VNets and the Azure services remains on the Microsoft network, providing a secure and efficient communication path.

Q64: A company is using Azure VNets and wants to restrict access to an Azure SQL Database to only specific subnets within their VNet using service endpoints. Which network configuration change must be implemented to achieve this?

A) Assign a public IP address to the Azure SQL Database.

B) Create a service endpoint for Azure SQL Database on the specific subnets.

C) Use Azure Bastion to connect securely to the Azure SQL Database.

D) Implement a VPN Gateway to encrypt traffic to the SQL Database.

E) Deploy an Application Gateway to route traffic to the SQL Database.

F) Set up a Load Balancer to distribute traffic to the SQL Database.

Answer: B

Explanation: To restrict access to an Azure SQL Database to specific subnets within a VNet using service endpoints, you need to enable service endpoints for Azure SQL Database on those specific subnets. By doing so, you extend the identity of the VNet to the Azure SQL Database service. This allows only the resources within the specified subnets to access the SQL Database, enhancing security by limiting exposure and access to the database to only the intended subnets. This is a common practice to secure access to PaaS services in Azure.

Q65: An organization is planning to use service endpoints to secure access to its Azure Blob Storage. They want to ensure that only traffic from their VNets can access the storage account, while any other traffic, including internet traffic, is denied. What should be configured on the storage account to fulfill this requirement?

A) Set the public access level to 'Private' on the storage account.

B) Implement a virtual network service endpoint for the storage account.

C) Enable a firewall rule on the storage account to allow traffic from specific IP ranges.

D) Use a private endpoint for the storage account.

E) Configure a shared access signature (SAS) with restricted permissions.

F) Enable traffic analytics to monitor access to the storage account.

Answer: B

Explanation: To secure Azure Blob Storage such that only traffic from specific VNets is allowed, service endpoints should be configured. By enabling a virtual network service endpoint for the storage account, the storage service will only accept traffic from the VNets that have been specified in the service endpoint configuration. This ensures that internet traffic is denied, and only the resources within those VNets can access the storage account. This approach leverages Azure's backbone network to secure the connection and restricts access to the storage account, ensuring compliance with security requirements.

Q66: A global e-commerce company is experiencing high latency issues with its web application, which serves customers from different continents. The company uses Azure Front Door to manage traffic efficiently. They have recently expanded their operations to include a new data center in Asia, but customers from Asia still experience significant delays. The company wants to optimize their Azure Front Door configuration to ensure lower latency and high availability for their global user base. They need to efficiently route user requests to the nearest and most responsive backend. Which feature of Azure Front Door should they configure to achieve this goal?

A) Caching rules

B) Session affinity

C) Health probes

D) Priority-based routing

E) Geo-filtering

F) Latency-based routing

Answer: F

Explanation: Azure Front Door offers several routing methods, and latency-based routing is specifically designed to direct user requests to the backend that provides the lowest latency. This is particularly useful for applications that serve a global audience, as it ensures that users are connected to the closest and most responsive data center. By configuring latency-based routing, the company can minimize the delay experienced by users, especially those in newly added regions like Asia. This approach balances the load across all available backends while prioritizing user experience by reducing latency.

Q67: You are tasked with setting up Azure Front Door for a multi-region application. The application must ensure high availability and automatically failover to another region if the primary region becomes unavailable. Which Azure Front Door configuration option should you use to ensure seamless failover?

A) WAF (Web Application Firewall) policies

B) URL rewrite

C) Session affinity

D) Custom domain configuration

E) Application Gateway integration

F) Priority-based routing

Answer: F

Explanation: Priority-based routing in Azure Front Door enables the configuration of multiple backends with assigned priorities. In this setup, the primary backend is given the highest priority, while secondary backends are assigned lower priorities. If the primary backend becomes unavailable due to failures or outages, Azure Front Door automatically routes the traffic to the next available backend based on the configured priorities. This ensures high availability and uninterrupted service for users. By using priority-based routing, you can effectively manage failover and ensure that your application remains accessible even in the event of regional failures.

Q68: While configuring Azure Front Door, you need to ensure that certain requests are directed to specific backends based on the country of origin of the request. Which feature should you implement to achieve this?

A) Path-based routing

B) Rate limiting

C) Geo-filtering

D) URL redirection

E) Health probes

F) Session persistence

Answer: C

Explanation: Geo-filtering in Azure Front Door allows you to create rules that direct traffic based on the geographical location of the client request. This is useful for scenarios where you want to comply with regional regulations, provide localized content, or optimize performance by directing users to region-specific backends. By configuring geo-filtering rules, you can control which backends serve requests from different countries, ensuring that users are routed according to your specified geographic logic. This feature enhances the flexibility and control over how traffic is managed in a global deployment scenario.

Q69: A multinational corporation uses Azure Front Door to manage its web traffic and wants to implement a strategy to cache static content closer to its users to improve load times. However, they need to ensure that dynamic content is always fetched directly from the backend. Which Azure Front Door feature should be configured to achieve this balance between caching and real-time data retrieval?

A) Caching rules

B) Geo-filtering

C) Health monitoring

D) Session affinity

E) Application Gateway integration

F) Custom domain configuration

Answer: A

Explanation: Caching rules in Azure Front Door allow you to specify how content is cached and served to users. By setting up caching rules, you can define which types of content should be cached and for how long. For static content like images, scripts, and stylesheets, caching can be enabled to reduce load times and bandwidth usage. For dynamic content, caching can be bypassed to ensure users receive the most up-to-date information directly from the backend. This combination of caching and real-time retrieval ensures that users have a fast and responsive experience while maintaining the accuracy of dynamic data.

Q70: True or False: Azure Front Door can be configured to perform SSL termination at the edge of Microsoft's global network, which helps reduce latency and offload SSL processing from your backend servers.

A) True

B) False

Answer: A

Explanation: Azure Front Door supports SSL termination at the edge of Microsoft's global network. This means that incoming SSL/TLS connections are decrypted at the edge locations, reducing the processing burden on your backend servers and potentially lowering latency by offloading encryption and decryption processes. By terminating SSL at the edge, Front Door can efficiently handle secure connections and serve content more quickly to users, improving overall performance and user experience. This feature is especially beneficial in scenarios where secure content delivery and low latency are critical requirements.

Q71: A multinational corporation is in the process of migrating its on-premises applications to Azure. They require a secure and efficient authentication mechanism that integrates with their existing Microsoft Entra ID (formerly Azure Active Directory) setup. The company has offices in multiple countries and needs to ensure that the authentication process is both resilient and respects regional data compliance regulations. Additionally, they wish to implement conditional access policies to enhance security. Which Azure service should they configure to best meet these requirements? ---

A) Azure Multi-Factor Authentication (MFA)

B) Azure AD Connect Health

C) Azure AD Application Proxy

D) Azure AD Privileged Identity Management

E) Azure AD Conditional Access

F) Azure AD B2C

Answer: E

Explanation: Azure AD Conditional Access is the most suitable service for this scenario as it provides a robust way to apply security policies based on user-specific conditions and signals. This service allows businesses to enforce policies based on user location, device state, and application sensitivity, thus ensuring compliance with regional data protection regulations. By integrating Conditional Access with Microsoft Entra ID, the company can ensure a secure authentication process while managing the requirements across different regions. Azure Multi-Factor Authentication, though enhancing security, does not directly handle conditional policies. Azure AD Application Proxy and other options do not specifically address the need for conditional and regional compliance authentication policies.

Q72: True or False? Microsoft Entra ID supports integrating with third-party identity providers to enable single sign-on (SSO) for non-Microsoft applications.

A) True

B) False

Answer: A

Explanation: Microsoft Entra ID does support integration with third-party identity providers through federation protocols such as SAML, OAuth, and OpenID Connect. This allows organizations to extend their single sign-on capabilities beyond Microsoft applications, enabling a seamless authentication experience for users across a wide range of applications. Through these integrations, companies can provide secure and efficient access to both on-premises and cloud applications, using a centralized identity management system.

Q73: A company wants to implement passwordless authentication for its Azure environment to enhance security and user experience. Which authentication method should they use to achieve this goal while leveraging Microsoft Entra ID? ---

A) Security Questions

B) Microsoft Authenticator App

C) Biometric Authentication through Windows Hello

D) Email Verification

E) SMS OTP (One-Time Password)

F) Hardware Tokens

Answer: C

Explanation: Biometric Authentication through Windows Hello is the recommended method for achieving passwordless authentication in Azure environments managed by Microsoft Entra ID. Windows Hello uses biometric data such as fingerprints or facial recognition, which enhances security by eliminating the reliance on passwords. This method not only increases security but also significantly improves user experience by providing a faster and more convenient authentication process. Other methods like SMS OTP or the Microsoft

Authenticator App require user actions that still involve passwords or additional steps, whereas Windows Hello provides a true passwordless experience.

Q74: An organization is setting up a conditional access policy in Microsoft Entra ID to require multi-factor authentication only when users access the corporate network from outside the trusted locations. Which setting should they configure to define trusted locations in the Conditional Access policy? ---

A) Named Locations

B) User Risk Policy

C) Sign-in Risk Policy

D) Device Platforms

E) Session Controls

F) Location-based Segmentation

Answer: A

Explanation: To define trusted locations in a Conditional Access policy, the organization needs to configure Named Locations. Named Locations are used in Conditional Access policies to specify the IP addresses or ranges that are considered safe or trusted. By setting up these locations, the organization can enforce multi-factor authentication only when users attempt to access resources from outside these defined trusted locations, ensuring security while minimizing unnecessary authentication prompts. The other options do not specifically configure trusted locations within Conditional Access policies.

Q75: A financial services company needs to ensure that all Azure resources are accessed securely using policies that consider user locations, device states, and sign-in risks. Which advanced feature of Microsoft Entra ID should they leverage to fulfill this requirement?

A) Azure AD Identity Protection

B) Azure AD Domain Services

C) Azure AD B2B

D) Azure AD Connect

E) Azure AD Conditional Access

F) Azure AD Self-Service Password Reset

Answer: E

Explanation: Azure AD Conditional Access is the advanced feature designed to handle complex security requirements by evaluating signals such as user location, device state, and sign-in risk before granting access to resources. This feature allows organizations like the financial services company to create policies that ensure secure access, taking into account various conditions and threats. It provides a dynamic and adaptive approach to security, allowing for the enforcement of appropriate access controls based on real-time risk assessment, which is crucial for industries with stringent security needs such as financial services. Azure AD Identity Protection focuses on detecting and responding to identity risks, but Conditional Access is specifically designed for enforcing access policies.

Q76: A multinational corporation, XYZ Corp, is in the process of setting up a hybrid cloud architecture. They have a primary data center in New York and have established an ExpressRoute connection to Azure. They now need to configure Azure private peering to securely extend their on-premises network into Azure with optimal performance. The network team has decided to use Azure Virtual Network Gateway for this purpose. They need to ensure that the routing is properly configured so that the traffic is routed through private peering instead of going over the public internet. What is the correct sequence of steps to configure Azure private peering for their ExpressRoute circuit?

A) Create a virtual network gateway, configure the routing table, provision ExpressRoute circuit, and then configure private peering.

B) Provision the ExpressRoute circuit, create a virtual network gateway, configure private peering, and then configure the routing table.

C) Configure private peering, provision ExpressRoute circuit, create a virtual network gateway, and then configure the routing table.

D) Create a virtual network gateway, provision ExpressRoute circuit, configure private peering, and then configure the routing table.

E) Provision the ExpressRoute circuit, configure the routing table, create a virtual network gateway, and then configure private peering.

F) Configure the routing table, provision the ExpressRoute circuit, create a virtual network gateway, and then configure private peering.

Answer: B

Explanation: Configuring Azure private peering involves several key steps to ensure the network traffic flows correctly between on-premises and Azure. The first step is to provision the ExpressRoute circuit, which provides a dedicated connection to Azure. Next, a virtual network gateway must be created in Azure to connect the on-premises network to the Azure Virtual Network. Once the gateway is established, private peering can be configured to allow private IP addresses to be used between Azure and on-premises resources. Lastly, the routing table needs to be configured to ensure that traffic is properly routed through the ExpressRoute connection rather than the public internet. This sequence ensures that all necessary components are correctly configured for seamless and secure connectivity.

Q77: When configuring Azure private peering, which of the following statements is true?

A) Private peering allows for IP address overlapping between Azure and on-premises resources.

B) You must use a separate ExpressRoute circuit for each Azure region.

Answer: B

Explanation: Azure private peering does not allow IP address overlapping; the IP address space used for Azure resources must be unique and not conflict with on-premises addresses. This is crucial to ensure proper routing and prevent any network issues. A single ExpressRoute circuit can indeed be used to connect to multiple Azure regions, but it requires enabling Global Reach and proper configuration. However, the question asks for a true statement, which is B, as without such configurations, separate circuits would typically be required.

Q78: To configure Azure private peering, a network engineer must assign a VLAN ID to the peering. What is the valid VLAN ID range that can be used for this configuration?

A) 0-4095

B) 1-4094

C) 2-4093

D) 1-4095

E) 1-4096

F) 2-4094

Answer: B

Explanation: When configuring Azure private peering, the VLAN ID is an integral part of the setup. Azure requires a VLAN ID in the range of 1-4094. This range is standard for VLAN configurations, where 0 and 4095 are reserved for specific purposes and are not typically used for customer-assigned VLANs. VLAN ID 0 is used for priority tagging, while 4095 is reserved for internal use.

Q79: An organization has set up Azure private peering, but they are experiencing unexpected traffic patterns where some traffic is still passing over the public internet. What could be a potential cause of this issue?

A) Incorrect VLAN ID assignment

B) Misconfigured routing table

C) Insufficient bandwidth allocation

D) Incorrect subnet mask configuration

E) Overlapping IP address spaces

F) Incorrect ExpressRoute circuit provisioning

Answer: B

Explanation: A misconfigured routing table is a common cause for unexpected traffic patterns in Azure private peering setups. If the routing table entries do not correctly prioritize the ExpressRoute paths or if there are missing routes, traffic may default to the public internet instead of using the private peering connection. This emphasizes the importance of ensuring that the routing table is meticulously configured to direct traffic through the desired paths, based on the organization's network design policies.

Q80: In the context of Azure private peering, which Azure PowerShell command is used to retrieve the details of an existing ExpressRoute circuit, including its private peering configuration?

A) Get-AzExpressRouteCircuit

B) Get-AzVirtualNetworkPeering

C) Get-AzExpressRouteCircuitPeering

D) Get-AzNetworkInterface

E) Get-AzVirtualNetworkGateway

F) Get-AzCircuitPeering

Answer: A

Explanation: The Get-AzExpressRouteCircuit command in Azure PowerShell is used to retrieve details about an existing ExpressRoute circuit, including its private peering configuration. It provides comprehensive information about the circuit, such as its provisioning state, service provider, and peering settings. This command is particularly useful for administrators who need to review the configuration or diagnose issues related to the ExpressRoute circuit. The other commands listed are related to different Azure networking components and do not provide the specific details required for ExpressRoute circuit peering.

Q81: Fabrikam, Inc. is an e-commerce enterprise experiencing performance issues with their online store, especially during peak traffic hours. They are leveraging Azure Front Door to improve their global reach. However, they notice that static content such as images and CSS files are not being delivered efficiently, resulting in increased load times. To address this, they intend to implement caching strategies that will optimize the delivery of static content. Fabrikam's IT team needs to configure caching rules to ensure that static content is cached at the edge locations for longer periods, reducing the load on the origin server and improving user experience. Which Azure Front Door feature should they utilize to achieve optimal caching for static content?

A) Configure session affinity

B) Enable dynamic site acceleration

C) Set custom caching rules

D) Use Web Application Firewall (WAF) policies

E) Enable global load balancing

F) Configure URL redirection

Answer: C

Explanation: To optimize the delivery of static content using Azure Front Door, custom caching rules should be configured. Custom caching rules allow the IT team to define how long specific content types should be cached at the edge locations. This is particularly beneficial for static content like images and CSS, which do not change frequently. By setting longer cache expiration times for these assets, Fabrikam can significantly reduce the load on the origin server and improve page load times for end-users. Custom caching rules in Azure Front Door provide granular control over cache settings, ensuring that the content delivery is efficient and tailored to the specific needs of the business while maintaining performance during peak traffic periods.

Q82: A system administrator wants to configure Azure Content Delivery Network (CDN) to cache content based on query string parameters. What method should be used to ensure the CDN caches different versions of a resource based on specific query strings?

A) Use the "No Query String" caching behavior

B) Implement "Cache Every Unique URL" setting

C) Enable global HTTP caching

D) Configure a custom domain

E) Utilize "Bypass Cache" mode

F) Set up priority caching rules

Answer: B

Explanation: To cache content based on query string parameters, the "Cache Every Unique URL" setting should be used. This setting allows the Azure CDN to treat each unique combination of URL and query string as a separate cacheable item. This is essential when different query string parameters result in different content, ensuring that users receive the correct version of the resource based on the query string they provide. This approach prevents cache collisions and delivers accurate content to the end-users by caching each unique URL with its associated query parameters separately.

Q83: True or False: Azure Front Door supports caching dynamic content by default.

A) True

B) False

Answer: B

Explanation: By default, Azure Front Door does not cache dynamic content. It is primarily designed to cache static content to improve performance and reduce the load on origin servers. Dynamic content, which changes frequently or is unique to user sessions, is not cached by default because caching it could result in delivering outdated or incorrect content to users. However, organizations can configure specific rules to cache certain types of dynamic content if it is deemed cacheable and does not compromise the integrity of the data being delivered.

Q84: An organization uses Azure Front Door for their web application. They want to ensure that certain sensitive content is never cached at the edge and is always fetched directly from the origin server. Which option should they choose to implement this requirement?

A) Configure caching rules with "Bypass Cache" mode

B) Set up a custom origin

C) Use a different content delivery network

D) Enable caching with short expiration

E) Implement global HTTPS caching

F) Utilize Azure Traffic Manager

Answer: A

Explanation: To ensure that certain sensitive content is never cached, the "Bypass Cache" mode should be configured in Azure Front Door's caching rules. This mode overrides the default caching behavior, ensuring that specific content types or paths are always fetched directly from the origin server and never stored at the edge. This approach is essential for content that must remain up-to-date and secure, such as user-specific data or frequently changing information. By utilizing the "Bypass Cache" mode, the organization can maintain data accuracy and compliance while leveraging the benefits of Azure Front Door for other content types.

Q85: A global company is using Azure CDN to distribute large media files. They notice that users in certain regions experience slower downloads compared to others. To address this issue, they want to implement a caching strategy that reduces latency and improves download speeds for those regions. Which configuration option should they consider?

A) Create a geo-filtering rule

B) Use Azure Traffic Manager

C) Implement a load-balancing policy

D) Enable large file optimization

E) Configure regional caching

F) Set up a custom domain for each region

Answer: E

Explanation: To reduce latency and improve download speeds in specific regions, the company should configure regional caching. Regional caching allows Azure CDN to store copies of files in multiple locations closer to the users, thereby reducing the distance that data must travel and improving access times. This approach is particularly effective for large media files, which can benefit from being cached at multiple geographically distributed points. By implementing regional caching, the company can ensure that users across different regions experience more consistent and faster download speeds, enhancing the overall performance of their CDN deployment.

Q86: Contoso Ltd. is setting up a new infrastructure in Azure and they want to ensure that their virtual network (VNet) can resolve hostnames within their network as well as on the internet. They have decided to use Azure DNS for external domain resolution and need to configure custom DNS settings for their VNet to use an on-premises DNS server for internal resolution. Which step should they take to implement this configuration in Azure?

A) Configure Azure DNS Private Resolver in the VNet.

B) Assign a Network Security Group (NSG) to the VNet.

C) Set up a DNS forwarder in Azure.

D) Define a custom DNS server under the VNet settings.

E) Use Azure Bastion for DNS traffic.

F) Enable Azure AD Domain Services for DNS management.

Answer: D

Explanation: To resolve hostnames both internally and externally, Contoso Ltd. needs to configure their VNet to use custom DNS settings. By defining a custom DNS server in the VNet settings, they can specify their on-premises DNS server for internal resolution. This allows their Azure VNet to forward DNS queries for internal domains to the on-premises DNS server, while external queries can be handled by Azure DNS or another specified external DNS service. Azure DNS Private Resolver is not necessary because it is primarily used for resolving private DNS zone records, and NSGs, Bastion, and Azure AD Domain Services do not directly manage DNS settings for VNets.

Q87: A company has set up multiple VNets across different Azure regions and wants to ensure consistent DNS resolution for their Azure resources. What is the most effective way to manage DNS settings across all VNets?

A) Use Azure Traffic Manager to manage DNS across VNets.

B) Deploy an Azure DNS Private Zone shared across all VNets.

C) Configure each VNet to use the default Azure-provided DNS.

D) Enable VNet peering and rely on automatic DNS resolution.

E) Implement Azure Front Door for DNS management.

F) Use Azure ExpressRoute to connect VNets for DNS resolution.

Answer: B

Explanation: The most effective method to ensure consistent DNS resolution across multiple VNets is to use an Azure DNS Private Zone. By deploying a private DNS zone and linking it to all VNets, a company can centrally manage DNS records and ensure that resources in any VNet can resolve names of resources in other VNets seamlessly. This approach avoids the need for external dependencies and ensures that DNS resolution is consistent and managed within the Azure environment. Azure Traffic Manager, Azure Front Door, and ExpressRoute do not directly manage DNS resolution across VNets.

Q88: True or False: Azure VNets can be configured to use both Azure-provided DNS and custom DNS servers simultaneously.

A) True

B) False

Answer: B

Explanation: Azure VNets cannot be configured to use both Azure-provided DNS and custom DNS servers at the same time. When a custom DNS server is specified in a VNet configuration, it overrides the Azure-provided DNS settings. Azure-provided DNS is automatically used if no custom DNS server is specified. This means that if you want to use a custom DNS server, you must specify it, and the built-in Azure DNS will not be used for that VNet unless you revert the settings.

Q89: Fabrikam Inc. needs to ensure DNS queries from their Azure VNet to their on-premises network are encrypted. Which solution should they implement to achieve this?

A) Configure a DNS-over-HTTPS (DoH) endpoint in Azure.

B) Set up a VPN connection between Azure and the on-premises network.

C) Use Azure ExpressRoute for secure DNS traffic.

D) Deploy an Azure DNS Private Resolver.

E) Enable Azure Firewall to filter DNS traffic.

F) Use Azure Bastion for secure DNS resolution.

Answer: B

Explanation: To encrypt DNS queries from an Azure VNet to an on-premises network, Fabrikam Inc. should set up a VPN connection. A VPN ensures that all traffic, including DNS queries, is encrypted between the Azure environment and on-premises networks. While DNS-over-HTTPS (DoH) is a method to encrypt DNS queries, it is not yet natively supported in Azure for VNet DNS queries. Azure ExpressRoute can also be used for a private connection, but VPNs are more commonly used for encryption purposes specifically for DNS traffic. Azure Firewall and Bastion do not provide DNS encryption capabilities.

Q90: Adventure Works is expanding its operations and has multiple VNets connected through VNet peering. They want to ensure that DNS resolution is consistent and seamless across these VNets. Which Azure feature should they use to achieve this?

A) Configure each VNet to use Azure DNS Private Resolver.

B) Set up a DNS conditional forwarder in each VNet.

C) Deploy an Azure DNS Private Zone and link it to all VNets.

D) Utilize Azure Traffic Manager for DNS queries.

E) Implement a custom DNS server in one VNet and peer it with others.

F) Use Azure Bastion to manage DNS settings centrally.

Answer: C

Explanation: Adventure Works can achieve seamless DNS resolution across multiple VNets by deploying an Azure DNS Private Zone and linking it to all VNets involved. This configuration allows them to manage DNS records centrally within Azure, ensuring that resources in any VNet can resolve names of resources across all other VNets. Azure DNS Private Resolver and Traffic Manager do not provide the necessary DNS resolution capabilities in this scenario, and relying on a single custom DNS server or Bastion for centralized DNS management is not an optimal solution.

Q91: A multinational corporation has deployed several mission-critical applications across its data centers in different continents. They utilize Azure ExpressRoute to ensure a stable and secure connection between their on-premises infrastructure and Azure services. The IT team is tasked with ensuring that data traffic over ExpressRoute is encrypted to meet compliance requirements for sensitive data transmission. They must choose a solution that integrates seamlessly with their existing setup and minimizes any potential latency issues. Which solution should the IT team implement to encrypt the data over ExpressRoute?

A) Use Azure Virtual WAN with IPsec encryption.

B) Configure Azure Point-to-Site VPN with RADIUS authentication.

C) Implement Azure Traffic Manager with SSL encryption.

D) Enable ExpressRoute Direct with MACsec encryption.

E) Configure Azure Site-to-Site VPN with dual redundancy.

F) Use Azure Application Gateway with TLS termination.

Answer: A

Explanation: Azure Virtual WAN with IPsec encryption provides a scalable solution to secure data across the network. By leveraging Virtual WAN, organizations can create a unified network architecture that efficiently manages traffic flow between Azure regions and on-premises data centers. IPsec encryption offers a robust method for encrypting data over ExpressRoute, ensuring compliance with regulatory standards without significantly impacting latency. This approach is particularly beneficial for multinational corporations where data privacy and speed are critical. Other options such as SSL or TLS encryption may not be directly applicable or efficient for encrypting traffic over ExpressRoute, and MACsec is typically used for layer 2 encryption on ExpressRoute Direct, which may not cater to all organizational setups.

Q92: You are an Azure network engineer responsible for ensuring all data transmitted over ExpressRoute circuits is encrypted. You read about a feature that allows you to encrypt data at the link layer (Layer 2) when using ExpressRoute Direct. Is this feature available for standard ExpressRoute circuits?

A) True

B) False

Answer: B

Explanation: The link layer encryption feature, known as MACsec, is exclusively available for ExpressRoute Direct circuits, not for standard ExpressRoute circuits. ExpressRoute Direct provides dedicated connectivity and allows organizations to establish a physical connection to Azure at 10 Gbps or 100 Gbps. It supports MACsec to encrypt data at Layer 2, offering an additional layer of security. Standard ExpressRoute circuits, which are shared connections through a service provider, do not support MACsec encryption. Instead, customers typically rely on IPsec encryption for data privacy over standard ExpressRoute circuits.

Q93: You are designing a solution to ensure encrypted traffic over Azure ExpressRoute for your company. The company has strict compliance requirements that necessitate using industry-standard encryption protocols. Which of the following services should you integrate with ExpressRoute to meet these encryption requirements?

A) Azure Firewall

B) Azure Load Balancer

C) Azure VPN Gateway

D) Azure Bastion

E) Azure Content Delivery Network (CDN)

F) Azure Front Door

Answer: C

Explanation: The Azure VPN Gateway is designed to establish secure network connections and can be used to encrypt traffic over Azure ExpressRoute through IPsec. By configuring a Site-to-Site VPN in conjunction with ExpressRoute, you can ensure that the data is encrypted end-to-end across the network. This setup is particularly useful for meeting stringent compliance requirements, as IPsec is a widely recognized industry standard for secure data transmission. Other services like Azure Firewall or Load Balancer are primarily focused on network security and load distribution rather than traffic encryption over ExpressRoute.

Q94: A global financial services firm is using Azure to host its applications and requires end-to-end encryption for all its data, including data transmitted over ExpressRoute. The firm has a dedicated ExpressRoute connection with high throughput requirements. They need a solution that not only encrypts data but also maintains high performance. What is the most suitable method to achieve this?

A) Implement an Azure Application Gateway with Web Application Firewall (WAF).

B) Utilize Azure ExpressRoute with a Site-to-Site VPN connection for IPsec encryption.

C) Set up Azure Traffic Manager to manage encrypted endpoints.

D) Use Azure Key Vault to encrypt data at rest.

E) Enable MACsec on ExpressRoute Direct.

F) Deploy Azure Security Center for network encryption.

Answer: B

Explanation: Setting up a Site-to-Site VPN connection in conjunction with Azure ExpressRoute is a proven method to achieve IPsec encryption of data traveling over the ExpressRoute. This approach ensures that all data traffic is encrypted end-to-end while traversing the network. It is particularly suitable for financial services firms with high throughput requirements, as it provides robust encryption without significantly impacting performance. While MACsec is an option for ExpressRoute Direct, it is not applicable for all ExpressRoute setups. Other solutions like Azure Application Gateway or Key Vault focus on different aspects of security, such as application-level protection or data-at-rest encryption, and do not address the need for encrypting traffic over ExpressRoute.

Q95: An organization has multiple branch offices connected to Azure via ExpressRoute. The IT security team needs to ensure that all data transmitted between branch offices and Azure is encrypted. They require a solution that can be centrally managed and offers flexibility in scaling with minimal impact on existing network architecture. Which Azure service or combination of services should they use?

A) Azure Site Recovery with encrypted replication.

B) Azure ExpressRoute with Network Security Groups (NSGs).

C) Azure Virtual WAN with IPsec-enabled branch connections.

D) Azure Backup with encrypted data transfer.

E) Azure Traffic Manager with global load balancing.

F) Azure DDoS Protection with encrypted data paths.

Answer: C

Explanation: Azure Virtual WAN with IPsec-enabled branch connections provides a centralized and scalable solution for encrypting data transmitted between branch offices and Azure over ExpressRoute. By leveraging Virtual WAN, organizations can manage network connectivity and encryption policies from a single interface, which simplifies the administration of secure connections across multiple locations. The use of IPsec ensures that all data traffic is encrypted, thereby meeting security and compliance requirements. This setup is ideal for organizations seeking a flexible and easily scalable network encryption solution that integrates seamlessly with their existing network architecture. Other options like Network Security Groups or Traffic Manager focus on different aspects of network management and do not directly address the need for encrypting data over ExpressRoute.

Q96: A multinational corporation is planning to migrate its on-premises data center to Azure. The company has a strict policy for all internet-bound traffic to be routed through their on-premises firewall for inspection before reaching the internet. During the migration phase, they intend to implement a hybrid network where their Azure VMs must send all outbound internet traffic through their on-premises data center. Given this requirement, which Azure configuration should be implemented to ensure compliance with their corporate policy?

A) Implement Azure Route Tables with a default route pointing to the on-premises VPN gateway.

B) Configure a User-Defined Route (UDR) with a next-hop type of Virtual Network Gateway.

C) Use Azure Traffic Manager to route outbound traffic through the on-premises network.

D) Create a Network Security Group (NSG) rule to allow all internet-bound traffic to the on-premises IP address.

E) Set up an Application Gateway with forced tunneling configured to route traffic to the on-premises network.

F) Enable Azure Firewall to forward all internet-bound traffic to the on-premises data center.

Answer: B

Explanation: Forced tunneling in Azure allows you to redirect all internet-bound traffic from Azure to on-premises, and the correct method to achieve this is to configure a User-Defined Route (UDR) with a next-hop type of Virtual Network Gateway. This configuration will ensure that all traffic destined for the internet is routed back through the on-premises data center, enabling the corporation to enforce its security policies. Azure Route Tables alone are not sufficient because they don't redirect internet-bound traffic by themselves. The Traffic Manager is for routing incoming traffic, not outbound. NSGs are used for filtering traffic but do not control routing. Application Gateway is primarily used for managing and securing incoming HTTP requests, and Azure Firewall would not provide the desired routing to on-premises without the correct UDR setup.

Q97: During the configuration of forced tunneling in Azure, what is the role of the BGP (Border Gateway Protocol) in the context of Azure VPN gateways?

A) BGP is used to automatically propagate default routes across all subnets.

B) BGP allows for dynamic routing between Azure and on-premises networks.

C) BGP is required for configuring forced tunneling on Azure Application Gateways.

D) BGP provides a backup route in case of primary route failure.

E) BGP is used to encrypt all traffic between Azure and on-premises.

F) BGP must be disabled for forced tunneling to function properly.

Answer: B

Explanation: BGP, or Border Gateway Protocol, is essential in Azure when setting up forced tunneling as it allows for dynamic routing between Azure and on-premises networks. With BGP, the Azure VPN gateway can advertise routes to the on-premises network, including the default route (0.0.0.0/0), ensuring that all internet-bound traffic is redirected through the on-premises network. This protocol facilitates automatic updates and changes in the network topology, making it ideal for hybrid cloud environments. BGP is not used for encryption or specifically required for Azure Application Gateways, nor does it inherently provide backup routes, but it does enable more complex, resilient routing configurations.

Q98: True or False? Forced tunneling can be used to route Azure VM traffic to a third-party cloud provider for specific inspection requirements.

A) True

B) False

Answer: B

Explanation: Forced tunneling in Azure is specifically designed to redirect outbound internet traffic from Azure VMs to an on-premises network, not to a third-party cloud provider. This configuration is intended for scenarios where organizations want to utilize their existing on-premises security infrastructure to inspect and filter traffic before it reaches the internet. Routing traffic to a third-party provider would require different configurations and is not the intended use case for Azure's forced tunneling capabilities. Instead, such requirements could potentially be handled by setting up a direct network connection or using a VPN to the third-party cloud, but this falls outside the scope of forced tunneling.

Q99: When setting up forced tunneling in Azure, which component is primarily responsible for defining the route that redirects internet-bound traffic from Azure to on-premises?

A) Azure Network Security Group (NSG)

B) Azure Load Balancer

C) User-Defined Routes (UDR)

D) Azure Traffic Manager

E) Azure Application Gateway

F) Azure Policy

Answer: C

Explanation: User-Defined Routes (UDR) are the primary component used in Azure to define custom routing rules, including those necessary for forced tunneling. By configuring a UDR with a route that directs 0.0.0.0/0 traffic to the Virtual Network Gateway, you effectively force all internet-bound traffic from the Azure virtual network to be forwarded to the on-premises network. NSGs are used for filtering traffic and do not control routing. The Azure Load Balancer and Traffic Manager are used for managing traffic distribution and failover, not routing. Application Gateway is for managing and securing web traffic, and Azure Policy is for governance and compliance, not routing.

Q100: A company has deployed several services within Azure and wants to ensure that all outbound traffic from these services is logged for compliance purposes. The traffic should be routed through their on-premises data center where they have advanced logging solutions. How can this requirement be achieved using Azure's networking features?

A) Configure a VPN Gateway with forced tunneling to direct traffic to the on-premises network.

B) Enable Diagnostics Logs on the Azure Application Gateway.

C) Use Azure Monitor to log all outbound traffic directly.

D) Set up an Azure Load Balancer with outbound rules to the on-premises data center.

E) Deploy an Azure Firewall and configure logging to an Azure Storage account.

F) Implement Azure Traffic Manager with logging enabled.

Answer: A

Explanation: To ensure that all outbound traffic from Azure services is routed through the on-premises data center for logging purposes, configuring a VPN Gateway with forced tunneling is the appropriate solution. Forced tunneling directs all outbound internet traffic from Azure services to the on-premises network, where the company can utilize its advanced logging solutions. While enabling diagnostics logs on Azure services and configuring Azure Monitor can provide logging capabilities, they do not address the requirement to route traffic through on-premises. Azure Load Balancer and Traffic Manager are not designed to route outbound traffic in this manner, and Azure Firewall, although useful for network security, does not inherently route traffic to on-premises without forced tunneling configuration.

Q101: Your company, Contoso Ltd., is deploying a web application in Azure that requires high availability and redundancy. The application is split across two Azure regions, and traffic is managed by an Azure Traffic Manager. To ensure the Traffic Manager routes users to the healthiest endpoint, you need to configure health probes. The traffic should be sent to the primary region unless there are issues, in which case, it should failover to the secondary region. The application endpoints are configured to respond with HTTP status codes 200-399. You need to set up a health probe for the Traffic Manager profile that can effectively monitor the endpoint health. Which configuration should you choose for the health probe?

A) Use an HTTP probe with a path to a specific file that returns a 200 status code.

B) Use a TCP probe on port 80 with a 10-second interval and 5-second timeout.

C) Use an HTTPS probe on port 443 with a path to a default page.

D) Use a custom probe with a 5-second interval and a 20-second timeout.

E) Use a UDP probe on port 123 with a 15-second interval.

F) Use a DNS probe to check the endpoint's domain resolution.

Answer: A

Explanation: In Azure Traffic Manager, HTTP or HTTPS probes are frequently used to check the health of an application endpoint. The probe path should point to a specific file or resource that your application can serve reliably and is expected to return a status code in the 200-399 range. This ensures that the Traffic Manager can accurately assess the health of the endpoint. Option A correctly describes using an HTTP probe with a path to a specific file returning a status code 200, which is ideal for monitoring the availability and health of the web application endpoints. TCP and UDP probes are not suitable for this context as they do not provide the same level of application-specific health information as HTTP/HTTPS probes. A DNS probe would not be applicable in this scenario, as it does not check the application layer health.

Q102: You have configured an HTTP health probe for an Azure Load Balancer. The probe is set to check a specific path on port 80 every 5 seconds with a timeout of 15 seconds and requires two consecutive successful responses to mark the endpoint as healthy. If the endpoint does not respond within 15 seconds for three consecutive checks, what is the state of the endpoint?

A) Healthy

B) Unhealthy

Answer: B

Explanation: In Azure Load Balancer, the health probe determines the health of the backend endpoint based on the criteria specified. The configuration states that the probe checks every 5 seconds and requires two successful responses to mark the endpoint as healthy. However, in this scenario, the endpoint fails to respond within the 15-second timeout for three consecutive checks. As a result, the load balancer deems the endpoint as unhealthy due to the lack of consecutive successful responses. This mechanism ensures that only healthy and responsive endpoints receive traffic, contributing to the overall reliability of the application.

Q103: An organization is utilizing Azure Application Gateway to distribute incoming traffic to a set of backend VMs hosting a web application. To ensure that the gateway routes requests only to healthy VMs, they need to configure a health probe. The application listens on port 8080 and returns a custom status page at "/status" that indicates the server's health with a 200 status code. Which of the following represents the best configuration for the health probe?

A) HTTP probe on port 80 with a path to "/status" and a 5-second interval.

B) TCP probe on port 8080 with a 10-second interval and 15-second timeout.

C) HTTP probe on port 8080 with a path to "/status" and a 30-second interval.

D) HTTPS probe on port 8080 with a path to "/status" and a 5-second interval.

E) HTTP probe on port 8080 with a path to "/" and a 5-second interval.

F) TCP probe on port 443 with a 5-second interval and 10-second timeout.

Answer: C

Explanation: Azure Application Gateway requires the configuration of health probes to monitor the health of backend resources. For a web application listening on port 8080, an HTTP probe is appropriate to inspect the specific status page returning a 200 status code, indicating the health of the server. The probe should be configured to check the "/status" path, as it directly provides health information. A 30-second interval is generally considered a balance between timely detection of failures and minimizing unnecessary probe traffic. Choosing an HTTP probe over TCP allows for more detailed checks at the application layer, ensuring that not just network connectivity but actual service health is verified.

Q104: In a distributed application deployment on Azure, you are tasked with configuring health probes for an Azure Load Balancer that distributes traffic to multiple instances of a service. The service listens on port 8443 and uses SSL/TLS for secure communication. The probe should ensure that it verifies the application-level health, not just network connectivity. What is the best way to configure the health probe?

A) HTTPS probe on port 443 with a path to "/" and a 10-second interval.

B) TCP probe on port 8443 with a 5-second interval and 5-second timeout.

C) HTTPS probe on port 8443 with a path to "/healthcheck" and a 15-second interval.

D) HTTP probe on port 80 with a path to "/healthcheck" and a 10-second interval.

E) UDP probe on port 8443 with a 20-second interval.

F) Custom probe with a 30-second interval and specific application checks.

Answer: C

Explanation: For a service using SSL/TLS on port 8443, the most effective health probe would be an HTTPS probe that checks an application-specific path, such as "/healthcheck". This ensures that the probe verifies not just connectivity but also the proper functioning of the application itself, which listens on the secure port. The HTTPS protocol is necessary to correctly handle SSL/TLS communication, ensuring that the probe can negotiate the proper encryption and receive a valid response. A 15-second interval strikes a reasonable balance between timely health checks and network overhead, making it suitable for production environments where both performance and reliability are critical.

Q105: A company is deploying a legacy application in Azure using an internal load balancer. The application does not have a built-in health check endpoint, and the team decides to use a TCP probe instead. The probe is configured on port 5500 with a 10-second interval and a 5-second timeout. Which statement accurately describes the probe's behavior and limitations?

A) The TCP probe will fail if the application does not return a 200 status code.

B) The TCP probe can only determine network connectivity, not application health.

C) The TCP probe will automatically adjust the interval based on network latency.

D) The TCP probe will provide detailed application-level health information.

E) The TCP probe cannot be used with an internal load balancer.

F) The TCP probe will balance traffic based on the least connections method.

Answer: B

Explanation: A TCP probe is suitable for scenarios where the application does not expose a specific health check endpoint. It operates by attempting to establish a TCP connection on the specified port. If the connection is successful, the endpoint is considered healthy. However, TCP probes only verify network connectivity and cannot assess application-level health, such as whether the application is correctly processing requests or returning the expected content. This limitation means that while a TCP probe can ensure the service is reachable, it cannot guarantee that the application is fully operational or returning the correct responses. This is an important consideration for ensuring high availability and reliability in production environments.

Q106: Contoso Ltd., a global e-commerce company, is leveraging Azure Application Gateway to manage web traffic for its online store. Their IT team needs to configure custom HTTP settings to improve security and performance. The team needs to enforce client certificate authentication, modify the request headers to include a custom header for tracking purposes, and ensure HTTP/2 is enabled for enhanced speed. What is the most appropriate configuration step the team should take to achieve these requirements?

A) Use Azure Policy to enforce HTTP/2 and manage custom headers.

B) Configure a listener with client certificate authentication and modify the backend HTTP settings to include a custom header.

C) Set up an Azure Front Door service to handle custom headers and enable HTTP/2.

D) Enable Web Application Firewall (WAF) on the Application Gateway and adjust HTTP settings.

E) Use Network Security Groups (NSGs) to enforce client certificate requirements and custom headers.

F) Deploy an Azure Load Balancer to handle the HTTP/2 and custom header configurations.

Answer: B

Explanation: Custom HTTP settings in Azure Application Gateway allow you to modify how requests are handled between the gateway and the backend pool. To enforce client certificate authentication, you configure the listener to require client certificates. You can also modify the HTTP settings to add custom request headers, which is useful for tracking and logging purposes. HTTP/2 can be enabled within the HTTP settings of the Application Gateway, ensuring the benefits of multiplexing and header compression. Azure Policy, NSGs, and Azure Load Balancer are not suitable for handling direct HTTP setting configurations on Application Gateway. Azure Front Door, while capable of handling HTTP/2 and custom headers, is a different service and not the focus for this particular setup.

Q107: A company needs to configure their Azure Application Gateway to handle sensitive data securely. They are required to disable the 'Use for App services' option in the HTTP settings to ensure traffic is only routed through their internal API endpoints. What is the primary reason for disabling this option?

A) To ensure that traffic is encrypted end-to-end using Azure's default certificates.

B) To prevent traffic from being routed to public App Service endpoints inadvertently.

C) To enable automatic scaling based on traffic load.

D) To support the use of custom domains for backend APIs.

E) To reduce latency by using the shortest routing path.

F) To enable access logging for compliance purposes.

Answer: B

Explanation: The 'Use for App services' option in Azure Application Gateway's HTTP settings allows traffic to be routed to Azure App Service endpoints directly. Disabling this option ensures that traffic is confined to internal API endpoints only, preventing any accidental routing to public App Service endpoints. This is crucial for maintaining the security of sensitive data by ensuring that it does not leave the internal network. This option does not directly impact encryption, scaling, domain support, or latency, but it does help maintain a controlled routing environment.

Q108: True or False? Enabling session affinity in Azure Application Gateway HTTP settings allows incoming requests from a client to be distributed evenly across multiple backend servers to optimize performance.

A) True

B) False

Answer: B

Explanation: Enabling session affinity, also known as "cookie-based session affinity," in Azure Application Gateway does not distribute requests evenly across multiple backend servers. Instead, it ensures that all requests from a specific client session are directed to the same backend server. This feature is useful for applications where user session data is stored on a particular server, allowing for a consistent user experience. It does not optimize performance through even distribution but rather maintains session state consistency.

Q109: The IT team at Fabrikam Inc. is configuring an Azure Application Gateway to support a new microservice architecture. They need to ensure that all backend services are reachable via HTTPS and that the gateway performs SSL offloading. Additionally, they want to add a custom health probe to monitor service availability. Which configuration should they implement in the HTTP settings?

A) Configure SSL offloading, enable session affinity, and use default health probes.

B) Enable HTTP/2, configure SSL offloading, and set up a custom health probe.

C) Enable session affinity, use default probes, and require server name indication (SNI).

D) Set up SSL bridging, enable HTTP/2, and use default health probes.

E) Configure SSL termination, add a custom health probe, and require SNI.

F) Enable SSL end-to-end encryption, use default health probes, and modify request headers.

Answer: E

Explanation: For Azure Application Gateway to support HTTPS connections to backend services while performing SSL offloading, SSL termination should be configured. This involves decrypting incoming SSL requests at the gateway and then forwarding them to the backend in unencrypted form (or optionally re-encrypting). Adding a custom health probe is essential to actively monitor the availability and health of specific backend services, allowing for more granular control compared to default probes. Requiring SNI ensures that proper certificates are used for communication with each backend service, especially in a multi-tenant or microservices environment.

Q110: A retail company is deploying an Azure Application Gateway to improve their web application's scalability and security. They are particularly concerned about the latency introduced by SSL handshakes during peak traffic times. Which HTTP setting configuration would be most effective in minimizing latency related to SSL handshakes?

A) Enable HTTP/2 to reduce latency through multiplexing.

B) Configure session affinity to maintain persistent connections.

C) Implement SSL offloading to terminate SSL sessions at the gateway.

D) Use backend pools with auto-scaling enabled.

E) Enable connection draining to balance traffic load.

F) Deploy multiple listeners to handle different SSL certificates.

Answer: C

Explanation: Implementing SSL offloading on Azure Application Gateway can significantly reduce latency associated with SSL handshakes. By terminating the SSL session at the gateway, the need to repeatedly perform SSL/TLS negotiations between the client and backend servers is eliminated. This not only reduces latency but also decreases the load on backend servers, allowing them to focus on processing application requests rather than handling SSL handshakes. While HTTP/2 and session affinity provide other performance benefits, they do not directly address SSL handshake latency. Connection draining and multiple listeners are not directly relevant to SSL handshake latency optimization.

Q111: Contoso Ltd. is expanding its cloud infrastructure to include more comprehensive load balancing solutions in Azure. They have an application that requires high availability across multiple regions. As part of their configuration, they need to set up Azure Front Door to manage traffic efficiently. The company has a requirement to inspect the incoming HTTP requests and route them based on the URL path specified. Which Azure Front Door feature should Contoso Ltd. leverage to achieve this URL-based routing? ---

A) Custom Domain HTTPS

B) Caching Rules

C) Session Affinity

D) URL Path-Based Routing Rules

E) Web Application Firewall (WAF)

F) Priority-based Routing

Answer: D

Explanation: URL Path-Based Routing Rules in Azure Front Door allow for routing decisions based on the URL path of the incoming request. This feature is crucial for applications that need to direct traffic to different back-end pools depending on specific segments of the URL path. By leveraging this feature, Contoso Ltd. can efficiently manage and direct their traffic to appropriate services or endpoints based on URL patterns, ensuring that requests are processed by the correct backend infrastructure.

Q112: A company is configuring an Azure Application Gateway with multiple listeners to manage HTTP and HTTPS traffic for their web applications. They need to set up a listener to handle secure traffic using a specific domain name and SSL certificate for secure communication. Which type of listener should they configure? ---

A) Basic Listener

B) Multi-site Listener

C) Path-based Listener

D) Redirection Listener

E) Default Listener

F) Priority Listener

Answer: B

Explanation: A Multi-site Listener in Azure Application Gateway is designed to handle secure traffic for multiple domain names. It allows the configuration of multiple site-specific listeners on a single Application Gateway, each associated with a specific domain name and SSL certificate. This is essential when managing secure communications (HTTPS) across various subdomains or distinct domain names, ensuring that the traffic is directed correctly while maintaining security through SSL.

Q113: A global e-commerce business utilizes Azure Traffic Manager to distribute user requests across multiple geographical locations. They need to configure Traffic Manager to direct users to the endpoint with the lowest latency. Which Traffic Manager routing method should they use to achieve this? ---

A) Priority Routing

B) Weighted Routing

C) Geographic Routing

D) Performance Routing

E) Subnet Routing

F) Round Robin Routing

Answer: D

Explanation: Performance Routing in Azure Traffic Manager is designed to improve the user experience by directing users to the closest endpoint in terms of network latency. This routing method is particularly beneficial for global applications, where minimizing the time it takes for users to connect to resources can significantly enhance performance. By using Performance Routing, the e-commerce business can ensure users are connected to the endpoint that offers the best response time based on their geographical location.

Q114: You are tasked with configuring an Azure Load Balancer to distribute traffic for a set of virtual machines that host the front-end of a web application. The company requires that the load balancer forwards traffic to the virtual machine with the least number of active connections. Which load-balancing algorithm should you select? ---

A) Round Robin

B) Least Connections

C) Source IP Affinity

D) Weighted Round Robin

E) Session Persistence

F) Hash-based Distribution

Answer: B

Explanation: The Least Connections algorithm is used in load balancing to distribute traffic by forwarding requests to the server with the fewest active connections at the time. This method helps balance the load more evenly across the servers by considering the current workload on each server rather than simply rotating requests (as in Round Robin). This is particularly useful for applications that may have varying processing times, ensuring that no single server becomes a bottleneck due to disproportionately high traffic loads.

Q115: True/False: In Azure, a listener configuration can include multiple custom rules for handling different types of HTTP requests, such as distinguishing between GET and POST methods.

A) True

B) False

Answer: A

Explanation: In Azure, particularly when configuring Application Gateway, a listener can be enhanced with custom rules that allow for the differentiation of HTTP requests based on methods like GET, POST, PUT, etc. These rules can be used to direct traffic to different back-end pools or apply specific processing logic depending on the HTTP method, path, or headers, providing a flexible and granular approach to traffic management within an application's architecture. This capability is crucial in designing sophisticated application delivery strategies that require tailored handling of different types of requests.

Q116: A multinational corporation, Contoso Ltd., is expanding its cloud infrastructure to improve connectivity between its European and North American data centers. They have decided to use Microsoft Azure's ExpressRoute service to establish a private connection. Contoso plans to configure Microsoft Peering to enable communication between their on-premises networks and Azure resources such as Azure Services and Office 365. Before proceeding, Contoso's network team must ensure that they meet all prerequisites and configure the routing domains correctly. They need to understand which address prefixes should be advertised to Microsoft and ensure compliance with Azure's requirements. What address prefixes should Contoso use for Microsoft Peering?

A) Public IP addresses owned by Contoso that are registered in an RIR and are not reserved by Azure.

B) Private IP addresses within the 10.0.0.0/8 range.

C) A mix of public and private IP addresses.

D) Public IP addresses that are not registered in any RIR.

E) Public IP addresses owned by Contoso that are registered in an RIR but are used in Azure Virtual Networks.

F) Any IP address, as long as it is not reserved by Azure.

Answer: A

Explanation: Microsoft Peering requires the use of public IP addresses that are owned by the customer and registered with a Regional Internet Registry (RIR). This ensures that the IP addresses are globally unique and routable over the internet. These addresses cannot be private IP addresses or IP addresses that are not registered, as this would violate Azure's policies and potentially lead to routing conflicts. The IP addresses must also not be reserved for Azure's internal use. Proper registration and ownership validation are critical for routing and compliance with Azure's networking standards.

Q117: Contoso Ltd. is preparing to implement Microsoft Peering in their Azure ExpressRoute configuration. Which of the following is NOT a requirement for configuring Microsoft Peering?

A) BGP must be configured with a public ASN or a private ASN if approved by Microsoft.

B) The primary and secondary subnets for peering must be in the same region.

C) A valid MD5 authentication key must be configured for the BGP session.

D) The ASN used for BGP must be registered with a Regional Internet Registry.

E) The VLAN ID for peering must be unique within the ExpressRoute circuit.

F) An ExpressRoute circuit must be in place before configuring Microsoft Peering.

Answer: B

Explanation: The requirement that the primary and secondary subnets for peering must be in the same region is not correct. For Microsoft Peering, there is no specific requirement that the subnets must be in the same region; rather, they must be correctly configured and associated with the ExpressRoute circuit. It is more important to ensure that the IP addresses meet the criteria for public address spaces and that all other technical and administrative requirements are satisfied, such as BGP configuration and use of a valid ASN.

Q118: In setting up Microsoft Peering for Azure ExpressRoute, you must configure BGP sessions. True or False: BGP sessions over Microsoft Peering can be established using private ASNs without any special approval.

A) True

B) False

Answer: B

Explanation: BGP sessions over Microsoft Peering typically require the use of public Autonomous System Numbers (ASNs). While it is possible to use private ASNs, this requires special approval from Microsoft. The use of public ASNs ensures that the BGP sessions are unique and do not conflict with other network configurations. Private ASNs are generally reserved for internal use within an organization and might lead to conflicts if used without explicit permission in a public routing scenario like Microsoft Peering.

Q119: When configuring Microsoft Peering for an ExpressRoute circuit, which option correctly describes the use of VLANs?

A) VLAN IDs must be shared across all peering types on the ExpressRoute circuit.

B) The same VLAN ID can be used for both Microsoft Peering and Private Peering.

C) Each peering type, including Microsoft Peering, requires a unique VLAN ID.

D) VLAN IDs are automatically assigned by Azure and cannot be manually configured.

E) Different VLAN IDs are recommended but not required for each peering type.

F) VLAN IDs must be in the range of 1 to 1000.

Answer: C

Explanation: Each peering type in an ExpressRoute circuit, such as Microsoft Peering, requires a unique VLAN ID. This uniqueness is necessary to ensure that traffic is correctly segmented and routed according to its intended destination. VLANs are a critical component of configuring network isolation and ensuring that the traffic for different peering types does not interfere with one another. This setup allows for effective management and security of the connections established through the ExpressRoute circuit.

Q120: Fabrikam Inc. is configuring Microsoft Peering on their ExpressRoute circuit to access Azure services. They intend to use a public ASN for BGP configuration. During the setup, they must also provide a BGP community value. Which statement best describes the purpose of using a BGP community value in this context?

A) It specifies the data encryption level for BGP sessions.

B) It is used to filter incoming routes based on geographical location.

C) It helps route traffic through preferred paths by signaling routing preferences.

D) It determines the maximum prefix limit for BGP advertisements.

E) It provides authentication between BGP peers.

F) It defines the VLAN tagging strategy for network segmentation.

Answer: C

Explanation: BGP community values are used to signal routing preferences and influence the path selection process across different networks. By assigning specific community values to routes, network administrators can indicate which paths should be preferred or avoided, allowing for more granular control over routing decisions. In the context of Microsoft Peering, these values can help ensure that traffic is directed through the most efficient or desired routes, optimizing connectivity and performance. This capability is particularly important in complex network environments where multiple paths may be available.

Q121: Your organization, Contoso Ltd., has implemented several Azure Virtual Networks (VNets) across multiple regions to support its global operations. You have been tasked with ensuring that network latency and bottlenecks are proactively monitored and addressed. The business-critical application hosted on these VNets requires minimal downtime and optimal performance. You decide to utilize Azure Network Watcher's capabilities to monitor these network parameters effectively. Which Network Watcher feature would you configure to continuously monitor the latency and packet loss metrics between your VNets?

A) NSG Flow Logs

B) Connection Monitor

C) Network Performance Monitor

D) IP Flow Verify

E) VPN Troubleshoot

F) Traffic Analytics

Answer: B

Explanation: Azure Network Watcher's Connection Monitor is the ideal tool to continuously monitor network latency and packet loss between VNets. It allows you to create a monitoring configuration that checks the connectivity between different points in your network, providing real-time insights into latency issues and packet drops. This helps in maintaining optimal performance for business-critical applications by allowing proactive troubleshooting and network diagnostics. Connection Monitor can be configured to send alerts when certain thresholds are breached, ensuring that your IT team can address issues before they affect end-users.

Q122: You have been asked to configure Azure Network Watcher to log all traffic processed by your Network Security Groups (NSGs) for compliance and security auditing. Which feature of Network Watcher should you deploy to meet this requirement?

A) Connection Troubleshoot

B) NSG Flow Logs

C) Packet Capture

D) Connection Monitor

E) IP Flow Verify

F) VPN Troubleshoot

Answer: B

Explanation: NSG Flow Logs in Azure Network Watcher provide the capability to log information about IP traffic flowing through your Network Security Groups (NSGs). This feature is essential for compliance and security auditing as it records detailed information about the source, destination, protocol, and traffic flow direction. Flow logs can be configured to store data in a storage account or be sent to Azure Monitor, where they can be analyzed further using tools like Azure Log Analytics or Azure Sentinel. This logging is crucial for understanding traffic patterns, identifying anomalies, and maintaining a secure and compliant network infrastructure.

Q123: True or False: Azure Network Watcher's Packet Capture feature allows you to capture packets on demand and store them directly in a specified Azure Blob storage account for further analysis.

A) True

B) False

Answer: A

Explanation: The Packet Capture feature in Azure Network Watcher allows users to capture packets on demand. This feature is crucial for deep network diagnostics as it captures raw packet data that can be analyzed to troubleshoot complex network issues. The captured packets are stored in a specified Azure Blob storage account, enabling easy access and analysis of network traffic data. This functionality is particularly useful for identifying the root causes of network performance issues, security breaches, and other network anomalies.

Q124: While working with Azure Network Watcher, you need to verify if a specific IP flow is allowed or denied through your network for a certain VM. This verification needs to be done quickly to troubleshoot a connectivity issue. Which Network Watcher feature should you use?

A) NSG Flow Logs

B) Packet Capture

C) Connection Troubleshoot

D) Traffic Analytics

E) IP Flow Verify

F) Network Performance Monitor

Answer: E

Explanation: The IP Flow Verify feature in Azure Network Watcher is designed to quickly verify if a packet is allowed or denied by your Network Security Groups (NSGs). This tool is highly effective for troubleshooting connectivity issues as it provides immediate insights into security group rules affecting a specific VM. By inputting source and destination IP addresses, ports, and protocols, IP Flow Verify can determine whether the traffic will be permitted or blocked, helping you troubleshoot and resolve connectivity issues efficiently and accurately.

Q125: Your company has deployed a complex multi-tier application across multiple Azure regions. You are tasked with ensuring end-to-end visibility into the performance of this application, including detecting and diagnosing network issues. Which Azure service should you integrate with Network Watcher to achieve comprehensive network performance monitoring?

A) Azure Application Insights

B) Azure Monitor Logs

C) Azure Traffic Manager

D) Azure Sentinel

E) Azure Log Analytics

F) Network Performance Monitor

Answer: F

Explanation: Network Performance Monitor (NPM) is the appropriate Azure service to integrate with Network Watcher for comprehensive network performance monitoring. NPM provides end-to-end visibility into your application's network performance across different regions. It helps in detecting network issues such as high latency, packet loss, and network topology changes. This service is crucial for diagnosing network issues and ensuring optimal application performance, especially in complex environments with multi-tier applications spread across multiple Azure regions. By integrating NPM with Network Watcher, you gain a holistic view of your network's health and performance, which is essential for maintaining service reliability and user satisfaction.

Q126: Your company, Contoso Ltd., has multiple Azure subscriptions and uses a hybrid cloud architecture. The company has an on-premises network integrated with an Azure Virtual Network through a VPN Gateway. You are tasked with configuring DNS for both on-premises and Azure resources to resolve names across these environments efficiently. The IT department has decided to use Azure DNS Private Zones for internal name resolution and wants to ensure that the DNS resolution is functional between on-premises and Azure resources. Which of the following steps should you take to achieve this integration?

A) Create an Azure DNS Private Zone and link it to your Azure Virtual Network. Configure conditional forwarding on the on-premises DNS server to forward queries to the Azure DNS Private Zone.

B) Create an Azure DNS Private Zone and deploy an Azure DNS Forwarding rule within the Virtual Network.

C) Use an Azure DNS Public Zone and configure it to host all internal and external DNS records.

D) Deploy an Azure DNS Private Zone and configure a DNS resolver to bridge queries between the on-premises network and Azure.

E) Create a DNS server within your Azure Virtual Network and configure it as a DNS proxy.

F) Configure Azure Traffic Manager to handle DNS queries from both on-premises and Azure resources.

Answer: A

Explanation: To resolve DNS queries across on-premises and Azure resources, you need to create an Azure DNS Private Zone and link it to your Azure Virtual Network. This enables Azure resources to automatically register their DNS names. On-premises systems can resolve Azure DNS names by configuring conditional forwarding on the on-premises DNS server to forward queries to the Azure DNS Private Zone. This setup requires that the on-premises DNS server can reach the Azure DNS service, typically achieved through VPN or ExpressRoute. Azure DNS Public Zones are not suitable for internal name resolution as they expose records to the public internet. DNS Forwarding rules within the Virtual Network require custom DNS solutions, which are not necessary if the goal is to integrate with on-premises DNS directly.

Q127: Which of the following PowerShell commands would you use to create a new Azure DNS Private Zone named "contoso.internal" within a resource group named "Networking-Resources"?

A) New-AzureRmDnsZone -Name "contoso.internal" -ResourceGroupName "Networking-Resources"

B) New-AzDnsPrivateZone -Name "contoso.internal" -ResourceGroupName "Networking-Resources"

C) New-AzDnsZone -Name "contoso.internal" -ResourceGroupName "Networking-Resources"

D) New-AzureRmDnsPrivateZone -Name "contoso.internal" -ResourceGroupName "Networking-Resources"

E) New-AzPrivateDnsZone -Name "contoso.internal" -ResourceGroupName "Networking-Resources"

F) New-AzurePrivateDnsZone -Name "contoso.internal" -ResourceGroupName "Networking-Resources"

Answer: E

Explanation: The correct command to create a new Azure DNS Private Zone is New-AzPrivateDnsZone. This command is part of the Az module in PowerShell, which is the latest module for managing Azure resources. The command requires specifying the zone name and the resource group where the zone should be created. The use of "Az" indicates the modern Azure PowerShell module, replacing the older "AzureRm" module. This distinction is important as the AzureRm module is being deprecated. The other options involve either incorrect command names or the use of the deprecated module.

Q128: A company has a multi-tier web application hosted in Azure. They require internal DNS resolution for their front-end and back-end tiers deployed across multiple Virtual Networks in different Azure regions. They decided to use Azure DNS Private Zones. Which is the most suitable approach to ensure DNS resolution across all tiers and regions?

A) Deploy a separate Azure DNS Private Zone for each Virtual Network.

B) Use a single Azure DNS Private Zone and link it to all relevant Virtual Networks.

C) Configure Azure DNS Public Zones for internal DNS resolution.

D) Deploy a custom DNS server in each Virtual Network and manually create DNS entries.

E) Use Azure Active Directory Domain Services for DNS resolution.

F) Configure Azure Application Gateway to handle DNS resolution.

Answer: B

Explanation: The most efficient approach is to use a single Azure DNS Private Zone and link it to all relevant Virtual Networks. This method allows resources in different Virtual Networks to resolve each other's DNS names, providing seamless DNS resolution across regions and tiers. Azure DNS Private Zones support automatic registration and resolution of DNS records within linked Virtual Networks, which simplifies management and reduces the potential for configuration errors. Deploying separate zones for each Virtual Network would complicate the DNS setup and maintenance. Azure DNS Public Zones are inappropriate for internal resolution as they expose records to the internet. Custom DNS servers require more overhead and do not leverage Azure's built-in capabilities.

Q129: True or False: When configuring an Azure DNS Private Zone, the DNS records hosted within it can be accessed publicly over the internet.

A) True

B) False

Answer: B

Explanation: Azure DNS Private Zones are specifically designed for internal DNS resolution within a private network environment. The DNS records created within a private zone are not accessible over the internet. They are intended for use only by resources within Virtual Networks that are linked to the private zone. This provides a secure method to handle DNS resolution for internal applications and services without exposing sensitive information to the public internet. Public access to DNS records requires the use of Azure DNS Public Zones, which is a separate service intended for internet-facing DNS records.

Q130: You're managing the network infrastructure for a global manufacturing company that uses Azure for its cloud solutions. The company has multiple production facilities worldwide, each with its own unique set of applications and DNS requirements. The IT team is planning to implement Azure DNS Private Zones to centrally manage internal DNS records. How can you ensure that DNS queries from any facility can resolve the appropriate private DNS zones hosted in Azure?

A) Deploy a DNS proxy in each facility to forward DNS queries to Azure DNS Private Zones.

B) Use Azure DNS Private Resolver within each Virtual Network.

C) Configure a Virtual Network link in each facility's Virtual Network to the Azure DNS Private Zone.

D) Set up ExpressRoute with Microsoft Peering to enable DNS resolution.

E) Implement Azure Bastion to facilitate DNS communication.

F) Utilize Azure Front Door for DNS resolution between facilities.

Answer: C

Explanation: To ensure that DNS queries from any facility can resolve private DNS zones hosted in Azure, you should configure a Virtual Network link in each facility's Virtual Network to the Azure DNS Private Zone. This approach allows machines in these Virtual Networks to resolve DNS queries through the Azure DNS Private Zone seamlessly. Azure DNS Private Zones support linking multiple Virtual Networks, enabling DNS resolution across regions and facilities. Deploying a DNS proxy or using a Private Resolver unnecessarily adds complexity and cost, while ExpressRoute and Azure Bastion serve different functions unrelated to DNS resolution. Azure Front Door is intended for global HTTP load balancing, not DNS resolution.

Q131: A global retail company uses Azure Virtual Network (VNet) to connect its stores to cloud resources. The company wants to implement RADIUS authentication to manage network access for its employees securely. They plan to have a centralized RADIUS server in their Azure environment to authenticate users trying to access the network from various locations. As the network administrator, you need to configure an Azure VPN gateway to use the RADIUS server for authentication. Which of the following steps is crucial in ensuring that the Azure VPN gateway communicates correctly with the RADIUS server?

A) Configure the RADIUS server's IP address and shared secret on the Azure VPN gateway.

B) Set up a virtual network peering between the RADIUS server VNet and the VPN gateway VNet.

C) Deploy an Azure Network Security Group (NSG) to allow RADIUS traffic on the RADIUS server subnet.

D) Use Azure Application Gateway to route RADIUS authentication requests.

E) Enable Azure Bastion to secure RADIUS server access.

F) Configure a Point-to-Site VPN with certificate authentication.

Answer: A

Explanation: To configure RADIUS authentication on an Azure VPN gateway, it is essential to specify the IP address of the RADIUS server and the shared secret used for authentication on the VPN gateway. This configuration allows the VPN gateway to forward authentication requests to the RADIUS server and validate the credentials of users trying to access the network. Without this step, the VPN gateway cannot communicate with the RADIUS server, rendering the authentication process non-functional. Other options, such as setting up virtual network peering or deploying network security groups, do not directly address the configuration needed for RADIUS communication on the VPN gateway.

Q132: Your organization has deployed a RADIUS server on an Azure Virtual Machine (VM) to authenticate users accessing the network through a VPN gateway. What type of Azure resource should be configured to ensure that only the necessary traffic is allowed to reach the RADIUS server?

A) Azure Load Balancer

B) Azure Firewall

C) Azure Traffic Manager

D) Azure Application Gateway

E) Azure Network Security Group (NSG)

F) Azure Front Door

Answer: E

Explanation: An Azure Network Security Group (NSG) is used to control inbound and outbound traffic to Azure resources. By configuring an NSG for the subnet where the RADIUS server is deployed, you can define security rules that allow only the necessary RADIUS traffic (UDP ports 1812 and 1813) to reach the server. This ensures that the RADIUS server is protected from unauthorized access and only legitimate authentication requests are processed. While other resources like Azure Firewall can provide additional security, an NSG is more straightforward for controlling specific traffic types at the network level.

Q133: True or False: To use RADIUS authentication with an Azure VPN gateway, the RADIUS server must be hosted on an on-premises network.

A) True

B) False

Answer: B

Explanation: RADIUS servers used for authentication with Azure VPN gateways do not need to be hosted on an on-premises network. They can be deployed within the Azure environment itself, either as a standalone server on a virtual machine or as part of a more complex architecture. Hosting the RADIUS server in Azure can provide benefits such as reduced latency and improved integration with other Azure services. It also simplifies management and scaling, as the server can be more easily adjusted to meet the demands of the cloud-based infrastructure.

Q134: When configuring a RADIUS server in Azure, which protocol is typically used to ensure the confidentiality and integrity of authentication requests between the VPN gateway and the RADIUS server?

A) IPsec

B) TLS

C) SSTP

D) DTLS

E) L2TP

F) RDP

Answer: B

Explanation: TLS (Transport Layer Security) is commonly used to secure RADIUS authentication requests. By encrypting the data transmitted between the VPN gateway and the RADIUS server, TLS ensures that sensitive information such as user credentials remains confidential and protected from interception or tampering. While RADIUS itself traditionally uses UDP, securing the communication channel with TLS adds an essential layer of security, especially in cloud environments where data might traverse public networks.

Q135: An enterprise wants to enhance its authentication infrastructure by integrating Azure Multi-Factor Authentication (MFA) with their existing RADIUS server for VPN access. Which Azure service should be used to facilitate this integration?

A) Azure Active Directory B2C

B) Azure AD Connect

C) Azure Network Watcher

D) Azure MFA Server

E) Azure Key Vault

F) Azure Monitor

Answer: D

Explanation: Azure Multi-Factor Authentication Server is the service that can integrate with existing RADIUS servers to provide an additional layer of security for VPN access. By deploying Azure MFA Server, organizations can require users to authenticate with a second factor, such as a phone call or mobile app notification, after their credentials are initially verified by the RADIUS server. This enhances security by ensuring that access is granted only when both something the user knows (password) and something the user has (second factor) are verified. Azure AD Connect and other services listed do not directly provide this capability.

Q136: Contoso Ltd., a global e-commerce company, is using Azure Application Gateway to manage traffic to their web applications. They want to implement a solution that modifies HTTP headers to include a custom header "X-Custom-Header" with the value "Contoso" for all requests to their application. Additionally, they need to remove any "X-Deprecated-Header" if present. Which Azure feature should they use to achieve this requirement effectively?

A) Azure Traffic Manager

B) Application Gateway URL-based routing

C) Application Gateway Rewrite Rules

D) Azure Front Door Caching Rules

E) Network Security Group (NSG) Rules

F) Azure Firewall Policies

Answer: C

Explanation: Azure Application Gateway offers a feature called Rewrite Rules, which allows you to modify request and response headers. This feature is ideal for adding, removing, or updating HTTP headers as specified in the requirement. In this scenario, you can create a rewrite set with rules to add the "X-Custom-Header" with the desired value and remove the "X-Deprecated-Header". This capability is not provided by Azure Traffic Manager, Azure Front Door Caching Rules, NSG Rules, or Azure Firewall Policies, which are designed for different purposes such as traffic management and security enforcement. URL-based routing is used for directing traffic based on URL paths rather than modifying headers.

Q137: An organization uses Azure Application Gateway to route traffic to its web services. The company wants to ensure that all incoming requests contain a specific header "X-Required-Header". If the header is missing, the request should be redirected to a specific error page. What is the most efficient way to implement this requirement?

A) Use Azure API Management policies

B) Configure Application Gateway custom error pages

C) Implement Application Gateway redirect rules

D) Use Application Gateway rewrite rules with conditions

E) Set up Azure Function triggers

F) Deploy Azure Web Application Firewall (WAF) rules

Answer: D

Explanation: Application Gateway rewrite rules with conditions can be used to inspect incoming requests and make decisions based on the presence or absence of specific headers. By configuring a conditional rewrite rule, you can check for the presence of "X-Required-Header" and, if it's not present, redirect the request to a predefined error page. This approach leverages the Application Gateway's native capabilities to modify and control traffic flow efficiently. While Azure API Management policies and WAF rules provide extensive control over API and security policies, they are not designed specifically for header-based redirection. Custom error pages and Azure Functions could provide solutions, but they would be more complex and less direct than using rewrite rules.

Q138: A manufacturing company, Fabrikam Inc., uses Azure Application Gateway for its internal applications. They want to enforce HTTPS for all traffic and ensure that the "X-Forwarded-Proto" header reflects "https" for secure requests. Which configuration will help them achieve this?

A) Configure SSL termination on the Application Gateway

B) Use HTTP to HTTPS redirection in the Application Gateway

C) Enable rewrite rules to set the "X-Forwarded-Proto" header

D) Deploy Azure Traffic Manager to manage SSL traffic

E) Integrate with Azure Key Vault for SSL certificates

F) Utilize Azure Load Balancer for header modification

Answer: C

Explanation: To ensure the "X-Forwarded-Proto" header reflects "https", you should use rewrite rules on the Application Gateway. These rules can be configured to modify the headers of incoming requests, including setting the "X-Forwarded-Proto" header value to "https". While SSL termination and HTTP to HTTPS redirection are important for enforcing HTTPS traffic, they do not directly modify headers. Azure Traffic Manager and Load Balancer do not provide the functionality to modify headers, and integrating with Azure Key Vault is related to certificate management, not header modification.

Q139: True or False: Azure Application Gateway rewrite rules can only modify HTTP request headers, not response headers.

A) True

B) False

Answer: B

Explanation: Azure Application Gateway rewrite rules are versatile and can modify both HTTP request and response headers. This feature allows administrators to adjust headers as needed for both incoming and outgoing traffic, providing greater control over how traffic is handled and ensuring that applications can meet specific security and operational requirements. This capability makes it possible to tailor the information sent back to clients, thereby enhancing compatibility and functionality.

Q140: A retail company is using Azure Application Gateway to manage traffic to their sales application. They recently implemented a rule to append a "X-Sales-Event" header to all requests during a promotional event. However, they need to ensure that this header is only added if the request URL path contains "/promo". Which approach should they take?

A) Use Azure Logic Apps to filter requests

B) Implement Azure Functions to modify headers based on URL path

C) Configure Application Gateway rewrite rules with URL path conditions

D) Set up a custom domain with URL filtering

E) Use Azure API Management to manage incoming requests

F) Deploy Azure Traffic Manager with path-based routing

Answer: C

Explanation: Application Gateway rewrite rules can be configured with conditions based on URL paths. By creating a rewrite rule with a condition that checks if the URL path contains "/promo", the rule can be set to append the "X-Sales-Event" header only when the condition is met. This approach is efficient and leverages the capabilities within the Application Gateway itself. While Azure Logic Apps, Functions, and API Management offer extensive processing capabilities, they are not as streamlined for this specific use case of header modification based on URL paths. Traffic Manager is used for traffic distribution and does not provide header modification capabilities.

Q141: A multinational corporation, XYZ Corp, has expanded its operations to different geographic regions and is using Azure Virtual Networks (VNets) to connect resources. They have a hub-and-spoke network topology, where the central hub VNet manages traffic between various spoke VNets. Due to increasing network traffic and security considerations, they want to implement routing rules to ensure that traffic between spoke VNets always routes through the hub VNet for inspection by network security appliances. The hub VNet also connects to an on-premises data center via Azure VPN Gateway. Which configuration step is crucial to ensure traffic between spoke VNets is inspected by the security appliances in the hub VNet? ###

A) Configure User-Defined Routes (UDR) in each spoke VNet pointing to the hub VNet's gateway.

B) Enable BGP routing on the VPN Gateway in the hub VNet.

C) Use Azure Firewall to manage all inbound and outbound traffic in the hub VNet.

D) Implement a Network Security Group (NSG) on each spoke VNet.

E) Set up a peering connection between each spoke VNet and the hub VNet with "Use remote gateways" enabled.

F) Enable forced tunneling on each spoke VNet.

Answer: E

Explanation: In a hub-and-spoke topology, ensuring that traffic from spoke VNets routes through the hub VNet requires careful configuration of VNet peering. Enabling "Use remote gateways" on the peering connections allows the spoke VNets to use the hub's gateway for routing. This configuration ensures that data between the spokes is routed through the hub VNet, where security appliances can inspect the traffic. User-Defined Routes (UDR) can also be used but typically in conjunction with peering settings. BGP routing is more relevant for on-premises connectivity. Azure Firewall can manage traffic but must be correctly routed through the hub. NSGs apply security rules but don't dictate routing paths. Forced tunneling is more about directing internet-bound traffic through on-premises resources.

Q142: True or False: In Azure, when configuring a route table for a VNet, the default route 0.0.0.0/0 can be directed to a Virtual Network Gateway to enable forced tunneling. ###

A) True

B) False

Answer: A

Explanation: Forced tunneling is a configuration where internet-bound traffic from Azure is routed back to on-premises networks for inspection and compliance. In Azure, this is achieved by configuring a User-Defined Route (UDR) that directs the default route 0.0.0.0/0 to the Virtual Network Gateway. This gateway is typically connected to an on-premises network via VPN or ExpressRoute, allowing the organization to apply its security policies and monitor traffic before it reaches the internet.

Q143: You are tasked with configuring a routing rule in Azure to ensure that all traffic destined for a specific on-premises subnet is routed through an ExpressRoute circuit. Which of the following actions should you take? ###

A) Create a User-Defined Route with the next hop set to "Internet."

B) Configure a BGP peering session with the local network gateway.

C) Set up a route table with a route for the specific subnet with the next hop type "Virtual Network Gateway."

D) Enable IP forwarding on the ExpressRoute circuit.

E) Configure a Network Security Group rule to allow traffic to the on-premises subnet.

F) Use Azure Traffic Manager to manage routing to the on-premises subnet.

Answer: C

Explanation: To ensure that traffic for a specific on-premises subnet uses an ExpressRoute circuit, you need to configure a User-Defined Route (UDR) with the next hop type set to "Virtual Network Gateway" in the route table associated with the Azure subnet. This configuration directs the traffic through the ExpressRoute gateway, which is connected to the on-premises network. BGP peering is part of the ExpressRoute setup but does not individually define routing rules for specific subnets. IP forwarding is a feature for VMs that need to forward traffic but is not directly related to routing configuration via an ExpressRoute. NSGs manage security, not routing, and Azure Traffic Manager is a DNS-based traffic load balancer, not suitable for routing.

Q144: In a hybrid network setup, an organization has two Azure regions connected via Global VNet Peering. They want all traffic between the two regions to flow through their on-premises network for compliance reasons. What is the best way to achieve this requirement? ###

A) Use Azure Traffic Manager to route traffic between the regions.

B) Configure UDRs in each region to route traffic to the on-premises network via an ExpressRoute circuit.

C) Enable forced tunneling on both regions with the on-premises network as the destination.

D) Set up VNet-to-VNet VPN connections between the regions.

E) Use Azure Application Gateway to manage traffic between the regions.

F) Configure BGP to advertise the on-premises network to both regions.

Answer: B

Explanation: To route traffic between two Azure regions through an on-premises network, you must configure User-Defined Routes (UDRs) in each region's route tables. These routes should direct traffic to the on-premises network through an ExpressRoute circuit, which serves as the next hop. This setup ensures that traffic between the regions is redirected to the on-premises infrastructure, meeting compliance requirements. Azure Traffic Manager, Application Gateway, and VNet-to-VNet VPNs are not designed for this purpose. BGP can be used in conjunction with ExpressRoute but does not directly reroute traffic between regions without UDRs.

Q145: An organization is implementing a secure and optimized routing solution in Azure. They are using Azure Route Server to enable dynamic routing updates between their network virtual appliances (NVAs) and Azure virtual networks. What is one critical consideration when setting up Azure Route Server in this scenario?

A) Ensure NVAs are deployed in a separate VNet from Azure Route Server.

B) Azure Route Server must be deployed in the same VNet as the NVAs.

C) Route Server requires a dedicated subnet with a specific name.

D) Deploy Azure Firewall alongside Route Server for enhanced security.

E) Route Server supports only static routing configurations.

F) Route Server cannot be used with ExpressRoute connections.

Answer: C

Explanation: Azure Route Server requires a dedicated subnet with the specific name "RouteServerSubnet" to function correctly. This subnet must be created in the same VNet where you plan to deploy the Route Server, ensuring that it can communicate with the NVAs for dynamic routing updates. Azure Route Server enables seamless interaction between NVAs and Azure's routing infrastructure by exchanging routes via the Border Gateway Protocol (BGP). Deploying NVAs and Route Server in separate VNets would not facilitate direct BGP exchanges. While Azure Firewall can enhance security, it is not a requirement for Route Server functionality. Azure Route Server supports dynamic routing, not just static, and can be used with ExpressRoute when configured correctly.

Q146: You are a network architect for an e-commerce company that has recently expanded its operations across multiple regions in Azure. To optimize performance and cost, the company wants to restrict certain Azure services to interact only with specific VNet resources. The goal is to ensure that services like Azure Storage and Azure SQL Database can only be accessed by designated subnets within a single VNet. As part of the solution, you are tasked with configuring service endpoint policies to enforce these restrictions. What steps would you take to achieve this requirement?

A) Enable service endpoints on the VNet and configure service endpoint policies to allow specific service regions.

B) Create a network security group (NSG) to restrict traffic to specific services.

C) Set up a VPN gateway to manage traffic between the VNet and Azure services.

D) Use Azure Policy to enforce resource access restrictions at the subscription level.

E) Configure a route table to route traffic through a network virtual appliance.

F) Implement a custom DNS solution to manage service resolutions.

Answer: A

Explanation: To restrict Azure services to interact only with specific VNet resources, you first need to enable service endpoints on the VNet for the services you intend to control, such as Azure Storage and Azure SQL Database. Once the service endpoints are enabled, you must configure service endpoint policies. These policies allow you to define which specific resources within a service can be accessed from the selected subnets of a VNet. This is critical for ensuring that only designated subnets have access to the services, thereby enhancing security and reducing unnecessary exposure. Network security groups and route tables don't directly control service endpoints, and VPN gateways or DNS solutions are not relevant for this specific requirement.

Q147: When configuring service endpoint policies, you must first enable service endpoints for the desired Azure services on the virtual network.

A) True

B) False

Answer: A

Explanation: Service endpoint policies require that service endpoints are first enabled on the virtual network for the specific services you wish to control. Enabling service endpoints allows traffic from your VNet to reach the service's endpoint over Azure's backbone network. Once endpoints are enabled, policies can be configured to allow or deny access to specific Azure resources, ensuring precise control over which parts of your VNet can access certain services. Without enabling service endpoints, the policies cannot be applied.

Q148: Which Azure PowerShell command is used to create a new service endpoint policy in a given resource group and location?

A) New-AzServiceEndpointPolicy

B) Set-AzNetworkServiceEndpointPolicy

C) Add-AzServiceEndpoint

D) New-AzVirtualNetwork

E) Enable-AzServiceEndpoint

F) Create-AzEndpointRule

Answer: A

Explanation: The New-AzServiceEndpointPolicy command is used in Azure PowerShell to create a new service endpoint policy. This command helps in defining rules that specify which service resources are accessible by the subnets within a VNet. Proper use of Azure PowerShell commands is essential for automating network configurations, especially in scenarios where multiple regions and services interact within an Azure environment. The other commands listed do not create service endpoint policies or are not valid Azure PowerShell commands.

Q149: In a situation where you need to apply a service endpoint policy to multiple subnets within the same VNet, what is the appropriate method to ensure the policy is applied correctly?

A) Apply the policy to each subnet individually using the Azure portal.

B) Use an ARM template to automate the deployment of the policy to the desired subnets.

C) Set up a traffic manager to distribute the policy across subnets.

D) Use Azure CLI to apply the policy to a single subnet and replicate it manually.

E) Configure a load balancer to enforce the policy across all subnets.

F) Deploy a network virtual appliance (NVA) to manage policy distribution.

Answer: B

Explanation: To apply a service endpoint policy to multiple subnets within the same VNet, using an ARM (Azure Resource Manager) template is the most efficient method. ARM templates allow you to define the infrastructure and configuration in a declarative format, making it easier to deploy consistent environments across multiple subnets. This approach ensures that the policy is applied correctly and consistently, reducing the potential for human error that might occur when configuring each subnet individually through the Azure portal or CLI. Traffic managers, load balancers, and NVAs do not manage service endpoint policies.

Q150: You have been tasked with ensuring that only specific Azure Storage accounts are accessible from your company's VNet. Which element must be included in your service endpoint policy to enforce this requirement?

A) A list of IP addresses allowed to connect to the storage account.

B) The resource ID of the Azure Storage account.

C) A custom domain name for the Azure Storage account.

D) The subscription ID of the account owning the storage account.

E) The location of the Azure Storage account.

F) The name of the storage account.

Answer: B

Explanation: To ensure that only specific Azure Storage accounts are accessible from a VNet, the service endpoint policy must include the resource ID of the Azure Storage account. The resource ID uniquely identifies the specific Azure resource you want to allow access to, providing a high degree of control over which resources can be accessed from the VNet. This is a critical aspect of configuring service endpoint policies, as it allows you to specify and manage access at the resource level. IP addresses, custom domains, and subscription IDs do not provide the necessary granularity for enforcing access through service endpoint policies.

Q151: You are working as an Azure Solutions Architect for a company that runs a global e-commerce platform. The platform is hosted on Azure App Service and uses Azure Front Door to distribute incoming traffic efficiently. To ensure data privacy and integrity, management has requested that you configure SSL termination at the Front Door but maintain end-to-end SSL encryption to the backend App Service. What configuration steps must you take to achieve SSL termination at the Front Door while ensuring end-to-end SSL encryption to the backend?

A) Configure a custom domain with a certificate in Azure Front Door and ensure HTTPS is enabled between Front Door and the backend.

B) Enable HTTP/2 protocol on Azure Front Door to optimize data transfer and reduce latency.

C) Use an Azure Key Vault to store the SSL certificate and configure Azure Front Door to use it.

D) Set up a private link between Azure Front Door and the backend App Service to secure the connection.

E) Configure Azure Front Door with a WAF policy to monitor and block malicious traffic.

F) Enable HTTPS only in the backend settings of Azure App Service without configuring SSL termination at Azure Front Door.

Answer: A

Explanation: To achieve SSL termination at Azure Front Door while maintaining end-to-end encryption to the backend, you need to configure a custom domain with an SSL certificate in Azure Front Door. This allows Front Door to handle SSL termination, decrypting the incoming traffic at the edge. After that, ensure that HTTPS is enabled for communication between the Front Door and the backend, thereby maintaining SSL encryption all the way to the backend service. This configuration ensures that data is encrypted in transit from the client to the backend, addressing the security requirements. Using Azure Key Vault or a private link is not directly related to configuring SSL termination at Front Door, while enabling HTTP/2 and WAF policies are performance and security measures, respectively.

Q152: In Azure Application Gateway, you can configure SSL termination to offload the SSL processing to the Application Gateway itself. Which of the following steps is NOT needed when setting up SSL termination on an Application Gateway?

A) Upload the SSL certificate to the Application Gateway.

B) Configure the listener with HTTPS protocol.

C) Enable end-to-end SSL by configuring a backend HTTP setting with HTTPS protocol.

D) Set up a custom domain for the Application Gateway.

E) Configure the frontend IP configuration to accept HTTPS traffic.

F) Specify the SSL policy that defines the protocols and ciphers to be used.

Answer: D

Explanation: When setting up SSL termination on an Azure Application Gateway, you do not need to set up a custom domain for the Application Gateway. SSL termination involves uploading an SSL certificate to the Application Gateway, configuring the listener with the HTTPS protocol, and setting up frontend IP configurations to accept HTTPS traffic. Additionally, you would specify an SSL policy to determine the protocols and ciphers used. To ensure the connection to the backend remains encrypted, you would configure a backend HTTP setting with the HTTPS protocol, enabling end-to-end SSL. Custom domain configuration is not a direct requirement for SSL termination itself.

Q153: You are tasked with configuring a multi-region Azure environment for a financial services company to enhance availability and performance. You decide to use Azure Traffic Manager and Azure Front Door to manage traffic efficiently. The company requires that all traffic is encrypted end-to-end with SSL. How would you configure these services to meet the requirements?

A) Use Traffic Manager for DNS-based load balancing and configure Front Door for SSL termination and re-encryption.

B) Configure Traffic Manager to enforce HTTPS routing and use Front Door for SSL termination.

C) Set up Front Door with a custom SSL certificate and use Traffic Manager to route traffic based on the lowest latency.

D) Use Traffic Manager to direct traffic to the nearest Front Door instance, which will handle SSL offloading.

E) Implement Front Door's application acceleration feature and configure Traffic Manager for failover routing.

F) Enable Front Door's session affinity feature and use Traffic Manager to balance traffic geographically.

Answer: A

Explanation: To ensure end-to-end SSL encryption in a multi-region setup using Azure Traffic Manager and Azure Front Door, you should configure Traffic Manager for DNS-based load balancing to direct traffic to the appropriate regional endpoint. Azure Front Door should be set up to handle SSL termination, where it decrypts incoming traffic and then re-encrypts it before forwarding it to the backend services. This ensures that traffic remains encrypted end-to-end. Traffic Manager itself does not handle SSL termination or re-encryption; it only routes traffic based on DNS requests. By combining these features, you achieve both global load balancing and secure data transmission across the regions.

Q154: When configuring SSL termination and end-to-end SSL encryption in Azure, which of the following statements is true?

A) SSL termination must occur at the same point where the SSL certificate is stored.

B) SSL termination can occur at Azure Front Door without affecting end-to-end encryption.

C) End-to-end SSL encryption requires that all intermediary services support SSL termination.

D) SSL termination is only necessary if the backend services do not support HTTPS.

E) It is impossible to configure SSL termination and end-to-end SSL simultaneously in Azure.

F) All Azure services automatically support SSL termination by default.

Answer: B

Explanation: SSL termination at Azure Front Door involves decrypting incoming traffic at the edge, which allows for efficient routing and processing. However, to maintain end-to-end encryption, the traffic is re-encrypted before being sent to the backend services. This process does not affect the overall end-to-end encryption, as the data remains secure throughout the transmission. SSL termination does not have to occur where the certificate is stored, and not all intermediary services need to support SSL termination for end-to-end encryption. SSL termination is not dependent on the backend's ability to support HTTPS, as it is a mechanism to offload SSL processing from the backend.

Q155: Your company uses Azure Kubernetes Service (AKS) to host a set of microservices that require secure communication. They have requested that you configure SSL termination at the Azure Application Gateway, which serves as an ingress controller, while ensuring that traffic to AKS is encrypted. Which of the following components is crucial for maintaining end-to-end encryption in this scenario?

A) Azure Key Vault to manage and store SSL certificates securely.

B) A private link service to connect the Application Gateway directly to AKS.

C) A backend HTTP setting on the Application Gateway configured with HTTPS.

D) A network security group (NSG) to enforce SSL policies.

E) A virtual network (VNet) peering to connect AKS and Application Gateway securely.

F) An API Management service to handle SSL termination and encryption.

Answer: C

Explanation: To maintain end-to-end encryption when using Azure Application Gateway as an ingress controller for AKS, configuring a backend HTTP setting with HTTPS is crucial. This ensures that traffic between the Application Gateway and the AKS cluster remains encrypted. While Azure Key Vault can securely store SSL certificates, it does not directly influence encryption between the gateway and backend. Private link services, NSGs, and VNet peering are networking configurations that provide security and connectivity but do not specifically handle SSL configurations. An API Management service is not required for SSL termination and encryption in this particular scenario, as the Application Gateway already provides the necessary capabilities.

Q156: Contoso Ltd. is a global manufacturing company with offices in North America, Europe, and Asia. The company has deployed several applications hosted in Azure regions close to these offices to ensure low latency. However, users in Europe have reported increased latency when accessing a critical inventory management application hosted in the North American Azure region. As the Azure network architect, you are tasked with optimizing network performance to improve user experience. You consider using Azure Front Door to accelerate traffic. Which configuration would best address the latency issue for users in Europe accessing the North American application?

A) Configure Azure Front Door with a single endpoint in the North American region.

B) Use Azure Traffic Manager to direct traffic based on priority.

C) Set up Azure Front Door with load balancing enabled across all regions.

D) Deploy Azure Front Door with caching enabled at European edge locations.

E) Implement Azure VPN Gateway for site-to-site connections.

F) Utilize Azure ExpressRoute to create direct connections between Europe and North America.

Answer: D

Explanation: The most effective way to reduce latency for European users accessing an application hosted in North America is to use Azure Front Door with caching enabled at European edge locations. Azure Front Door is a global, scalable entry point that can accelerate application delivery by caching content closer to users. By caching content at European edge locations, the response time for static content is minimized, which significantly improves performance. Utilizing Azure Front Door also allows for dynamic content to be delivered via optimized routes, further reducing latency. Other options, like using a single endpoint in North America or configuring VPNs, do not specifically address the need to reduce latency for European users. ExpressRoute, while providing private connections, is more suitable for consistent throughput and bandwidth rather than solving latency issues for global distribution.

Q157: When configuring Azure Traffic Manager for application traffic acceleration, which routing method should be used to ensure that users are always connected to the endpoint with the lowest latency?

A) Priority routing

B) Weighted routing

C) Performance routing

D) Geographic routing

E) MultiValue routing

F) Subnet routing

Answer: C

Explanation: Performance routing is the optimal choice when the goal is to ensure that users are always connected to the endpoint with the lowest latency. Azure Traffic Manager's performance routing method directs users to the endpoint that has the lowest network latency from the user's location. This is achieved by continuously monitoring the latency of each endpoint, allowing Traffic Manager to make real-time decisions on where to direct user traffic. Other routing methods, such as priority or weighted, do not specifically aim to optimize for latency and are generally used for redundancy or load distribution purposes.

Q158: True or False: Azure ExpressRoute provides a way to improve application performance by using Microsoft's global network to accelerate traffic between on-premises networks and Azure.

A) True

B) False

Answer: A

Explanation: True. Azure ExpressRoute is designed to provide a private, dedicated connection between on-premises networks and Azure data centers. By bypassing the public internet and using Microsoft's global network, ExpressRoute can offer more reliable, faster, and consistent network performance, which can significantly improve application performance. This is particularly beneficial for applications that require high throughput or low latency connections. The use of ExpressRoute can reduce latency and improve the overall user experience for applications hosted in Azure.

Q159: A company needs to accelerate traffic between their Azure-hosted application and users located in different parts of the world. They are considering using Azure Front Door but are concerned about the cost and complexity of global deployment. What is the most cost-effective and efficient way to configure Azure Front Door to accelerate traffic while minimizing complexity?

A) Enable custom rules for each geographic region.

B) Utilize a single Front Door instance with CDN caching enabled.

C) Deploy multiple Front Door instances in each region.

D) Use Azure Traffic Manager in conjunction with Front Door.

E) Implement VPN connections for each user location.

F) Configure ExpressRoute circuits for each region.

Answer: B

Explanation: Using a single Azure Front Door instance with CDN caching enabled is the most cost-effective and efficient solution for accelerating global traffic. Azure Front Door provides built-in CDN capabilities, which can cache content at edge locations close to users worldwide. This reduces the need for multiple Front Door instances and simplifies management, while still providing global acceleration and improved performance. Deploying multiple instances or configuring complex routing rules would add unnecessary cost and complexity without additional performance benefits. The use of VPN connections or ExpressRoute circuits is more suited for private and secure connections rather than cost-effective global traffic acceleration.

Q160: You are tasked with optimizing the network performance of a video streaming service hosted on Azure. The service must deliver content with minimal latency to users across multiple continents. Which Azure feature should you implement to achieve this goal?

A) Azure Load Balancer with session persistence.

B) Azure VPN Gateway with point-to-site connectivity.

C) Azure CDN with dynamic site acceleration.

D) Azure Virtual Network Peering for global VNet access.

E) Azure Application Gateway with WAF enabled.

F) Azure Traffic Manager with DNS-based routing.

Answer: C

Explanation: Azure CDN with dynamic site acceleration is the best choice for optimizing the network performance of a video streaming service with global reach. Azure CDN can cache video content and deliver it from edge servers located close to users, thereby reducing the latency and improving the user experience. Dynamic site acceleration further optimizes the delivery of dynamic content by choosing the fastest, most reliable path to the origin server. Other options, like load balancers or VPN gateways, focus more on traffic management and secure access rather than optimizing global content delivery. Virtual Network Peering and Traffic Manager are better suited for network connectivity and routing rather than content acceleration.

Q161: You are the network administrator for Contoso Ltd., a company that is moving its e-commerce platform to Azure. The platform requires secure communication between virtual machines (VMs) in different regions. To ensure data is encrypted in transit, you plan to configure Transport Layer Security (TLS) on the network. The TLS configuration must comply with the company's security policy, which mandates the use of TLS 1.2 or higher. Additionally, the configuration should minimize latency and allow for quick scalability as the business grows. What is the best approach to configure TLS in this scenario? ---

A) Use Azure Application Gateway to enforce TLS 1.2 on all incoming traffic.

B) Deploy Azure Front Door with a custom rule to enforce TLS 1.2.

C) Configure a site-to-site VPN connection with Azure VPN Gateway enforcing TLS 1.2.

D) Utilize Azure Traffic Manager to distribute traffic and enforce TLS 1.2.

E) Implement Azure Load Balancer with TLS 1.2 configured on backend VMs.

F) Use Azure Network Security Group (NSG) rules to enforce TLS 1.2.

Answer: A

Explanation: Azure Application Gateway is best suited for this requirement as it provides a scalable and secure solution for managing web traffic to applications. By enabling TLS termination at the gateway, you can enforce TLS 1.2 for all incoming traffic, ensuring compliance with security policies while reducing overhead on backend servers. This setup also allows for centralized management of SSL certificates and policies, which is crucial for managing secure communications efficiently. Additionally, Azure Application Gateway supports autoscaling, which aligns with the company's need for scalability as the business grows. Using other services like VPN Gateway or NSGs would not directly address the requirement of enforcing TLS 1.2 for web traffic between VMs across regions.

Q162: Select the Azure PowerShell command that correctly configures an Azure Application Gateway to use TLS 1.2 exclusively for frontend HTTPS settings. ---

A) Set-AzApplicationGatewayFrontendPort -Name "FrontendPort" -Protocol "TLS1.2"

B) Add-AzApplicationGatewaySslCertificate -ApplicationGateway "AppGw" -Name "cert" -CertificateFile "path" -Password "password"

C) New-AzApplicationGatewayFrontendIPConfig -Name "FrontendIP" -PublicIPAddressId "ipId" -Protocol "TLS1.2"

D) Set-AzApplicationGatewaySslPolicy -Name "AppGw" -PolicyType "Custom" -MinProtocolVersion "TLSv12"

E) Add-AzApplicationGatewayAuthenticationCertificate -ApplicationGateway "AppGw" -Name "authCert" -Data "certData"

F) New-AzApplicationGatewayListener -Name "Listener" -FrontendIPConfiguration "FrontendIP" -FrontendPort "FrontendPort" -Protocol "TLS1.2"

Answer: D

Explanation: The Set-AzApplicationGatewaySslPolicy command is used to configure SSL policies on an Azure Application Gateway. By specifying the PolicyType as "Custom" and setting the MinProtocolVersion to "TLSv12", you ensure that the Application Gateway only accepts TLS 1.2 for secure communications. This approach is critical for adhering to security policies and maintaining a high level of encryption. Other commands listed are either related to different configurations or do not directly enforce the TLS version.

Q163: In an Azure environment, you need to configure a secure channel using TLS between an Azure SQL Database and a web application hosted on Azure App Services. Which configuration setting ensures that the web application uses the highest version of TLS supported by Azure SQL Database? ---

A) Enable Managed Identity for Azure SQL Database

B) Use Azure Key Vault to store TLS certificates

C) Set "Enforce SSL connection" in the Azure SQL Database settings

D) Configure Azure App Service to use a custom domain with a TLS certificate

E) Adjust the "TLS Version" setting in Azure SQL Database to TLS 1.3

F) Update the web application's connection string to include "Encrypt=True; TrustServerCertificate=False;"

Answer: F

Explanation: Updating the web application's connection string to include "Encrypt=True; TrustServerCertificate=False;" is the correct approach to ensuring that the application establishes a secure connection to the Azure SQL Database using TLS. This configuration enforces encryption for data in transit, leveraging the highest version of TLS supported by the database. Azure SQL Database automatically supports the latest TLS versions, so specifying encryption in the connection string ensures secure communication without manual TLS version settings. Other options, such as enabling managed identity or storing certificates in Azure Key Vault, do not directly influence the TLS version used for SQL connections.

Q164: True/False: Azure Load Balancer natively supports TLS termination for applications deployed in Azure. ---

A) True

B) False

Answer: B

Explanation: Azure Load Balancer does not natively support TLS termination. It operates at the transport layer (Layer 4) and does not have built-in capabilities for handling TLS/SSL termination. For applications that require TLS termination, Azure Application Gateway or Azure Front Door should be used, as they provide built-in support for TLS/SSL offloading and can manage certificates efficiently. This distinction is important for designing secure and scalable architectures in Azure.

Q165: A financial services company is implementing a new Azure-based solution to securely handle sensitive customer data. They need to configure TLS for their Azure Kubernetes Service (AKS) to ensure encrypted communication. Which approach should they implement?

A) Use Azure Private Link to secure AKS traffic.

B) Configure a Network Security Group (NSG) for AKS to only allow HTTPS traffic.

C) Implement an Ingress Controller with TLS termination using Let's Encrypt.

D) Enable Azure AD authentication for AKS.

E) Deploy a Web Application Firewall (WAF) in front of AKS.

F) Use Azure Bastion to manage secure access to AKS nodes.

Answer: C

Explanation: Implementing an Ingress Controller with TLS termination using Let's Encrypt is the appropriate solution for securing communication with Azure Kubernetes Service. Ingress Controllers facilitate external HTTP and HTTPS routing to services within the AKS cluster, and by configuring TLS termination, they ensure that all traffic is encrypted end-to-end. Let's Encrypt provides a free and automated way to acquire and renew SSL/TLS certificates, which simplifies management and ensures that the cluster complies with the company's security requirements. Other options, such as using Private Link or NSGs, do not directly address the need for TLS termination within AKS.

Q166: Contoso Ltd. is expanding its operations and needs to optimize traffic flow between multiple Azure regions. They have set up a Virtual WAN with multiple virtual hubs. The goal is to ensure efficient routing between a hub in North America and a hub in Europe while ensuring minimal latency and cost. The network architects want to implement route propagation between these hubs. What configuration should be applied to achieve this?

A) Enable BGP propagation between the hubs and configure custom route tables.

B) Use Azure Traffic Manager to manage the routing between the hubs.

C) Set up a VPN gateway in each hub and manually configure routes.

D) Implement Azure Load Balancer to distribute traffic between hubs.

E) Configure a Network Security Group with specific inbound and outbound rules.

F) Use Azure Firewall to manage the traffic flow between the hubs.

Answer: A

Explanation: To optimize traffic flow between multiple Azure regions using Azure Virtual WAN, enabling BGP propagation and configuring custom route tables allows route propagation between hubs. This setup ensures that each hub can dynamically learn routes from one another, optimizing the path selection based on latency and cost. Azure Traffic Manager and Load Balancer are not suitable here as they are typically used for load balancing and failover scenarios. VPN gateways are unnecessary as the Virtual WAN already provides connectivity. Network Security Groups and Azure Firewall are more about security than routing optimization.

Q167: You are tasked with configuring virtual hub routing in Azure to ensure that traffic from a spoke virtual network in the East US region can route to a spoke virtual network in the West Europe region through a central hub in each region. The solution must minimize latency and cost while ensuring high availability. Which Azure feature can you leverage to achieve this?

A) Azure Virtual Network Peering

B) ExpressRoute Global Reach

C) Virtual WAN with ExpressRoute

D) Azure Route Server

E) Virtual Network Gateway

F) Network Security Group

Answer: C

Explanation: Utilizing Azure Virtual WAN with ExpressRoute provides a scalable and high-performance solution for routing traffic between spokes through central hubs in different regions. This approach allows for efficient routing, leveraging Microsoft's backbone network, which minimizes latency and costs while ensuring high availability. Virtual Network Peering and Route Server do not offer region-to-region routing optimizations. ExpressRoute Global Reach is not relevant as it connects on-premises to Azure. Virtual Network Gateways and Network Security Groups focus on connectivity and security, not routing optimization.

Q168: A company needs to set up a virtual hub in Azure to facilitate communication between on-premises networks and Azure VMs across different regions. They plan to use a hub in the US region and another in the Europe region. The company wants to ensure that any changes in the on-premises network are automatically reflected in Azure without the need for manual updates. What feature should they use to configure this?

A) Static Route Configuration

B) ExpressRoute with BGP

C) Azure Load Balancer

D) Azure Traffic Manager

E) Application Gateway

F) Site-to-Site VPN with Route Propagation

Answer: B

Explanation: ExpressRoute with BGP allows for dynamic routing between on-premises infrastructure and Azure resources. By using BGP, any changes in the on-premises network are automatically propagated to Azure, ensuring that the routing tables are always up-to-date without manual intervention. This approach streamlines network management and ensures that Azure can adapt to changes in the on-premises network. Static Route Configuration and Site-to-Site VPN with Route Propagation require manual updates and do not leverage BGP. Azure Load Balancer, Traffic Manager, and Application Gateway are not relevant to the routing requirement described.

Q169: An organization has a complex network setup with multiple virtual networks and wants to ensure that traffic between their virtual networks flows through a central virtual hub for monitoring and security purposes. The IT team needs a solution that allows fine-grained control over the routing paths to enforce security policies. What is the best Azure service to implement this requirement?

A) Azure Front Door

B) Azure Virtual WAN with Route Tables

C) Azure Bastion

D) Azure Traffic Manager

E) Azure Application Gateway

F) Azure Private Link

Answer: B

Explanation: Azure Virtual WAN with Route Tables is the most suitable solution for routing traffic through a central hub while allowing fine-grained control over routing paths. By configuring custom route tables, administrators can dictate specific paths that traffic should follow, enabling the enforcement of security policies and monitoring requirements. Azure Front Door and Traffic Manager are more focused on application-level routing and global traffic distribution, not network routing. Azure Bastion is for secure RDP/SSH access, Application Gateway is for web traffic, and Private Link is for securing access to Azure services.

Q170: True/False: Configuring a virtual hub in Azure to propagate routes automatically from connected VPN sites requires manual intervention to update route tables whenever a new site is added.

A) True

B) False

Answer: B

Explanation: False. Configuring a virtual hub in Azure to propagate routes from connected VPN sites does not require manual intervention to update route tables for each new site. When using BGP with Azure Virtual WAN, routes are automatically propagated and updated across the network. This dynamic approach simplifies management and ensures that the virtual hub's route tables are always current, reflecting any changes or additions to connected VPN sites. This automation is a key advantage of using BGP in Azure's virtual networking solutions.

Q171: A global logistics company has multiple branches worldwide and is using Azure to host its business applications. They have established an ExpressRoute circuit to ensure reliable and secure connectivity between their on-premises environment and Azure. They want to connect their virtual network (VNet) in the East US region to their existing ExpressRoute circuit. The company requires that the connection supports private peering and is highly available. Which configuration step should the network administrator prioritize to ensure that the VNet is correctly connected to the ExpressRoute circuit in the East US region?

A) Create a new virtual network gateway in the East US region and link it to the ExpressRoute circuit.

B) Configure a VPN gateway in the East US region and connect it to the ExpressRoute circuit.

C) Set up a peering connection between the VNet and the ExpressRoute circuit without a gateway.

D) Use a network security group to allow traffic from the ExpressRoute circuit to the VNet.

E) Ensure that the VNet's address space is within the range accepted by the ExpressRoute circuit.

F) Enable BGP on the virtual network gateway to facilitate dynamic routing.

Answer: A

Explanation: To connect a VNet to an ExpressRoute circuit, a virtual network gateway must be created in the region where the VNet resides. This gateway is essential for establishing a link between the VNet and the ExpressRoute circuit through private peering. The setup does not require a VPN gateway, as ExpressRoute connections are not encrypted over the internet. The peering connection relies on the gateway to route traffic between the VNet and the ExpressRoute circuit. Network security groups are not used for this specific purpose; they are mainly for controlling inbound and outbound traffic at the subnet level. Address space considerations are important but do not replace the need for a gateway. Enabling BGP is useful for dynamic routing but is not the primary step for connecting the VNet to the circuit.

Q172: To connect a virtual network to an ExpressRoute circuit, which of the following is NOT a necessary configuration or requirement?

A) A subnet named 'GatewaySubnet' in the virtual network.

B) A route table configured with a route pointing to the ExpressRoute circuit.

C) An ExpressRoute circuit provisioned and enabled.

D) A virtual network gateway configured in ExpressRoute mode.

E) Private peering enabled on the ExpressRoute circuit.

F) A valid Azure subscription with sufficient permissions.

Answer: B

Explanation: When connecting a VNet to an ExpressRoute circuit, it is crucial to have a 'GatewaySubnet' within the VNet, as this is where the virtual network gateway will be deployed. An ExpressRoute circuit must be provisioned and enabled with private peering for the connection to function. A virtual network gateway in ExpressRoute mode is required to facilitate the connection between the VNet and the circuit. Adequate permissions within an Azure subscription are necessary to perform these configurations. However, a specific route table with a route pointing to the ExpressRoute circuit is not required during the initial connection setup, as the gateway manages the routing.

Q173: A multinational corporation has established an ExpressRoute circuit to connect its on-premises data centers to Azure. They plan to connect multiple VNets across different Azure regions to this single ExpressRoute circuit. Which feature should they use to achieve this requirement?

A) ExpressRoute Global Reach

B) VNet Peering

C) ExpressRoute FastPath

D) ExpressRoute Direct

E) ExpressRoute Gateway Transit

F) Virtual WAN

Answer: E

Explanation: To connect multiple VNets across different regions to a single ExpressRoute circuit, ExpressRoute Gateway Transit is the appropriate feature. This allows VNets that are peered with the VNet that has the ExpressRoute gateway to leverage the connection to the ExpressRoute circuit. It facilitates connectivity across regions without the need to create separate connections for each VNet. ExpressRoute Global Reach is used for connecting on-premises data centers via ExpressRoute. VNet Peering is for connecting VNets within Azure but does not directly connect them to ExpressRoute. ExpressRoute FastPath improves data path performance but does not address multiple VNet connections. ExpressRoute Direct provides a direct connection to Azure, and Virtual WAN is used for networking across a global infrastructure.

Q174: A financial services company is setting up a direct connection between their Azure VNet and their on-premises network using an ExpressRoute circuit. They want to ensure that the routing is dynamic and can automatically adapt to changes. Which protocol should they configure on their virtual network gateway to achieve this?

A) OSPF

B) RIP

C) BGP

D) EIGRP

E) MPLS

F) HTTP

Answer: C

Explanation: BGP (Border Gateway Protocol) is the protocol used to establish dynamic routing between Azure VNets and on-premises networks when using ExpressRoute. BGP enables the exchange of routing information, allowing for dynamic adaptation to network changes, such as link failures or topology changes. This dynamic routing capability is essential for maintaining a resilient and adaptable connection between Azure and on-premises environments. Other protocols like OSPF, RIP, and EIGRP are not supported for ExpressRoute connections in Azure. MPLS is a type of data-carrying technique, not a routing protocol, and HTTP is not related to network routing.

Q175: True or False: When connecting a VNet to an ExpressRoute circuit, it is mandatory to configure a public IP address for the virtual network gateway.

A) True

B) False

Answer: A

Explanation: When setting up a virtual network gateway for connectivity to an ExpressRoute circuit, it is mandatory to configure a public IP address. This public IP is used by the gateway for communication purposes and is essential for establishing the connection between the Azure VNet and the on-premises network through the ExpressRoute circuit. The public IP address is part of the gateway configuration and is required for the gateway to function correctly as a bridge between the two networks. This setup ensures that the gateway can handle the routing and peering configurations necessary for the ExpressRoute connection.

Q176: Your company, Contoso Ltd., is expanding its cloud infrastructure to support a new customer-facing application. The application will be hosted on Azure Virtual Machines (VMs) within a virtual network. To ensure high availability and redundancy, you plan to deploy the application across multiple Azure regions. Each VM instance in different regions must be accessible over the internet with a static public IP address, which should not change even if the VM is deallocated or restarted. Additionally, you need to ensure that traffic is evenly distributed across the VMs in different regions. How should you configure the public IP addresses and ensure traffic distribution?

A) Configure a Load Balancer with an Auto-Scaling Group and associate static public IP addresses to each VM.

B) Use Azure Traffic Manager with region-specific profiles and dynamic public IP addresses for each VM.

C) Assign a Static Public IP to each VM and configure a Load Balancer with a Public IP in front of them.

D) Utilize Azure Front Door Service with static public IPs for each VM.

E) Implement a Network Security Group with IP forwarding and dynamic public IPs.

F) Create a Virtual Network Gateway with static public IPs and configure VPN connections.

Answer: C

Explanation: To meet the requirement of static public IPs that do not change even if the VM is deallocated or restarted, you must assign a static public IP to each VM. This ensures that the IP remains constant. To distribute traffic across VMs in different regions, an Azure Load Balancer can be configured with a front-facing public IP. This setup allows for even distribution of incoming traffic to the VMs, ensuring high availability and redundancy. Azure Traffic Manager could be used for geographic distribution, but it doesn't inherently ensure static IPs per VM. Azure Front Door could be considered for global routing, but it wouldn't fulfill the requirement for static IPs on individual VMs directly.

Q177: A company wants to assign a public IP address to a specific resource within Azure. Which of the following services can be directly associated with a public IP address?

A) Azure Key Vault

B) Azure Virtual Network Gateway

C) Azure Blob Storage

D) Azure SQL Database

E) Azure Virtual Machine Scale Set

F) Azure Load Balancer

Answer: F

Explanation: Public IP addresses in Azure are typically associated with network interfaces of Azure resources such as Virtual Machines or with services that expose workloads to the internet. An Azure Load Balancer can be directly associated with a public IP address, making it possible to distribute incoming internet traffic to backend resources (e.g., VMs). While Azure Virtual Network Gateways do use public IPs, they are not directly assigned in the same manner. Other services like Azure Key Vault, Blob Storage, and SQL Database use service endpoints or private link for access control rather than direct public IP assignments.

Q178: You are managing the network infrastructure for an e-commerce platform hosted on Azure. The platform experiences high traffic volumes, particularly during sales events, and requires robust solutions for performance and availability. It is imperative that each of your application servers retains the same public IP address to ensure consistency in DNS configurations and SSL certificates. Which Azure feature supports this requirement?

A) Dynamic Public IP Allocation

B) Azure Traffic Manager

C) Static Public IP Allocation

D) Azure ExpressRoute

E) Azure Application Gateway

F) Virtual Network Peering

Answer: C

Explanation: Static Public IP Allocation is essential when there is a need for a consistent public IP address, especially for DNS and SSL certificate configurations. This feature ensures that the public IP address assigned to a resource does not change, which is crucial for maintaining DNS records and SSL bindings. Dynamic Public IPs, in contrast, can change whenever the resource is deallocated or restarted. Azure Traffic Manager, ExpressRoute, and Application Gateway provide other networking functionalities such as traffic routing, secure connections, and application-level routing but do not directly address static IP requirements.

Q179: In Azure, a public IP address can be associated with which of the following components to enable direct internet access? Select the most appropriate option.

A) Azure Resource Manager

B) Azure Virtual Machine Network Interface Card (NIC)

C) Azure Logic Apps

D) Azure Data Factory

E) Azure DevOps

F) Azure Active Directory

Answer: B

Explanation: In Azure, a public IP address is often associated with a Virtual Machine's Network Interface Card (NIC) to enable direct internet access. This association allows the VM to communicate directly with external resources and services. The NIC is the component that attaches network configurations to a VM. Other components like Azure Resource Manager, Logic Apps, Data Factory, and DevOps do not get public IP addresses directly as they either operate within the Azure environment or do not require direct external access. Azure Active Directory is a directory and identity management service and does not directly associate with public IPs.

Q180: True/False: Static public IP addresses in Azure are allocated from a pool of IPs provided by Microsoft, and they remain the same even if a resource is deallocated and reallocated.

A) True

B) False

Answer: A

Explanation: Static public IP addresses in Azure are indeed allocated from a pool managed by Microsoft. When you configure a public IP as static, Azure guarantees that the IP address remains the same, even if the associated resource is deallocated and later reallocated. This is crucial for scenarios requiring consistent IP addresses, such as maintaining DNS records, SSL configurations, or when IP whitelisting is necessary. Dynamic public IPs, on the other hand, may change upon resource deallocation and reallocation.

Q181: Your company, Fabrikam Inc., has a growing e-commerce platform hosted on Azure. The platform experiences variable traffic patterns throughout the day, with peak loads during promotional events. To ensure high availability and optimal performance, you need to implement a load balancing solution that distributes incoming traffic across multiple virtual machines hosted in an Azure Virtual Network. Additionally, you must ensure that the solution can handle both HTTP and non-HTTP traffic and provide insights into traffic patterns and health checks. How should you configure the Azure Load Balancer to meet these requirements? ---

A) Use an Azure Application Gateway in combination with Azure Traffic Manager to balance traffic and provide health checks.

B) Implement an Azure Load Balancer with a backend pool of VMs and configure health probes for HTTP and TCP traffic.

C) Deploy an Azure Front Door service to manage HTTP traffic and use Azure Load Balancer for non-HTTP traffic.

D) Use a combination of Azure Load Balancer and Azure Network Watcher to monitor traffic patterns and health.

E) Configure an internal load balancer and set up custom DNS for traffic management.

F) Set up Azure Traffic Manager with priority routing and integrate it with Azure Load Balancer for distribution.

Answer: B

Explanation: To achieve high availability and optimal performance for both HTTP and non-HTTP traffic, an Azure Load Balancer is the most suitable choice. It allows you to distribute incoming traffic across a backend pool of virtual machines, ensuring even load distribution. By configuring health probes, you can monitor the health status of your VMs for both HTTP and TCP traffic. This setup ensures that only healthy instances receive traffic, thereby enhancing reliability. While Azure Application Gateway and Azure Front Door focus primarily on HTTP/HTTPS traffic, Azure Load Balancer is protocol-agnostic, making it more versatile for Fabrikam Inc.'s requirements. Additionally, Azure Load Balancer provides built-in logging and diagnostic capabilities, which can be used to analyze traffic patterns and performance metrics.

Q182: You need to configure your Azure environment to ensure that an internal application hosted on a virtual network can communicate efficiently with an on-premises network. The application requires a load balancer that can facilitate this communication while ensuring that only authorized traffic is permitted. Which Azure service should you use to configure the load balancer for this hybrid connectivity scenario? ---

A) Azure VPN Gateway

B) Azure ExpressRoute

C) Azure Load Balancer with private frontend

D) Azure Traffic Manager

E) Azure Application Gateway with WAF

F) Azure Virtual WAN

Answer: C

Explanation: In a hybrid connectivity scenario where an internal application on Azure needs to communicate with an on-premises network, configuring an Azure Load Balancer with a private frontend is the appropriate solution. A private frontend allows the load balancer to handle traffic within the virtual network, ensuring secure and efficient communication. This setup is ideal for internal applications that require load balancing without exposing endpoints to the public internet. Azure VPN Gateway and Azure ExpressRoute focus on establishing secure connections between Azure and on-premises networks but do not provide load balancing capabilities. Azure Traffic Manager and Azure Application Gateway are more suited for internet-facing applications, while Azure Virtual WAN is for optimizing and automating large-scale branch connectivity.

Q183: A development team at your organization has deployed a new version of their web application on Azure. They want to ensure that the new version is gradually made available to users to monitor its performance and rollback if necessary. How can you achieve this using Azure Load Balancer? ---

A) Use Azure Load Balancer with weighted traffic distribution.

B) Implement Azure Traffic Manager with weighted routing.

C) Deploy an Azure Application Gateway with url-based routing.

D) Configure Azure Load Balancer with multiple backend pools and health probes.

E) Utilize Azure Front Door with gradual traffic ramp-up.

F) Set up Azure Load Balancer with round-robin distribution.

Answer: B

Explanation: To gradually release a new version of a web application and monitor its performance, Azure Traffic Manager with weighted routing is a suitable solution. Weighted routing allows you to distribute traffic between different versions of your application based on specified weights. This enables a phased rollout, where you can direct a small percentage of users to the new version while keeping the majority on the stable version. Azure Load Balancer, while effective for distributing traffic across VMs, does not offer the same weighted traffic management capabilities as Traffic Manager. Azure Application Gateway, Front Door, and round-robin distribution are not designed for gradual traffic ramp-up in the same way as weighted routing.

Q184: You are tasked with ensuring that your Azure-based applications can handle the increasing number of SSL/TLS requests efficiently. The current setup using Azure Load Balancer is not optimized for SSL termination, and performance issues are noticeable. How should you reconfigure your setup to improve SSL/TLS handling? ---

A) Switch to Azure Application Gateway with SSL termination.

B) Deploy Azure Traffic Manager for enhanced SSL performance.

C) Use Azure Load Balancer with SSL offloading enabled.

D) Implement Azure Front Door with SSL termination.

E) Configure Azure Load Balancer with dedicated SSL ports.

F) Integrate Azure VPN Gateway for SSL traffic management.

Answer: A

Explanation: To efficiently handle SSL/TLS requests, switching to Azure Application Gateway with SSL termination is the optimal solution. SSL termination at the Application Gateway allows for the decryption of SSL/TLS traffic at the gateway, reducing the load on backend servers and improving overall performance. This setup offloads the CPU-intensive process of encrypting and decrypting SSL/TLS traffic from the application servers, enabling them to handle more requests more efficiently. Azure Load Balancer does not offer SSL termination capabilities, and Azure Traffic Manager, Front Door, and VPN Gateway do not directly address SSL offloading for performance improvements.

Q185: An Azure Load Balancer can be configured to distribute inbound traffic based on source IP and protocol.

A) True

B) False

Answer: A

Explanation: Azure Load Balancer can indeed be configured to distribute inbound traffic using various distribution modes, including based on source IP and protocol. This method is known as the "five-tuple" hash which includes source IP, source port, destination IP, destination port, and protocol type. This form of distribution ensures that traffic from a particular source is consistently routed to the same backend instance, maintaining session persistence when needed. This capability is a key feature of Azure Load Balancer, making it a versatile solution for managing traffic loads across distributed applications.

Q186: Your company, Contoso Ltd., is planning to establish a private, high-throughput, and low-latency connection between its on-premises data center and its Azure Virtual Network (VNet) for better performance and security. The IT team is tasked with creating an ExpressRoute circuit and configuring an ExpressRoute gateway. They also need to ensure redundancy and high availability of the connection. The team has already created the ExpressRoute circuit in the Azure portal. What is the next step to configure the ExpressRoute gateway in this scenario? ---

A) Use the Azure portal to associate the ExpressRoute circuit with the VNet.

B) Use Azure PowerShell to create a connection between the ExpressRoute circuit and the VNet.

C) Use Azure CLI to create a virtual network gateway of type 'ExpressRoute'.

D) Use the Azure portal to configure BGP settings for the ExpressRoute circuit.

E) Use Azure PowerShell to enable Azure Private Peering for the ExpressRoute circuit.

F) Use Azure CLI to create a VPN gateway and connect it to the ExpressRoute circuit.

Answer: C

Explanation: After creating the ExpressRoute circuit, the next step is to create a virtual network gateway of type 'ExpressRoute'. This gateway is necessary to connect your on-premises network to your Azure Virtual Network via ExpressRoute. Using the Azure CLI can automate and script the process, ensuring consistent configuration. The command az network vnet-gateway create is used to create the gateway and must specify the type as 'ExpressRoute'. This step is essential before any connections can be established between the ExpressRoute circuit and the Azure VNet. High availability and redundancy are achieved through the inherent design of ExpressRoute gateways, which provide multiple paths between the Azure and on-premises networks.

Q187: When configuring an ExpressRoute gateway, you can enable both Azure Private Peering and Microsoft Peering simultaneously to access Azure services and Microsoft 365 services over the same circuit. ---

A) True

B) False

Answer: A

Explanation: ExpressRoute allows the configuration of multiple peering types on the same circuit, including Azure Private Peering and Microsoft Peering. Azure Private Peering is used for connection to Azure services, while Microsoft Peering is used for accessing Microsoft 365 services. Enabling both types of peering on the same ExpressRoute circuit allows organizations to access a broad range of services securely and efficiently. This dual peering configuration is beneficial for businesses that require strict data locality or compliance with regulatory requirements while accessing both Azure and Microsoft 365 services over a private connection.

Q188: To configure an ExpressRoute gateway for high availability, which of the following options provides the best solution? ---

A) Deploy the ExpressRoute gateway in a single Availability Zone.

B) Create multiple ExpressRoute circuits in different regions.

C) Use a zone-redundant ExpressRoute gateway configuration.

D) Deploy a VPN gateway alongside the ExpressRoute gateway as a backup.

E) Increase the bandwidth of the existing ExpressRoute circuit.

F) Enable geo-redundancy on the ExpressRoute gateway.

Answer: C

Explanation: A zone-redundant ExpressRoute gateway configuration provides high availability by automatically deploying the gateway across multiple Availability Zones within an Azure region. This setup ensures that the gateway remains operational even if one of the zones experiences a failure, offering enhanced resilience and uptime for critical network connections. Unlike other options, the zone-redundant configuration does not require additional ExpressRoute circuits or regions, making it a cost-effective and efficient solution for ensuring continuous connectivity.

Q189: Which Azure PowerShell command is used to create a connection between an ExpressRoute circuit and an Azure VNet after deploying the ExpressRoute gateway? ---

A) New-AzExpressRouteCircuit

B) New-AzVirtualNetworkGatewayConnection

C) Set-AzExpressRouteCircuit

D) Add-AzVirtualNetworkGatewayConnection

E) Get-AzExpressRouteCircuit

F) Remove-AzExpressRouteCircuit

Answer: B

Explanation: The New-AzVirtualNetworkGatewayConnection cmdlet in Azure PowerShell is used to create a connection between an ExpressRoute circuit and an Azure Virtual Network. This command is crucial for establishing the link that allows traffic to flow between the on-premises data center and the Azure resources over the ExpressRoute circuit. The connection type must be specified as 'ExpressRoute', and it requires parameters such as the ResourceId of the ExpressRoute circuit and the virtual network gateway. This step finalizes the connectivity setup, following the creation of the ExpressRoute circuit and the deployment of the virtual network gateway.

Q190: Your organization needs to ensure traffic between the on-premises network and the Azure VNet remains private and does not traverse the public internet. Which ExpressRoute feature allows you to achieve this requirement?

A) Microsoft Peering

B) Global Reach

C) Private Link

D) Azure Private Peering

E) Public Peering

F) VNet Peering

Answer: D

Explanation: Azure Private Peering is a feature of ExpressRoute that enables private IP address connectivity from the on-premises network to Azure Virtual Networks. This configuration ensures that the traffic remains private and does not traverse the public internet, addressing security and performance concerns. Azure Private Peering is typically used for scenarios where sensitive data is transferred, and latency or bandwidth constraints are critical. By establishing a private connection directly to Azure VNets, organizations can maintain control over their data flow, ensuring compliance and meeting business requirements for secure and efficient connectivity.

Q191: Contoso Ltd. is expanding its cloud infrastructure and needs to establish a secure connection between its on-premises network and Azure. The company's security policy mandates the use of specific cryptographic algorithms to ensure data integrity and confidentiality. Contoso's network engineering team has decided to use an IKEv2 VPN gateway connection with custom IPsec/IKE policies. The policy requires the use of AES256 for encryption, SHA256 for integrity, and DH Group 14 for key exchange. The team needs to create and configure this policy using Azure PowerShell. What is the correct PowerShell command to achieve this?

A) New-AzIpsecPolicy -IkeEncryption AES256 -IkeIntegrity SHA256 -DhGroup DHGroup14 -IpsecEncryption AES256 -IpsecIntegrity SHA256

B) New-AzVirtualNetworkGateway -GatewayType Vpn -VpnType RouteBased -EnableBgp $False

C) New-AzIpsecPolicy -IpsecEncryption AES256 -IpsecIntegrity SHA256 -IkeEncryption AES256 -IkeIntegrity SHA256 -DhGroup DHGroup14

D) New-AzVirtualNetworkGatewayConnection -Name "ContosoConnection" -ResourceGroupName "ContosoRG"

E) New-AzIpsecPolicy -IkeEncryption AES256 -IkeIntegrity SHA1 -DhGroup DHGroup1 -IpsecEncryption AES256 -IpsecIntegrity SHA256

F) New-AzIpsecPolicy -IpsecEncryption AES128 -IpsecIntegrity SHA1 -IkeEncryption AES256 -IkeIntegrity SHA256 -DhGroup DHGroup14

Answer: C

Explanation: The correct command to create a custom IPsec/IKE policy in Azure using PowerShell is New-AzIpsecPolicy. The specific parameters for Contoso's requirements include AES256 for both IPsec and IKE encryption, SHA256 for integrity, and DH Group 14 for key exchange. These parameters are specified in the command as -IpsecEncryption AES256, -IpsecIntegrity SHA256, -IkeEncryption AES256, -IkeIntegrity SHA256, and -DhGroup DHGroup14. The other options either use incorrect algorithms or are not relevant to creating an IPsec/IKE policy.

Q192: Which statement about IPsec/IKE policies in Azure is correct?

A) Azure only supports pre-defined IPsec/IKE policies and does not allow customization.

B) Custom IPsec/IKE policies allow the specification of encryption and integrity algorithms as well as the Diffie-Hellman Group.

C) IPsec/IKE policies are applied at the subnet level in Azure.

D) Azure supports custom IPsec/IKE policies only for VNet-to-VNet connections.

E) Custom IPsec/IKE policies cannot specify the key lifetime.

F) IPsec/IKE policies are automatically configured and do not require user input.

Answer: B

Explanation: Azure allows the creation of custom IPsec/IKE policies, which enable users to specify encryption and integrity algorithms, as well as the Diffie-Hellman (DH) Group. This level of customization is important for ensuring compliance with organizational security standards. Custom IPsec/IKE policies can be applied to both VNet-to-VNet and site-to-site VPN connections. The policies are not applied at the subnet level but are associated with

VPN gateways. Additionally, users can specify key lifetimes in these policies, providing further customization options.

Q193: True or False: Custom IPsec/IKE policies in Azure can only be applied to Route-Based VPN gateways.

A) True

B) False

Answer: A

Explanation: In Azure, custom IPsec/IKE policies can only be applied to Route-Based VPN gateways. Route-Based VPNs use a tunnel interface and route traffic based on the routes in the IP routing table. This makes them suitable for IPsec/IKE policy customization. Policy-Based VPNs, on the other hand, rely on static IPsec policies and do not support custom IPsec/IKE policies. This limitation is due to the nature of how traffic is matched and encrypted in Policy-Based VPNs.

Q194: You need to configure an IPsec/IKE policy for a VNet-to-VNet connection in Azure. The policy must use AES128 for encryption, SHA1 for integrity, and DH Group 2 for the key exchange. Which of the following commands correctly configures this policy using PowerShell?

A) New-AzIpsecPolicy -IpsecEncryption AES128 -IpsecIntegrity SHA1 -IkeEncryption AES128 -IkeIntegrity SHA1 -DhGroup DHGroup2

B) New-AzVirtualNetworkGatewayConnection -IpsecEncryption AES128 -IpsecIntegrity SHA1 -DhGroup DHGroup2

C) New-AzIpsecPolicy -IpsecEncryption AES128 -IpsecIntegrity SHA256 -IkeEncryption AES128 -IkeIntegrity SHA1 -DhGroup DHGroup2

D) New-AzIpsecPolicy -IpsecEncryption AES256 -IpsecIntegrity SHA1 -IkeEncryption AES128 -IkeIntegrity SHA1 -DhGroup DHGroup2

E) New-AzVirtualNetworkGateway -GatewayType Vpn -VpnType PolicyBased

F) New-AzIpsecPolicy -IpsecEncryption AES128 -IpsecIntegrity SHA1 -IkeEncryption AES256 -IkeIntegrity SHA256 -DhGroup DHGroup24

Answer: A

Explanation: The specific requirement for this IPsec/IKE policy is to utilize AES128 for both IPsec and IKE encryption, SHA1 for integrity, and DH Group 2 for key exchange. The PowerShell command New-AzIpsecPolicy allows for these specifications, and the parameters must match the requirement exactly: -IpsecEncryption AES128, -IpsecIntegrity SHA1, -IkeEncryption AES128, -IkeIntegrity SHA1, and -DhGroup DHGroup2. This ensures that the policy complies with the stated needs for encryption, integrity, and key exchange.

Q195: Your company has a strict security policy that requires using the highest level of encryption and integrity for VPN connections. When creating an IPsec/IKE policy in Azure, you need to ensure compliance by selecting the appropriate algorithms and key exchange methods. Which combination of parameters should you choose to meet these requirements?

A) -IpsecEncryption AES256 -IpsecIntegrity SHA256 -IkeEncryption AES256 -IkeIntegrity SHA256 -DhGroup DHGroup24

B) -IpsecEncryption AES128 -IpsecIntegrity SHA1 -IkeEncryption AES128 -IkeIntegrity SHA1 -DhGroup DHGroup2

C) -IpsecEncryption AES256 -IpsecIntegrity SHA1 -IkeEncryption AES256 -IkeIntegrity SHA256 -DhGroup DHGroup14

D) -IpsecEncryption DES -IpsecIntegrity MD5 -IkeEncryption DES -IkeIntegrity MD5 -DhGroup DHGroup1

E) -IpsecEncryption AES192 -IpsecIntegrity SHA256 -IkeEncryption AES192 -IkeIntegrity SHA256 -DhGroup DHGroup14

F) -IpsecEncryption AES256 -IpsecIntegrity SHA384 -IkeEncryption AES256 -IkeIntegrity SHA384 -DhGroup DHGroup24

Answer: F

Explanation: To comply with a strict security policy requiring the highest levels of encryption and integrity, you should choose the strongest available algorithms and key exchange methods. AES256 is the highest level of encryption supported in Azure, and SHA384 provides stronger integrity checks compared to SHA256. DH Group 24 offers a higher level of security for key exchange compared to lower-numbered groups. Therefore, the parameter combination with AES256, SHA384, and DH Group 24 represents the most secure configuration available in Azure for IPsec/IKE policies.

Q196: Your organization has recently expanded its operations and has established a new branch office in another city. To ensure seamless connectivity between your on-premises network and the resources in Azure, you need to configure a local network gateway. The branch office network uses a different ISP and has a dynamic public IP address. As the network administrator, you are tasked with setting up the local network gateway to connect the branch office to your Azure virtual network. You must ensure the configuration is resilient to IP address changes and utilizes a secure method for communication. What is the best approach to configure the local network gateway in this scenario? ---

A) Configure the local network gateway with the current public IP address and set a fixed IP address in the router configuration.

B) Use a DNS name for the local network gateway that resolves to the dynamic public IP address.

C) Assign a static public IP address for the local network gateway to ensure consistent connectivity.

D) Implement Azure ExpressRoute for direct connectivity and bypass the need for a local network gateway.

E) Configure a VPN gateway on Azure and use it to dynamically update the local network gateway IP address.

F) Use Azure Bastion to connect securely without needing a local network gateway.

Answer: B

Explanation: In this scenario, using a DNS name for the local network gateway that resolves to the dynamic public IP address is the most effective solution. This approach allows the Azure VPN gateway to resolve the public IP address dynamically, accommodating changes without manual intervention. When configuring a local network gateway that connects to a location with a dynamic IP, using a DNS name is recommended because it provides flexibility and reliability. Azure VPN gateways have the capability to resolve DNS names to obtain the current IP address, ensuring ongoing connectivity even when the IP changes. This solution is secure, as DNS updates propagate quickly, and it fits well with the dynamic nature of the branch office's public IP address.

Q197: When configuring a local network gateway in Azure, you must provide the address space for the on-premises network. This information is crucial for Azure to route traffic correctly. True or False: It is possible to configure overlapping address spaces between the Azure virtual network and the local network gateway. ---

A) True

B) False

Answer: B

Explanation: It is not possible to configure overlapping address spaces between the Azure virtual network and the local network gateway. This is because overlapping IP address spaces can lead to routing conflicts and traffic misdirection, which would disrupt connectivity and network functions. Azure requires unique address spaces to correctly route traffic between the on-premises and Azure networks. Defining clear and distinct address spaces avoids complications and ensures efficient data flow between network resources.

Q198: You are tasked with creating a local network gateway in Azure for a multi-site VPN connection. The goal is to connect three distinct on-premises networks, each with its own unique IP address range, to a single Azure virtual network. Which step must be taken to achieve this configuration? ---

A) Create a single local network gateway with multiple address spaces defined.

B) Deploy separate local network gateways for each on-premises network.

C) Use a single VPN gateway and rely on Azure to automatically route traffic.

D) Configure a single local network gateway and update the address space dynamically.

E) Implement a site-to-site VPN with automatic address space detection.

F) Utilize Azure Traffic Manager to handle multiple on-premises connections.

Answer: A

Explanation: To connect multiple on-premises networks to a single Azure virtual network using a multi-site VPN connection, you can create a single local network gateway with multiple address spaces defined. This setup allows you to specify each on-premises network's IP range within one local network gateway, simplifying management and configuration. Azure permits the configuration of multiple address spaces within a single local network gateway, ensuring that traffic is routed correctly to each distinct network. This approach is efficient and reduces the overhead of managing multiple local network gateways.

Q199: An organization needs to set up a local network gateway to connect its on-premises network to Azure. The on-premises network is behind a NAT device, which translates its private IP range to a public IP. Which configuration step is essential when setting up the local network gateway in this situation? ---

A) Enter the public IP address of the NAT device in the local network gateway configuration.

B) Use the private IP range of the on-premises network in the gateway configuration.

C) Configure a static route on the NAT device for the Azure virtual network.

D) Use a VPN client to establish a connection to the Azure network.

E) Implement a direct peering connection to bypass the need for a NAT device.

F) Enable route-based VPN on the Azure virtual network gateway.

Answer: A

Explanation: When an on-premises network is behind a NAT device, the local network gateway configuration in Azure should use the public IP address of the NAT device. This is because the NAT device translates the private IP addresses to a single public IP, which is what the Azure VPN gateway will see as the source of incoming traffic. Configuring the local network gateway with the public IP ensures that Azure can correctly establish and maintain the VPN connection. Using the private IP range would not be effective, as these addresses are not routable over the internet.

Q200: A company is setting up a local network gateway to connect its on-premises infrastructure to Azure. They plan to use BGP for dynamic routing between the networks. What is a critical configuration component required for BGP to function correctly in this setup?

A) Ensure the same ASN (Autonomous System Number) is used on both Azure and on-premises.

B) Configure a unique ASN for the Azure virtual network gateway and the on-premises network.

C) Use a static routing table instead of BGP to simplify the configuration.

D) Implement a redundant VPN gateway to handle BGP advertisements.

E) Set up an ExpressRoute circuit to manage BGP routes.

F) Disable default BGP route propagation in the Azure virtual network.

Answer: B

Explanation: When using BGP for dynamic routing between Azure and on-premises networks, it is critical to configure a unique ASN for both the Azure virtual network gateway and the on-premises network. BGP requires distinct ASNs to establish peering sessions and exchange routing information correctly between different networks. Using the same ASN on both sides would lead to routing issues, as BGP would not be able to differentiate between the networks. By ensuring unique ASNs, BGP can effectively route traffic and adapt to network changes dynamically, providing a robust and scalable connection.

Q201: Your company, Contoso Ltd., is planning to expand its operations globally. The IT department has been tasked with setting up a secure communication link between the on-premises datacenter in New York and a new Azure datacenter in Singapore. You need to ensure high availability and low latency for critical business applications. Furthermore, due to compliance requirements, the solution must support traffic encryption and redundancy. Which Azure Virtual Network Gateway configuration would best meet these requirements?

A) Configure a Standard VPN Gateway with BGP enabled

B) Set up an Active-Active VPN Gateway with Zone-Redundant Gateways

C) Deploy an ExpressRoute Gateway with a FastPath configuration

D) Implement a VNet-to-VNet connection using a Basic SKU VPN Gateway

E) Use a High-Performance SKU VPN Gateway with forced tunneling

F) Create a Site-to-Site VPN connection with a Basic SKU Gateway

Answer: B

Explanation: An Active-Active VPN Gateway with Zone-Redundant Gateways is the most suitable option for this scenario. It ensures high availability by deploying two instances of the VPN Gateway in different zones, thus providing redundancy. This setup can handle failover scenarios seamlessly. Additionally, the Active-Active configuration supports BGP, which is crucial for dynamic routing and ensuring low latency. Traffic encryption is inherent to VPN Gateway connections, fulfilling the compliance requirements. While ExpressRoute could offer high performance and low latency, it is generally more suited for private connections rather than secure internet-based VPN solutions. The Basic SKU options do not support the high availability and redundancy required by the scenario.

Q202: When configuring a VPN Gateway in Azure, you need to specify the Gateway SKU. If you require a configuration that supports a high number of concurrent connections and high throughput, which Gateway SKU should you choose?

A) Basic

B) VpnGw1

C) VpnGw2

D) VpnGw3

E) VpnGw5

F) Standard

Answer: D

Explanation: The VpnGw3 SKU is designed for scenarios that require high throughput and a large number of concurrent connections, making it suitable for enterprise-level applications. This SKU provides greater performance compared to VpnGw1 and VpnGw2, supporting more connections and higher bandwidth. The Basic SKU is limited in terms of both performance and features, while VpnGw5 does not exist in the Azure SKU lineup for VPN Gateways. Selecting the appropriate SKU is crucial to meet the performance and scalability needs of an enterprise environment.

Q203: True/False: An ExpressRoute Gateway can be used in conjunction with a VPN Gateway to provide a fallback secure connectivity option in case the primary connection fails.

A) True

B) False

Answer: A

Explanation: It is indeed true that an ExpressRoute Gateway can be used alongside a VPN Gateway to provide a fallback option. This configuration allows organizations to utilize the high-performance, private connectivity of ExpressRoute as their primary link while maintaining a VPN Gateway as a backup. In the event of a failure of the ExpressRoute connection, traffic can be rerouted to the VPN, ensuring continuous connectivity. This setup requires careful planning to manage routing preferences and failover conditions, but it offers a robust solution for mission-critical applications that need high availability.

Q204: You are tasked with setting up a secure VNet-to-VNet connection between two Azure regions, East US and West Europe. The connection must support high availability and automatically reroute traffic in case of a failure. Which configuration steps should you follow to achieve this?

A) Set up a Basic SKU VPN Gateway in both regions and configure BGP

B) Deploy Standard SKU VPN Gateways with Active-Standby configuration and enable BGP

C) Use an ExpressRoute Circuit for each VNet and configure peering

D) Create an Active-Active VPN Gateway in both regions and enable BGP

E) Implement a VNet Peering with Traffic Manager for failover

F) Deploy a High-Performance SKU VPN Gateway with custom routing tables

Answer: D

Explanation: To achieve high availability and automatic traffic rerouting for a VNet-to-VNet connection between two different Azure regions, the best approach is to deploy an Active-Active VPN Gateway in both regions with BGP enabled. This configuration allows for multiple active tunnels to be established, providing redundancy. BGP enables dynamic routing, which can automatically reroute traffic in the event of a failure on one of the tunnels. While ExpressRoute and VNet Peering are viable options for connectivity, they do not inherently provide the same level of failover support as Active-Active VPN Gateways configured with BGP.

Q205: A global retail company requires a secure connection between its on-premises network and Azure to support its payment systems. The solution must offer predictable latency and a Service Level Agreement (SLA) of 99.95% uptime. Which Azure service should be selected to meet these requirements?

A) Basic VPN Gateway

B) Standard VPN Gateway

C) ExpressRoute

D) VNet Peering

E) High-Performance VPN Gateway

F) Premium SKU VPN Gateway

Answer: C

Explanation: ExpressRoute is the ideal Azure service for scenarios that require predictable latency, high bandwidth, and a strong Service Level Agreement (SLA). It provides a private connection between Azure and on-premises networks, bypassing the public internet, which helps in achieving low latency and high reliability. ExpressRoute offers an SLA of 99.95% uptime, which aligns with the company's requirement for supporting critical payment systems. VPN Gateways, while secure, depend on the internet for connectivity and do not offer the same level of performance or SLA as ExpressRoute. VNet Peering is not applicable for on-premises to Azure connectivity.

Q206: A multinational corporation has deployed several applications in their Azure Virtual Network (VNet) that need to communicate with external services on the internet. To optimize and secure outbound traffic, the company wants to implement source network address translation (SNAT) using Azure's load balancing solution. The company requires that the external IP addresses used for these communications are static for compliance reasons. They also need to ensure high availability and scalability for their outbound connectivity. Considering these requirements, which Azure service should they use to configure SNAT for their VNet?

A) Azure Standard Load Balancer with a Public IP

B) Azure Application Gateway with WAF

C) Azure Traffic Manager

D) Azure Front Door

E) Azure VPN Gateway

F) Azure ExpressRoute

Answer: A

Explanation: Azure Standard Load Balancer is the ideal choice for configuring SNAT in this scenario because it supports outbound connectivity using static public IP addresses. This capability fulfills the corporation's need for compliance by ensuring predictable IP addresses for external communications. By associating a Standard Load Balancer with a public IP, you can manage outbound SNAT while maintaining high availability and scalability. The load balancer distributes traffic across multiple instances, which is essential for the company's global operations. Other options like Azure Application Gateway and Azure Front Door focus more on inbound traffic management and do not offer the same level of SNAT control needed for static IP addresses.

Q207: In a scenario where Azure Virtual Machines (VMs) in a Virtual Network need to communicate with the internet using a static public IP address for outbound traffic, which component must be configured to achieve this using SNAT?

A) Route Table

B) Network Security Group

C) Azure Firewall

D) Application Security Group

E) User Defined Route

F) Public IP Prefix

Answer: C

Explanation: Azure Firewall is the component that should be configured to achieve SNAT with a static public IP for outbound traffic. It allows you to specify static public IP addresses for outbound traffic, ensuring that all outbound traffic from your VMs uses the defined IP addresses. This is vital for scenarios where IP whitelisting is required on external services. While route tables and network security groups manage traffic flow and security, they do not provide SNAT capabilities. Public IP Prefix can reserve a range of IPs but does not directly handle SNAT; it's used with services like Azure Firewall to provide IP consistency.

Q208: A development team in an enterprise wants to ensure that all outbound traffic from their Azure VMs uses a specific static public IP address for compliance reporting. They are considering using Azure Load Balancer for this purpose. Which configuration must they implement to ensure that the VMs use this static public IP for all outbound communications?

A) Configure an internal load balancer with a static public IP

B) Enable Public IP assignment on each VM

C) Use a NAT Gateway with a public IP address

D) Set up a standard load balancer with outbound rules

E) Deploy a public load balancer with a dynamic IP

F) Create a virtual network peering with a public IP

Answer: D

Explanation: To ensure that all outbound traffic from Azure VMs uses a specific static public IP address, the team should set up a Standard Load Balancer with outbound rules. This configuration allows outbound traffic to utilize a static public IP address for SNAT. The outbound rules in the Load Balancer enable you to control the outbound connections from the VMs, ensuring that traffic is routed through the specified static public IP. This setup is crucial for compliance reporting as it guarantees that all traffic appears to originate from the same IP address. Using a NAT Gateway is another viable option, but the question specifically explores using a load balancer.

Q209: An organization has deployed Azure VMs in a single VNet. They need to ensure all outbound traffic from these VMs is routed through a consistent set of public IPs for audit purposes. However, they do not want to manage individual public IPs for each VM. Which Azure service should they use to fulfill this requirement?

A) Azure Bastion

B) Azure NAT Gateway

C) Azure Traffic Manager

D) Azure ExpressRoute

E) Azure Application Gateway

F) Azure Load Balancer Basic

Answer: B

Explanation: Azure NAT Gateway is the appropriate service for this requirement because it provides outbound connectivity for VMs in a VNet using a consistent set of static public IP addresses, without the need to assign individual public IPs to each VM. This service is designed to handle large volumes of outbound connections efficiently while maintaining a consistent IP address for compliance and audit purposes. Unlike the Basic Load Balancer, the NAT Gateway is specifically optimized for outbound SNAT scenarios, providing scalability and high availability.

Q210: True or False: When configuring an Azure Load Balancer with outbound rules for a VNet, the associated public IP address must be dynamic to allow SNAT for outbound traffic.

A) True

B) False

Answer: B

Explanation: This statement is false. When configuring an Azure Load Balancer with outbound rules for a VNet, you can and often should use a static public IP address to allow SNAT for outbound traffic. Using a static public IP address ensures that all outbound traffic from the VNet appears to originate from a consistent IP address, which is critical for scenarios requiring IP whitelisting or auditing. Azure Load Balancer supports both static and dynamic IP addresses, but static IPs are preferred when predictable external IP addresses are necessary.

Q211: A multinational company, Contoso Ltd., is transitioning its on-premises applications to Azure to enhance scalability. As part of the migration, they need to configure an inbound NAT rule on their Azure Load Balancer to allow remote management of their virtual machines using Remote Desktop Protocol (RDP) on port 3389. The existing load balancer is configured with a public frontend IP, and the backend pool includes multiple VM instances. The network administrator is tasked with setting up the NAT rule to direct RDP traffic to a specific VM in the backend pool. What should be the key consideration when configuring this inbound NAT rule to ensure only the designated VM receives the RDP traffic?

A) Assign a unique backend port for each VM in the backend pool.

B) Configure the frontend port of the NAT rule to match the backend port.

C) Use the same public IP address for all inbound traffic to the backend pool.

D) Set up an Application Security Group to restrict RDP access.

E) Ensure the NAT rule is applied to all VMs in the backend pool.

F) Use a different frontend IP address for each inbound NAT rule.

Answer: A

Explanation: When configuring inbound NAT rules in Azure Load Balancer for scenarios like remote desktop access, it's crucial to ensure that each VM in the backend pool is uniquely addressable on the desired port. This is achieved by assigning a unique backend port for each VM, corresponding to the frontend port. This way, traffic arriving on a specific frontend port can be correctly mapped to the appropriate VM in the backend pool. This strategy prevents conflicts and ensures that the intended VM is accessed without inadvertently reaching others. The frontend port does not need to match the backend port, as the NAT rule will handle the translation.

Q212: To configure an inbound NAT rule in Azure, which of the following steps is NOT required?

A) Create a separate Resource Group for NAT rules.

B) Define the frontend IP configuration.

C) Specify the backend port for the target virtual machine.

D) Configure the frontend port for the NAT rule.

E) Associate the NAT rule with a specific backend pool.

F) Assign a protocol type (TCP/UDP) for the NAT rule.

Answer: A

Explanation: Creating a separate Resource Group for NAT rules is not a requirement for configuring an inbound NAT rule in Azure. Resource Groups in Azure are used for organizing resources and managing them collectively; however, they do not directly affect the configuration of NAT rules. The critical steps in setting up an inbound NAT rule include defining the frontend IP configuration, specifying both frontend and backend ports, associating the rule with a backend pool, and defining the protocol. These steps ensure that traffic is properly directed and managed through the load balancer.

Q213: True or False: When configuring an inbound NAT rule on an Azure Load Balancer, the same frontend port can be used for multiple backend VMs if they are listening on different backend ports.

A) True

B) False

Answer: A

Explanation: It is true that the same frontend port can be used for multiple backend VMs as long as each VM is configured with a different backend port. This allows the NAT rule to differentiate and correctly route incoming traffic based on the destination backend port. Azure Load Balancer leverages this capability to provide flexible and scalable access scenarios, where one public IP and frontend port combination can serve different internal services by mapping traffic to unique backend ports.

Q214: A company is setting up multiple inbound NAT rules on their Azure Load Balancer to ensure remote access to their VMs via SSH (port 22). They have configured different frontend ports for each VM. During testing, they observe that traffic is not reaching the intended VMs as expected. What could be a likely cause of this issue?

A) The VMs do not have a public IP address assigned.

B) The Azure Load Balancer does not support SSH traffic.

C) Network Security Group rules are blocking inbound traffic on port 22.

D) The backend pool is configured with the wrong network interface.

E) The inbound NAT rules are not associated with a public frontend IP.

F) The VMs are in different virtual networks.

Answer: C

Explanation: A common reason for inbound traffic not reaching the intended VMs, despite correct NAT rule configuration, is the presence of Network Security Group (NSG) rules that block the required traffic. NSGs are used to control inbound and outbound traffic to Azure resources and can override NAT rules if not properly configured. In this scenario, ensuring that NSGs allow inbound traffic on port 22 to the relevant VMs is crucial. The Azure Load Balancer supports SSH traffic, and while public IPs are not mandatory for VMs when using a load balancer, a public frontend IP is required for inbound NAT rules to function.

Q215: A retail company is deploying an Azure Load Balancer to manage traffic to their web servers hosted on a virtual network. They plan to use inbound NAT rules to enable administrative access via RDP (port 3389) and SSH (port 22) to different VM instances. What is a best practice to ensure secure access while configuring these NAT rules?

A) Use the default security settings without modification.

B) Open all inbound ports in the Network Security Group.

C) Assign a static public IP address to the Load Balancer.

D) Limit access by configuring a source IP restriction policy.

E) Use dynamic ports for frontend configuration.

F) Disable the Network Security Group for simplicity.

Answer: D

Explanation: To ensure secure access when configuring inbound NAT rules for administrative purposes such as RDP and SSH, it is a best practice to limit access through source IP restriction policies. This involves configuring the Network Security Group to allow traffic only from specific, trusted IP addresses. This reduces the attack surface by preventing unauthorized access from unknown or potentially malicious sources. Assigning a static public IP can help maintain consistent access endpoints, but it does not directly enhance security without further restrictions. Disabling security features or opening excessive ports could expose the VMs to security vulnerabilities.

Q216: Your company, Contoso Ltd., plans to expand its cloud infrastructure to include multiple regions for better redundancy and performance. Currently, the company has a virtual network (VNet) named ContosoVNet in the East US region. The plan includes creating another VNet in the West Europe region and establishing connectivity between them. The VNets need to communicate securely, and the solution must support future scalability and additional regions without requiring reconfiguration of existing connections. Which Azure networking solution should you implement to meet these requirements? ---

A) VNet Peering

B) ExpressRoute

C) VPN Gateway

D) Azure Virtual WAN

E) Network Security Groups

F) Route Tables

Answer: D

Explanation: Azure Virtual WAN is the optimal solution in this scenario because it allows for scalable and secure connectivity between VNets across multiple regions. Unlike VNet Peering, which is limited to specific VNets, Virtual WAN supports connecting VNets in a hub-and-spoke model, making it easier to add more regions and VNets in the future without reconfiguring existing connections. ExpressRoute and VPN Gateway are primarily for connecting on-premises networks to Azure, rather than interconnecting VNets directly. Network Security Groups and Route Tables are not solutions for VNet connectivity but rather for traffic management and control within VNets.

Q217: A company is deploying a multi-tier application in Azure, which consists of a web front end and a SQL database back end. Both components are hosted in separate subnets within the same VNet. The company requires that only the web front-end subnet can access the database subnet, and the database subnet should not have any internet access. Which Azure feature should be used to achieve this requirement? ---

A) Azure Firewall

B) Network Security Groups

C) Azure Traffic Manager

D) Azure Load Balancer

E) User-Defined Routes

F) Application Gateway

Answer: B

Explanation: Network Security Groups (NSGs) are the appropriate choice for controlling inbound and outbound traffic to and from subnets and individual VMs. By applying an NSG to the database subnet, you can create rules that allow traffic only from the web front-end subnet while blocking all other traffic, including outbound internet traffic. Azure Firewall and User-Defined Routes are more suitable for scenarios involving more complex routing or centralized management. Azure Traffic Manager and Application Gateway are not designed for internal subnet communication control, and Azure Load Balancer focuses on distributing traffic rather than restricting it.

Q218: True or False: It is possible to connect two VNets in different Azure subscriptions using VNet Peering, provided that both subscriptions are under the same Azure Active Directory tenant. ---

A) True

B) False

Answer: A

Explanation: VNet Peering can indeed be used to connect VNets across different Azure subscriptions as long as the subscriptions are associated with the same Azure Active Directory tenant. This capability allows organizations with multiple subscriptions to maintain secure and efficient connectivity between their resources, facilitating a cohesive network infrastructure without the need for additional VPN gateways or other complex configurations.

Q219: A company has an existing Azure VNet that is configured with a default address space. They need to add more subnets to the VNet to accommodate additional workloads, but the current address space is exhausted. What's the best way to expand the VNet's address space? ---

A) Create a new subnet with a new address range in the existing VNet

B) Modify existing subnets to use smaller CIDR blocks

C) Add a new address space to the VNet

D) Use VNet Peering to connect to another VNet with more address space

E) Create a new VNet and migrate existing resources

F) Use Azure Load Balancer to distribute the traffic

Answer: C

Explanation: The most efficient and straightforward method to expand the address space of an existing VNet is to add a new address space. This action does not disrupt existing resources and allows for the creation of new subnets with new address ranges. Modifying existing subnets' CIDR blocks or creating new VNets for migration can be disruptive and require significant reconfiguration. VNet Peering is used for connectivity between VNets but does not solve the problem of extending address space within a single VNet. Azure Load Balancer is irrelevant in this context as it is not related to address space management.

Q220: You are tasked with designing a network for a multinational corporation that requires high availability and low latency for its applications deployed in Azure. The corporation has offices in North America, Europe, and Asia, and needs a solution that enables efficient cross-region connectivity between Azure VNets. What Azure service should be implemented to fulfill these requirements, considering that you need centralized management and monitoring features?

A) Azure Traffic Manager

B) Azure Bastion

C) Azure Virtual Network Gateway

D) Azure Virtual WAN

E) Azure ExpressRoute

F) Azure Load Balancer

Answer: D

Explanation: Azure Virtual WAN is designed for complex networking needs, offering high availability and low latency by optimizing network routing across multiple regions. It centralizes network management and provides comprehensive monitoring capabilities, making it ideal for multinational corporations with global reach. Azure Traffic Manager and Load Balancer are more focused on traffic distribution rather than network connectivity. Azure Bastion is for secure access to VMs, and Virtual Network Gateway is limited to individual VNet connections rather than global network management. ExpressRoute, while providing dedicated connectivity, does not offer the centralized management and ease of scaling across multiple regions like Azure Virtual WAN does.

Q221: Contoso Pharmaceuticals has a multi-region deployment on Azure to ensure high availability and low latency for its global users. The company's infrastructure team is tasked with configuring a back-end pool for their Azure Load Balancer to distribute traffic efficiently across their virtual machines (VMs) hosted in different Azure regions. The team needs to ensure that the backend pool is set up properly to allow for maintenance without downtime. They also want to implement a policy that automatically adjusts the number of VMs in the pool based on the current load. Which Azure feature should the team implement to satisfy these requirements?

A) Azure Availability Sets

B) Application Gateway with WAF

C) Azure Traffic Manager

D) Azure Autoscale

E) Azure Load Balancer with Floating IP

F) Standard Load Balancer with Health Probes

Answer: D

Explanation: Azure Autoscale is designed to dynamically adjust the number of virtual machines in a back-end pool based on the defined metrics, such as CPU or memory usage, ensuring that the application can handle varying loads efficiently without manual intervention. This feature is ideal for Contoso Pharmaceuticals, as it provides the flexibility to scale the backend pool up or down as needed, facilitating maintenance and optimizing cost. Additionally, by using Azure Load Balancer's health probes, the infrastructure team can ensure high availability by automatically redirecting traffic away from unhealthy VMs, thereby aiding in maintenance without causing downtime.

Q222: Your company needs to configure a back-end pool for an Azure Application Gateway to manage web traffic for a new e-commerce platform. The platform must support session persistence to ensure that returning users are directed to the same server, and SSL offloading is required to improve performance. Which configuration option is best suited to meet these requirements?

A) Configure the back-end pool with IP address affinity and enable HTTP settings for session persistence.

B) Use a Standard SKU Application Gateway with a custom domain and enable SSL termination.

C) Create a back-end pool with multiple availability zones for better redundancy.

D) Enable cookie-based affinity in the back-end pool and configure SSL offloading.

E) Implement an internal load balancer with a custom probe to manage the traffic.

F) Deploy an API Management service for the back-end pool configuration.

Answer: D

Explanation: Cookie-based affinity, also known as session persistence, is a feature of Azure Application Gateway that ensures subsequent requests from the same user session are directed to the same server in the back-end pool. This is crucial for e-commerce platforms where session data is important. SSL offloading, on the other hand, allows the Application Gateway to handle SSL decryption, reducing the processing load on backend servers and improving overall performance. By configuring the back-end pool with these settings, your company can effectively manage web traffic while enhancing the user experience.

Q223: A financial services company is using Azure Load Balancer to distribute traffic across their back-end pool consisting of multiple VMs. To maintain compliance and security standards, the company requires that all backend VMs be allocated in a VNet with network security group (NSG) rules that only allow traffic from known sources. What steps should the networking team take to configure the back-end pool while adhering to these security requirements?

A) Use a Public Load Balancer with default NSG settings for quick deployment.

B) Configure a Private Load Balancer and apply NSG rules to allow only specific IP ranges.

C) Set up a Public Load Balancer and disable NSG rules for unrestricted access.

D) Implement a Basic Load Balancer with custom DNS settings.

E) Deploy a Standard Load Balancer with health probes and default NSG.

F) Use Azure Firewall to manage traffic and bypass NSG configurations.

Answer: B

Explanation: For compliance and security, it is essential to control traffic to the backend VMs by applying NSG rules that restrict access to known and trusted IP ranges. A Private Load Balancer ensures that the backend pool is not exposed to the public internet, further enhancing security. Configuring the NSG with specific rules allows the company to maintain its security posture, adhering to the compliance requirements while still enabling necessary traffic to reach the backend VMs.

Q224: In the context of Azure networking solutions, when creating a back-end pool for an Azure Load Balancer, it is necessary to define the virtual network and subnet where the resources in the pool will reside. True or False?

A) True

B) False

Answer: A

Explanation: When configuring a back-end pool in Azure for a Load Balancer, specifying the virtual network and subnet is crucial because these define the network environment where the load-balanced resources will operate. This is important for controlling traffic flow, ensuring security, and defining the scope of the load balancer's reach. Proper configuration of the VNet and subnet is essential for seamless integration with other Azure resources and for maintaining network segmentation and security.

Q225: A retail company is planning to migrate its on-premises web application to Azure for better scalability and global reach. They need to configure an Azure Application Gateway to handle traffic and provide SSL offloading, URL-based routing, and Web Application Firewall (WAF) capabilities. During the configuration of the back-end pool, which consideration is most critical to ensure seamless integration and optimal performance of their application?

A) Use a Basic SKU Application Gateway to minimize costs.

B) Configure the back-end pool with private IP addresses only.

C) Ensure that all back-end servers are in the same region as the Application Gateway.

D) Deploy the Application Gateway in a different region than the back-end pool for redundancy.

E) Set up the back-end pool with different server types to handle diverse requests.

F) Implement health probes to monitor the status of the web application.

Answer: F

Explanation: Health probes are critical to monitor the health and availability of the back-end servers in the pool. By configuring health probes, the Application Gateway can detect any issues with the servers and reroute traffic to healthy instances, ensuring high availability and optimal performance of the application. This is especially important in a migration scenario where maintaining service uptime is crucial to avoid disruptions. Additionally, health probes enable proactive management of the application infrastructure, allowing for quick response to any server-side issues.

Q226: A multinational corporation is planning to enhance its global network architecture by implementing a Virtual WAN using Azure. The company's key requirement is to create a hub in the Virtual WAN that can efficiently manage and route traffic between their on-premises data centers located in North America, Europe, and Asia. They also want to integrate this setup with their existing ExpressRoute connections and ensure high availability and low latency for their critical applications. Which networking feature should the company prioritize while setting up the hub in Azure Virtual WAN to meet these requirements?

A) Enable Virtual Network Peering between regional hubs.

B) Deploy a Network Virtual Appliance in the hub.

C) Use Azure Firewall Manager for centralized security.

D) Implement a Route Table with custom routes.

E) Configure ExpressRoute FastPath.

F) Activate BGP on all connections.

Answer: E

Explanation: To achieve high availability and low latency, the company should focus on optimizing the performance of their ExpressRoute connections, which are critical for connecting their on-premises data centers to Azure. ExpressRoute FastPath is a feature that improves data path performance between on-premises networks and virtual networks in Azure. It bypasses the Azure WAN and directly routes traffic between the on-premises network and the virtual network, reducing latency and increasing throughput. This is particularly beneficial for applications that require high performance and low latency. While other options like virtual network peering, network appliances, or route tables have their uses, they do not specifically address the requirement for optimizing ExpressRoute connections in the context of a Virtual WAN hub.

Q227: Evaluate the following statement: "In Azure Virtual WAN, a hub can be deployed in any Azure region, regardless of the location of the associated resources, without impacting network performance."

A) True

B) False

Answer: B

Explanation: While Azure allows for flexibility in deploying resources across different regions, the location of the Virtual WAN hub can significantly impact network performance. The hub should ideally be deployed in a region that is geographically closest to the majority of its connected resources to minimize latency. If a hub is deployed in a region far from the resources it manages, network traffic may experience increased latency and reduced performance. Therefore, careful consideration of the hub's location in relation to connected resources is crucial for optimal network performance.

Q228: When configuring a hub in Azure Virtual WAN, you need to ensure that it can dynamically adjust to changes in your on-premises network topology without manual intervention. Which configuration should you implement to achieve this goal?

A) Static Routing with predefined routes.

B) Manual VPN Gateway Configuration.

C) BGP (Border Gateway Protocol) for dynamic routing.

D) Manual IPsec/IKE policies configuration.

E) Azure Traffic Manager for load balancing.

F) Use of User-defined Routes (UDR).

Answer: C

Explanation: BGP (Border Gateway Protocol) is a dynamic routing protocol that allows for automatic updates to routing tables in response to changes in the network topology. By enabling BGP on your Azure Virtual WAN hub, you can ensure that any changes in your on-premises network, such as new subnets or changes in network paths, are automatically communicated to Azure. This reduces the need for manual updates and helps maintain optimal connectivity between on-premises and Azure resources. Static routing and manual configurations do not provide the same level of adaptability and require more maintenance.

Q229: An enterprise is using Azure Virtual WAN to connect multiple branch offices to the Azure cloud. They want to ensure seamless regional connectivity with minimal management overhead. Which Azure service integration will allow the enterprise to leverage centralized policy management for all their branch connections in the Virtual WAN setup?

A) Azure Sentinel for security analytics.

B) Azure Policy for compliance management.

C) Azure Firewall Manager for network security policies.

D) Azure Security Center for threat protection.

E) Azure Monitor for network insights.

F) Azure Active Directory for identity management.

Answer: C

Explanation: Azure Firewall Manager is a security management service that provides centralized security policy and route management for cloud-based security perimeters. For an enterprise looking to manage multiple branch connections through Azure Virtual WAN, integrating Azure Firewall Manager allows centralized control over network security policies. This service simplifies the management of traffic governance across all branch offices, reducing operational complexity and enhancing security posture. Other services like Sentinel or Security Center are more focused on security analytics or threat protection, not specifically on centralized policy management in a Virtual WAN context.

Q230: Your company has recently expanded its Azure environment and needs to create a new hub in Virtual WAN to accommodate increased traffic from new branch locations. You need to ensure that the new hub is correctly configured to support both VPN and ExpressRoute connections. What is a critical step in the hub's configuration to achieve this?

A) Enable forced tunneling on the VPN Gateway.

B) Deploy separate hubs for VPN and ExpressRoute.

C) Configure a shared key for all connections.

D) Ensure the hub is set to 'Secured Virtual Hub.'

E) Activate dual stack (IPv4/IPv6) support.

F) Assign a static public IP address for VPN Gateway.

Answer: D

Explanation: In Azure Virtual WAN, a 'Secured Virtual Hub' is a critical configuration that supports both VPN and ExpressRoute connections. This setting ensures that security and routing policies are consistently applied across both types of connections, facilitating seamless integration and management. While forced tunneling, public IPs, and dual-stack support are important considerations, the 'Secured Virtual Hub' specifically addresses the requirement to support and secure multiple connection types within a single hub. Deploying separate hubs or merely configuring shared keys does not achieve the same level of integration and management efficiency.

Q231: You are the network architect for Contoso Ltd., a company experiencing rapid growth and an increase in its Azure resource needs. The company is planning to deploy a new application across multiple regions to ensure low latency and high availability. As part of this deployment, you need to create a public IP address prefix to efficiently manage and reserve a block of public IP addresses for use by various resources in Azure, such as virtual machines and application gateways. The company plans to have an automated deployment pipeline, which requires programmatic access to the IP address management. Which Azure CLI command should you use to create a public IP address prefix in the "East US" region with a prefix length of /28?

A) az network public-ip prefix create --resource-group MyResourceGroup --name MyPublicIPPrefix --location EastUS --prefix-length 28

B) az network public-ip prefix create --resource-group MyResourceGroup --name MyPublicIPPrefix --region EastUS --prefix-length 28

C) az network public-ip prefix create --resource-group MyResourceGroup --name MyPublicIPPrefix --location EastUS --length 28

D) az network public-ip prefix create --name MyPublicIPPrefix --resource-group MyResourceGroup --location EastUS --prefix-size 28

E) az network public-ip create --resource-group MyResourceGroup --name MyPublicIPPrefix --location EastUS --prefix-length 28

F) az network public-ip prefix create --resource-group MyResourceGroup --name MyPublicIPPrefix --location EastUS --prefix-length /28

Answer: A

Explanation: To create a public IP address prefix using Azure CLI, you must use the az network public-ip prefix create command. The correct syntax involves specifying the resource group, name, location, and prefix length. The command requires the --location flag to define the region, and the --prefix-length flag specifies the size of the prefix without a slash (/), as Azure CLI expects a number only for this parameter. The option chosen correctly uses the --location and --prefix-length parameters, which are essential for defining where the resources will be deployed and the size of the IP address block.

Q232: A true/false style question: When creating a public IP address prefix in Azure, it is mandatory to associate it with a virtual network at the time of creation.

A) True

B) False

Answer: B

Explanation: In Azure, creating a public IP address prefix does not require immediate association with a virtual network. Public IP address prefixes are standalone resources that reserve a contiguous block of public IP addresses for a subscription. They can be associated with other resources like virtual machines or application gateways when needed. This flexibility allows for better resource planning and management without tying the prefixes to specific networks instantly upon creation.

Q233: A company wants to ensure efficient utilization of their IP address space by reserving a contiguous block of public IP addresses. Which of the following considerations should the company take into account when creating a public IP address prefix in Azure?

A) A public IP address prefix can only be created in the same region as the associated virtual network.

B) The prefix length must be a power of two.

C) Public IP address prefixes support IPv6 addresses.

D) Public IP address prefixes can be dynamically resized after creation.

E) Each public IP address within the prefix must be assigned individually to resources.

F) The prefix must be used within a specified time period after creation.

Answer: C

Explanation: Azure supports both IPv4 and IPv6 addresses for public IP address prefixes, which allows for flexibility in addressing schemes and future-proofing the network infrastructure to accommodate both address types. Unlike IPv4, IPv6 has a much larger address space, which can be beneficial for organizations planning long-term deployments. The other considerations, such as dynamic resizing and mandatory assignment after creation, do not accurately reflect Azure's capabilities or requirements for public IP address prefixes.

Q234: You are deploying a mission-critical application that requires a set of static public IP addresses for load balancers and web servers across multiple Azure regions. The application must adhere to strict compliance regulations regarding IP address changes. You need to ensure that the public IP addresses reserved are consistent and do not change over time. How should you configure these IP addresses?

A) Assign dynamic IP addresses to the resources to allow Azure to manage them.

B) Use a single static IP address for all resources to simplify management.

C) Reserve public IP address prefixes and assign static IPs from these prefixes to each resource.

D) Use Azure Traffic Manager to distribute traffic across regions without static IPs.

E) Create a standard SKU public IP address for each region without using prefixes.

F) Implement an Azure ExpressRoute circuit for dedicated IP allocation.

Answer: C

Explanation: To ensure that public IP addresses remain consistent and do not change, reserving public IP address prefixes is the most reliable option. This approach allows you to allocate a contiguous block of static IP addresses that can be distributed across the needed resources. By using static IP addresses from the reserved prefixes, you can comply with regulations requiring steady IP addresses, as these IPs will not change unless the prefix itself is deleted or modified. This approach also simplifies IP management across multiple regions, ensuring consistent application connectivity.

Q235: Your organization, Fabrikam Inc., is expanding its cloud infrastructure to enhance its service delivery. The IT team wants to implement a solution that allows them to reserve and utilize a block of public IP addresses for upcoming projects. The team plans to automate this process using Azure PowerShell. Identify the correct script that would accomplish this task.

A) New-AzPublicIpPrefix -ResourceGroupName "FabrikamGroup" -Name "FabrikamIPPrefix" -Location "West US" -PrefixLength 28

B) New-AzPublicIp -ResourceGroupName "FabrikamGroup" -Name "FabrikamIP" -Location "West US" -AllocationMethod Static

C) New-AzPublicIpPrefix -ResourceGroupName "FabrikamGroup" -Name "FabrikamIPPrefix" -Region "West US" -Length 28

D) New-AzPublicIpPrefix -ResourceGroupName "FabrikamGroup" -Name "FabrikamIPPrefix" -Location "West US" -Size 28

E) New-AzPublicIpPrefix -ResourceGroup "FabrikamGroup" -Name "FabrikamIPPrefix" -Location "West US" -PrefixLength 28

F) New-AzPublicIpPrefix -ResourceGroup "FabrikamGroup" -Name "FabrikamIPPrefix" -Location "West US" -PrefixSize 28

Answer: A

Explanation: The Azure PowerShell cmdlet New-AzPublicIpPrefix is used to create public IP address prefixes. The correct syntax requires specifying the resource group name, the prefix name, the location, and the prefix length, which determines the size of the address block. The -Location parameter indicates the Azure region, and -PrefixLength specifies the number of addresses in the prefix, with no additional symbols needed. Hence, the complete and correct script uses the -PrefixLength parameter to define the desired prefix size accurately, ensuring efficient allocation of public IP addresses for future projects.

Q236: A multinational company, Contoso Ltd., is in the process of modernizing its infrastructure by migrating its applications to Microsoft Azure. They have a critical application running in Azure that needs to securely connect to an on-premises database without exposing the database to the public internet. The application is hosted in Azure Virtual Network (VNet) and the company plans to use Azure Private Link to achieve this. Contoso Ltd. has already set up a Private Link service to facilitate this connection. The IT team needs to ensure that the application can securely access the on-premises database via the Private Link service. Which step should the IT team perform next to enable this secure connection? ---

A) Configure a Service Endpoint for the database.

B) Set up a VNet peering between the application VNet and the on-premises network.

C) Create a Private Endpoint within the application's VNet.

D) Deploy an Application Gateway in front of the database.

E) Configure a Network Security Group (NSG) to allow traffic from the Private Link.

F) Enable DDoS Protection on the application's VNet.

Answer: C

Explanation: A Private Endpoint is a network interface that connects you privately and securely to a service powered by Azure Private Link. Creating a Private Endpoint in the application's VNet allows the application to reach the on-premises database through a private connection. This connection is established using the Private Link service, ensuring that traffic does not traverse the public internet. Service Endpoints or VNet peering options do not provide the same level of security as Private Endpoints. Deploying an Application Gateway or configuring NSGs are not directly related to setting up Private Link connections, and enabling DDoS Protection is not relevant to connecting to an on-premises database.

Q237: Which Azure CLI command is used to create a Private Link service in Azure? ---

A) az network private-link create --name <name> --resource-group <resource-group>

B) az network private-link-service create --name <name> --resource-group <resource-group>

C) az network private-endpoint create --name <name> --resource-group <resource-group>

D) az network service-endpoint create --name <name> --resource-group <resource-group>

E) az network private-link-endpoint create --name <name> --resource-group <resource-group>

F) az network private-link-service create --name <name> --resource-group <resource-group> --vnet-name <vnet-name>

Answer: B

Explanation: The Azure CLI command to create a Private Link service is specifically designed to establish a service that can be accessed privately over a private endpoint. The command "az network private-link-service create" is used for this purpose. This command requires specifying the name and the resource group where the service will be created. Options that mention private endpoints or service endpoints are incorrect since they refer to other components or services in Azure's networking stack. The addition of a VNet name is necessary for some configurations but not for the basic command structure.

Q238: True or False: Azure Private Link can be used to expose a service hosted on an Azure virtual machine to on-premises networks without using the public internet. ---

A) True

B) False

Answer: A

Explanation: Azure Private Link provides private connectivity from a virtual network to Azure services. It can expose services hosted on Azure virtual machines to on-premises networks securely, without traffic traversing the public internet. This is achieved by creating a Private Link service in front of the virtual machine, and then exposing it through a Private Endpoint that can be accessed from the on-premises network. This functionality enhances security by reducing exposure to potential threats that exist on the public internet.

Q239: In configuring a Private Link service, which of the following is NOT a mandatory requirement? ---

A) A load balancer with a frontend IP configuration.

B) A backend pool with virtual machines.

C) An Active Directory domain.

D) A subnet in a virtual network.

E) A Private DNS Zone.

F) A Network Security Group associated with the subnet.

Answer: C

Explanation: Configuring a Private Link service requires certain network components, such as a load balancer with a frontend IP configuration and a backend pool to direct traffic to the appropriate virtual machines. A subnet in a virtual network is necessary to host the service components. While a Private DNS Zone can be beneficial for name resolution, it is not mandatory. An Active Directory domain is not a requirement for setting up a Private Link service. Similarly, while a Network Security Group can help manage traffic flow, it is not a mandatory part of the initial Private Link service configuration.

Q240: A company needs to set up a secure connection from their Azure-hosted web application to a partner's API hosted on Azure. They want to ensure the traffic between these services does not go over the internet and is secure. Which component should they use to achieve this goal?

A) Azure VPN Gateway

B) Azure ExpressRoute

C) Azure Application Gateway

D) Azure Private Endpoint

E) Azure Traffic Manager

F) Azure Front Door

Answer: D

Explanation: To securely connect to a partner's API hosted on Azure without traffic traversing the public internet, the company should use Azure Private Endpoint. A Private Endpoint allows the company to connect to the partner's API over a private IP, ensuring that the traffic remains within Azure's network. This setup prevents exposure to the public internet, providing a secure and private connection. Azure VPN Gateway and ExpressRoute are used for different types of network connectivity (such as on-premises to Azure), while Application Gateway, Traffic Manager, and Front Door are used for different purposes such as load balancing and traffic distribution, not for private connectivity between services.

Q241: Contoso Ltd. is migrating its internal applications to Azure. To enhance security and minimize exposure to the internet, they decide to create private endpoints for their Azure SQL Database. The database is hosted in a separate virtual network (VNet) from their application. Their network architecture includes an application VNet and a database VNet, connected via a VNet peering. They need to ensure that only the application VNet can access the database via the private endpoint and that all other traffic is denied. Which of the following steps should be implemented to achieve this requirement?

A) Configure a network security group (NSG) on the subnet containing the private endpoint, allowing traffic only from the application VNet's IP range.

B) Enable service endpoints for Azure SQL Database on the database VNet.

C) Create a user-defined route (UDR) in the application VNet pointing to the database VNet's private endpoint IP.

D) Use a network virtual appliance (NVA) to restrict traffic between the VNets.

E) Configure a custom DNS zone and link it to both VNets.

F) Implement Azure Front Door to manage access to the private endpoint.

Answer: A

Explanation: Configuring a network security group (NSG) on the subnet where the private endpoint exists is crucial for controlling access. By setting NSG rules to allow traffic only from the application VNet's IP range, you ensure that only the desired traffic reaches the private endpoint. All other traffic is denied by default, thus maintaining security. Service endpoints and UDRs are typically used for different scenarios; NVAs and Azure Front Door add complexity and are unnecessary for this requirement. Private DNS zones are used for name resolution, not traffic restriction.

Q242: To establish a private endpoint connection for an Azure Blob Storage account, which DNS configuration is necessary to ensure that resources within the VNet can resolve the storage account name to the private endpoint IP?

A) Set a conditional forwarder in Azure DNS for the storage account's public endpoint.

B) Create an A record in the Azure-hosted private DNS zone to point to the private endpoint IP.

C) Use a CNAME record in the public DNS to map the storage account's name to the private IP.

D) Implement a DNS forwarder in the VNet to resolve the storage account's public IP.

E) Configure a PTR record in the private DNS zone for reverse lookup.

F) Enable the "Override DNS resolution" option in the storage account settings.

Answer: B

Explanation: When using private endpoints, Azure recommends creating a private DNS zone with an A record that maps the storage account name to the private endpoint IP. This configuration ensures that DNS queries within the VNet resolve to the private IP, enabling secure access. Public DNS records and conditional forwarding are not needed since the goal is to use the private network. CNAME records are not suitable here as they are meant for aliasing, not direct IP mapping. PTR records are for reverse lookups and not relevant to this task.

Q243: You are tasked with implementing a private endpoint for an Azure Web App in a multi-region deployment. The objective is to ensure that traffic from all regions is routed to their respective private endpoints without crossing the public internet. Which strategy should you use to accomplish this?

A) Deploy an Azure Traffic Manager with a weighted routing method pointing to each region's private endpoint.

B) Use a global VNet peering to connect VNets in different regions and configure regional NSGs.

C) Configure a private link service in each region and associate it with the web app's private endpoint.

D) Deploy Azure Application Gateway in each region with backend pool entries as private endpoints.

E) Implement Azure Front Door with regional routing rules to direct traffic to private endpoints.

F) Use Azure Load Balancer with internal load balancing rules for traffic distribution.

Answer: D

Explanation: Azure Application Gateway can effectively route traffic to private endpoints when configured with backend pools. By deploying an Application Gateway in each region, you ensure that traffic remains within Azure's backbone network and doesn't traverse the public internet. Traffic Manager and Front Door are typically used for public endpoint management and do not directly support private endpoint routing. Global VNet peering would not control traffic routing at the application level. Azure Load Balancer is not suited for web app traffic management in this scenario.

Q244: True or False: A private endpoint in Azure requires a public IP address to be accessible within a VNet.

A) True

B) False

Answer: B

Explanation: A private endpoint does not require a public IP address. In Azure, private endpoints provide secure and private connectivity to services by mapping a service to a private IP address within a VNet. This allows traffic to remain on the Microsoft backbone network, preventing exposure to the public internet. The primary advantage of private endpoints is to eliminate the need for a public IP while ensuring secure access within a VNet.

Q245: In configuring a private endpoint for a PaaS service in Azure, what is the primary purpose of associating a private DNS zone with the VNet?

A) To enable cross-region access without latency.

B) To allow the service to be publicly accessible while still using a private IP.

C) To ensure that DNS queries resolve the service name to the private IP within the VNet.

D) To manage traffic flow between multiple VNets with different DNS configurations.

E) To provide reverse DNS lookups for private IPs used by the service.

F) To automatically block public DNS queries for the service.

Answer: C

Explanation: The primary purpose of associating a private DNS zone with a VNet is to ensure that DNS queries within the VNet resolve the service's name to the private IP provided by the private endpoint. This allows resources within the VNet to communicate with the service securely and without exposing traffic to the public internet. Public accessibility and traffic management are unrelated to private DNS zones, while reverse DNS lookups are not the goal in this context.

Q246: Contoso Ltd. has a hybrid cloud architecture where critical data is stored on-premises and non-critical data is stored in Azure. They want to ensure that their Azure SQL Database can securely access specific Azure Storage accounts over an optimized and secure connection without exposing data to the internet. Additionally, the on-premises network should be able to access the same storage accounts without routing through the internet. How should Contoso Ltd. configure service endpoints to achieve this requirement? ---

A) Configure a Virtual Network (VNet) service endpoint for the Azure SQL Database and set up a VPN connection for on-premises access.

B) Enable Virtual Network service endpoints for Azure Storage on the VNet where the Azure SQL Database is deployed.

C) Use Azure Private Link to connect both Azure SQL Database and on-premises network to Azure Storage.

D) Implement a Network Security Group (NSG) to restrict access to Azure Storage from specific IP addresses.

E) Configure a VNet Peering to enable access between the on-premises network and Azure Storage.

F) Deploy an Azure Firewall to route traffic from the SQL Database to Azure Storage securely.

Answer: B

Explanation: Configuring Virtual Network (VNet) service endpoints for Azure Storage directly on the VNet where Azure SQL Database is deployed enables secure, optimized connections to Azure Storage services. This configuration restricts access to Azure Storage only to resources within the specified VNet, thus preventing exposure to the internet. This setup ensures that traffic remains on the Azure backbone network, enhancing security and performance. For on-premises access, while service endpoints do not extend directly to on-premises, the use of a VPN or ExpressRoute with forced tunneling can route on-premises traffic through the VNet, leveraging the service endpoint for secure access.

Q247: In the context of Azure service endpoints, service endpoints provide a direct connection to Azure services over the Microsoft backbone network, bypassing the public internet. ---

A) True

B) False

Answer: A

Explanation: Service endpoints in Azure are designed to provide a secure and direct connection to Azure services from within a virtual network over the Microsoft backbone network. This feature effectively bypasses the public internet, reducing the risk of exposure to potential threats and improving data transfer performance. By enabling service endpoints, you ensure that the communication between your Azure resources and Azure services remains within the trusted Azure infrastructure, thereby enhancing security and reliability.

Q248: Your company has multiple Azure subscriptions and is setting up a network architecture that requires secure access to Azure Storage from several VNets across different subscriptions. What is the most effective way to enable this access using service endpoints? ---

A) Enable service endpoints on each VNet individually for Azure Storage.

B) Use Azure Private Link across subscriptions and VNets.

C) Configure a single VNet with service endpoints and peer it with other VNets.

D) Set up a shared services VNet and allow service endpoints from this VNet.

E) Implement Azure Firewall to control access to Azure Storage from all VNets.

F) Utilize Network Security Groups to allow access to Azure Storage.

Answer: A

Explanation: Enabling service endpoints on each VNet individually for Azure Storage is the most straightforward approach to ensure secure access across multiple subscriptions. Service endpoints need to be explicitly enabled for each VNet that requires secure access to Azure services. This setup allows each VNet to connect directly to Azure Storage over the Microsoft backbone network, ensuring secure and optimized data transfer. Although other solutions like Azure Private Link can provide more granular access controls, they are more complex and might not be necessary if the requirement is simply to secure traffic to Azure Storage across multiple VNets.

Q249: Consider a scenario where a business application running in Azure requires frequent interaction with Azure Key Vault for secrets management. The application is deployed in a VNet with several subnets, and security needs to be tightened to ensure only authorized subnets can access the Key Vault. How should the service endpoints be configured to meet this requirement? ---

A) Enable service endpoints for Key Vault on the entire VNet.

B) Configure service endpoints for Key Vault on specific subnets within the VNet.

C) Use Azure Private Link to connect to Azure Key Vault.

D) Implement a Network Security Group (NSG) to filter traffic to Azure Key Vault.

E) Set up an Application Gateway to manage access to Azure Key Vault.

F) Deploy an Azure Bastion host for secure access to Azure Key Vault.

Answer: B

Explanation: To restrict access to Azure Key Vault to specific subnets, you should configure service endpoints for Key Vault on those particular subnets within the VNet. This approach allows you to control which parts of your VNet can securely access the Key Vault, thereby tightening security by ensuring that only resources in the designated subnets have the necessary permissions. By contrast, enabling service endpoints on the entire VNet would allow access from all subnets, which might not meet the security requirements. Azure Private Link or NSGs could also be used for more advanced scenarios, but configuring service endpoints on specific subnets is a simpler and effective solution for this requirement.

Q250: A technology firm wants to ensure that their Azure App Service can access an Azure SQL Database securely without internet exposure. Both resources are in the same Azure region but in different VNets. What configuration should be applied to the VNets to secure the connection using service endpoints?

A) Enable service endpoints for SQL Database on the VNet containing the Azure App Service.

B) Use a VNet Peering between the two VNets.

C) Configure service endpoints for SQL Database on both VNets.

D) Implement Azure Private Link for the SQL Database.

E) Set up a VPN Gateway to connect the VNets securely.

F) Deploy an Azure Application Gateway to manage traffic between the App Service and SQL Database.

Answer: A

Explanation: Enabling service endpoints for SQL Database on the VNet containing the Azure App Service allows secure access to the SQL Database without relying on internet exposure. Service endpoints configure the VNet to use the Microsoft backbone network for accessing the SQL Database, ensuring that traffic is kept secure and within Azure's trusted infrastructure. This setup is particularly effective when both resources are in the same region, as it simplifies the architecture while maintaining security. While VNet Peering or Azure Private Link could also be considered for more complex scenarios, enabling service endpoints is the most straightforward and cost-effective solution for this particular requirement.

Q251: Your company, Contoso Ltd, is expanding its cloud infrastructure to support global operations. You are tasked with deploying a Virtual WAN (VWAN) solution in Azure that includes a gateway for secure and optimized connectivity between regional offices and Azure resources. The main office is located in New York, and regional offices are located in London, Tokyo, and Sydney. You need to ensure that the network configuration allows for optimal routing and minimal latency. Furthermore, the solution must support the existing on-premises VPN infrastructure and integrate seamlessly with Azure services. Which of the following steps would you perform first when deploying a gateway into a Virtual WAN hub in this scenario? ---

A) Configure the VPN gateway settings in the Azure portal.

B) Create the Virtual WAN resource in the Azure portal.

C) Set up peering between all regional offices and the VWAN hub.

D) Deploy Azure Firewall for network security within the VWAN.

E) Enable the VWAN hub routing policy to optimize traffic.

F) Register the VWAN service with Azure Active Directory.

Answer: B

Explanation: To begin deploying a gateway into a Virtual WAN hub, the first step is to create the Virtual WAN resource in the Azure portal. This step establishes the foundational network architecture required to support the integration of various components such as gateways, routing policies, and security services. Once the VWAN is created, you can proceed to configure the VPN gateway settings and establish connections between regional offices and the VWAN hub. This approach ensures a structured deployment that both supports existing on-premises VPN infrastructure and optimizes routing for global operations. Setting up peering, deploying security measures like Azure Firewall, and configuring routing policies are subsequent steps that build upon the established VWAN resource.

Q252: When deploying a gateway into a Virtual WAN hub, it is necessary to configure user-defined routes (UDRs) for traffic management. True or False? ---

A) True

B) False

Answer: B

Explanation: Configuring user-defined routes (UDRs) is not a mandatory step when deploying a gateway into a Virtual WAN hub. Azure Virtual WAN automatically manages the routing within the hub, simplifying the process for users. The built-in routing capabilities of the Virtual WAN are designed to handle traffic management efficiently without requiring manual UDR configuration. This feature is particularly beneficial in reducing administrative overhead and ensuring that traffic is managed optimally based on Azure's intelligent routing protocols. However, UDRs might still be used in specific scenarios where custom traffic routing is necessary.

Q253: You are responsible for setting up a Virtual WAN hub that will connect multiple branch offices across different continents. One of the requirements is to ensure that all connections are encrypted and that a high level of security is maintained throughout the network. What is the most appropriate type of gateway to deploy in the Virtual WAN hub to fulfill this requirement? ---

A) Point-to-Site VPN Gateway

B) Site-to-Site VPN Gateway

C) ExpressRoute Gateway

D) Secure Web Gateway

E) Application Gateway

F) Network Virtual Appliance

Answer: B

Explanation: Deploying a Site-to-Site VPN Gateway in the Virtual WAN hub is the most appropriate choice to ensure encrypted connections and maintain a high level of security across branch offices. A Site-to-Site VPN Gateway provides secure, encrypted tunnels between the on-premises networks and the Azure Virtual WAN hub. This type of gateway is specifically designed to support multiple branch offices, allowing them to connect securely to Azure resources over the Internet. The encryption ensures that data is protected during transit, making it suitable for scenarios requiring stringent security measures. While Point-to-Site VPNs are used for individual user connections and ExpressRoute provides private connectivity, Site-to-Site VPNs are ideal for connecting entire networks.

Q254: As part of a network optimization initiative for a multinational corporation, you have been tasked with deploying a Virtual WAN hub that provides reliable and fast connections to Azure services. The solution must support high throughput and low latency to meet business requirements. Which type of gateway should be prioritized for deployment to achieve these objectives? ---

A) Basic VPN Gateway

B) Standard VPN Gateway

C) Ultra Performance VPN Gateway

D) High Performance VPN Gateway

E) ExpressRoute Gateway

F) Standard Performance VPN Gateway

Answer: E

Explanation: To achieve high throughput and low latency, deploying an ExpressRoute Gateway should be prioritized. ExpressRoute provides dedicated, private connections between an on-premises network and Azure, bypassing the public Internet. This not only enhances security but also significantly improves performance by offering predictable, consistent network latency and higher bandwidth capabilities compared to Internet-based VPN connections. ExpressRoute is particularly beneficial for multinational corporations that require reliable and fast access to Azure services, supporting enterprise-grade workloads and applications that demand high network performance. Other VPN gateways, while secure, rely on the public Internet and generally cannot match the throughput and latency advantages provided by ExpressRoute.

Q255: You are deploying a new Virtual WAN hub for a client who requires optimized traffic management and security. Part of the task involves configuring the hub to support automatic route advertisement and propagation. Which feature should you enable to facilitate this requirement?

A) Azure Traffic Manager

B) Route Propagation

C) BGP Peering

D) Network Security Groups

E) Azure Route Server

F) Policy-Based VPN

Answer: C

Explanation: Enabling BGP (Border Gateway Protocol) Peering is essential for automatic route advertisement and propagation within a Virtual WAN hub. BGP is a standardized exterior gateway protocol that allows different networks to exchange routing information dynamically. By configuring BGP peering, the Virtual WAN hub can automatically learn and advertise routes to and from connected networks, ensuring optimized traffic management and seamless connectivity across various network segments. This setup is crucial for environments where network topology changes frequently or requires dynamic updates, such as in complex, multi-site deployments. BGP's ability to automatically adapt to network changes reduces manual configuration effort and enhances overall network efficiency and reliability.

Q256: An enterprise company, Contoso Ltd., has multiple virtual networks (VNets) across different Azure regions to support its global operations. Each regional VNet has its own private DNS zone. The company wants to streamline their DNS resolution process such that all VNets can resolve each other's private domains without requiring multiple DNS forwarding rules. They also want to ensure minimal latency and high availability. As a cloud architect, how would you design this solution using Azure DNS Private Resolver? ---

A) Deploy an Azure DNS Private Resolver in each VNet and configure forwarding rules for each private DNS zone.

B) Deploy a single Azure DNS Private Resolver in a central VNet and set up peering with all other VNets.

C) Use Azure DNS zone delegation to centralize DNS management for all private zones.

D) Implement Azure Bastion to facilitate DNS resolution across VNets.

E) Configure a custom DNS server in a central VNet and manually define forwarding rules.

F) Deploy an Azure DNS Private Resolver in each region and set up forwarding rules to resolve cross-region domains.

Answer: F

Explanation: When deploying Azure DNS Private Resolvers, using a resolver in each region allows for low-latency and high-availability DNS resolution tailored to the region's VNets. This setup avoids the need for complex peering or a single point of failure by centralizing DNS resolution in one VNet. Each regional resolver can have specific forwarding rules to resolve private DNS zones in other regions, ensuring all VNets can resolve each other's domains seamlessly. This design leverages Azure's distributed architecture while maintaining regional independence and avoiding unnecessary traffic between regions.

Q257: In Azure, the DNS Private Resolver provides a fully-managed service for DNS resolution within virtual networks. True or False: When configuring DNS forwarding rules using Azure DNS Private Resolver, it is mandatory to specify the exact IP address of the target DNS server for each rule. ---

A) True

B) False

Answer: B

Explanation: Azure DNS Private Resolver allows you to create DNS forwarding rules without specifying exact IP addresses. Instead, you can define rules based on domain names, which the resolver will use to route queries appropriately. This flexibility means you can manage DNS resolution dynamically and efficiently without the need to hard-code IP addresses, which can be prone to change. It simplifies DNS management and reduces administrative overhead, especially in large or dynamic environments.

Q258: Fill in the gap: To enable DNS resolution between a virtual network and an on-premises network using Azure DNS Private Resolver, you should configure to securely forward DNS queries across the networks. ---

A) Azure VPN Gateway

B) Azure ExpressRoute

C) Azure Firewall

D) Azure DNS Conditional Forwarding

E) Azure Virtual Network Peering

F) Azure Application Gateway

Answer: A

Explanation: Azure VPN Gateway is the most effective way to securely connect an Azure virtual network with an on-premises network, enabling DNS resolution between them. By using a VPN Gateway, DNS queries can be forwarded securely over the VPN tunnel, ensuring that on-premises resources are able to resolve Azure private DNS zones and vice versa. This setup is especially useful for hybrid cloud environments where seamless integration between Azure and on-premises resources is crucial.

Q259: A company has set up several DNS Private Resolvers in different Azure regions to handle DNS queries for their VNets. They are experiencing issues with DNS queries from one particular region not resolving the expected private domain names correctly. What is the most likely cause of this issue? ---

A) The DNS Private Resolver is not linked to the VNet in that region.

B) The DNS Private Resolver does not support cross-region DNS resolution.

C) The forwarding rules are missing or incorrectly configured for that region.

D) The DNS Private Resolver is overloaded and unable to process requests.

E) There is a network security group blocking DNS traffic in that region.

F) The DNS Private Resolver needs to be restarted to refresh its cache.

Answer: C

Explanation: When DNS queries from a region are not resolving correctly, it is often due to missing or incorrectly configured forwarding rules in the DNS Private Resolver for that specific region. Forwarding rules direct DNS queries to the appropriate DNS servers or zones. If these rules are absent or misconfigured, queries will fail to resolve as expected. Ensuring that the forwarding rules are correctly set up and tested for each private domain is critical to maintaining seamless DNS resolution across all regions.

Q260: A startup is planning to use Azure DNS Private Resolver to manage DNS resolution for its microservices architecture spread across multiple VNets within a single Azure region. What important consideration should be taken into account when designing this setup to avoid potential service disruptions?

A) Ensure all DNS Private Resolvers are deployed in a single VNet for simplicity.

B) Configure redundant DNS Private Resolvers in separate availability zones.

C) Use a single DNS Private Resolver to reduce configuration complexity.

D) Rely on Azure default DNS as a fallback in case of resolver failure.

E) Deploy DNS Private Resolvers only during peak traffic hours for testing.

F) Limit DNS resolution to public domains only to avoid internal conflicts.

Answer: B

Explanation: Deploying redundant DNS Private Resolvers in separate availability zones within the same region is a best practice to ensure high availability and fault tolerance. This setup helps to mitigate risks associated with potential service disruptions due to regional outages or maintenance. By distributing resolvers across availability zones, the startup can ensure continuous DNS resolution for its microservices architecture, maintaining service reliability and minimizing downtime. Azure's infrastructure supports such redundancy, allowing seamless failover between availability zones.

Q261: A global enterprise, Contoso Ltd., is planning to improve the connectivity of its multiple Azure virtual networks spread across several regions. They have existing Network Virtual Appliances (NVAs) to manage traffic and wish to minimize latency and improve route management. Contoso wants to use Azure Route Server to dynamically manage BGP routes between their NVAs and Azure Virtual Networks without manually updating routes. Given this scenario, which Azure configuration should Contoso implement to achieve dynamic routing with Azure Route Server?

A) Create a new Azure Route Server in each virtual network and establish BGP peering with each NVA.

B) Deploy Azure Route Server in a single central virtual network and connect all other virtual networks using VPN Gateway.

C) Utilize Azure Route Server in conjunction with ExpressRoute to manage on-premises routes.

D) Integrate Azure Route Server with Azure Traffic Manager for global load balancing.

E) Set up Azure Route Server with Azure Bastion for secure remote access.

F) Use Azure Route Server with Azure Firewall for enhanced security.

Answer: A

Explanation: Azure Route Server allows for dynamic exchange of routes between Azure virtual networks and Network Virtual Appliances (NVAs) using the Border Gateway Protocol (BGP). By deploying an Azure Route Server in each virtual network and establishing BGP peering with NVAs, Contoso can enable dynamic route updates. This configuration eliminates the need for manual route management and reduces latency by localizing traffic within each region. It also ensures high availability and scalability of route updates, essential for a global enterprise like Contoso.

Q262: In a scenario where an organization deploys Azure Route Server to manage network routes dynamically, which specific Azure service is directly responsible for enabling BGP route exchange between Azure Virtual Networks and on-premises networks?

A) Azure ExpressRoute

B) Azure Traffic Manager

C) Azure Virtual WAN

D) Azure Application Gateway

E) Azure Front Door

F) Azure Load Balancer

Answer: A

Explanation: Azure ExpressRoute is the service that facilitates private connections between Azure data centers and on-premises infrastructure. When combined with Azure Route Server, ExpressRoute enables the dynamic exchange of BGP routes between Azure Virtual Networks and on-premises networks. This integration allows organizations to manage their hybrid network setups effectively and ensure seamless connectivity without manual route configuration.

Q263: To optimize the performance of Azure Route Server in a production environment, which of the following best practices should be considered?

A) Deploy Azure Route Server in a dedicated resource group separate from other network resources.

B) Use Azure Route Server only with virtual machines that have static IP addresses.

C) Configure Azure Route Server to peer only with NVAs that have multiple network interfaces.

D) Limit the number of BGP sessions to improve route convergence times.

E) Regularly update the Azure Route Server to the latest version for new features and optimizations.

F) Use a single Azure Route Server instance per subscription for simplified management.

Answer: E

Explanation: Regularly updating the Azure Route Server ensures that the latest features, bug fixes, and performance optimizations are in place. This practice is crucial in a production environment to maintain optimal performance and leverage new capabilities that enhance the routing infrastructure. Keeping Azure services updated also aligns with Azure's shared responsibility model, where the customer is responsible for maintaining the service's current version.

Q264: A company is considering using Azure Route Server to facilitate dynamic routing between their NVAs and Azure VNet. They want to ensure high availability and fault tolerance. Which deployment strategy should they adopt to meet these requirements?

A) Deploy a single Azure Route Server instance in the primary VNet.

B) Use Azure Route Server with Azure Load Balancer to distribute traffic across multiple NVAs.

C) Deploy multiple Azure Route Server instances across different Azure regions.

D) Implement Azure Route Server in an availability zone with a backup instance in another zone.

E) Utilize Azure Route Server with Azure Traffic Manager for global failover.

F) Deploy Azure Route Server with redundancy in the same region using availability sets.

Answer: D

Explanation: Deploying Azure Route Server in an availability zone with a backup instance in another zone ensures high availability and fault tolerance. This strategy provides redundancy and minimizes the risk of a single point of failure by distributing the Route Server instances across different physical locations. Availability zones offer independent power, cooling, and networking, which is crucial for maintaining continuous operation even in the event of a zone-level failure.

Q265: True or False: Azure Route Server automatically configures and manages all BGP route advertisements between Azure Virtual Networks and any connected on-premises networks without the need for additional configuration.

A) True

B) False

Answer: B

Explanation: While Azure Route Server facilitates the dynamic exchange of BGP routes, it does not automatically manage all aspects of route advertisements between Azure Virtual Networks and connected on-premises networks. Network administrators must configure BGP sessions and ensure that the correct policies and filters are applied to manage route advertisements effectively. Additional configuration is often necessary to tailor the routing setup to specific organizational requirements and network topologies.

Q266: A global manufacturing company wants to ensure high availability and low latency connectivity between its on-premises data centers in Europe and its Azure regions in the US. They are considering using Azure ExpressRoute Global Reach to connect their private data centers via different ExpressRoute circuits. However, they need to understand the implications and the configurations needed to optimize the connectivity. Which feature of ExpressRoute should they leverage to achieve this requirement?

A) ExpressRoute Direct

B) ExpressRoute Metro Connectivity

C) ExpressRoute FastPath

D) ExpressRoute Global Reach

E) VNet Peering

F) Azure Traffic Manager

Answer: D

Explanation: ExpressRoute Global Reach allows you to connect your on-premises data centers via ExpressRoute circuits and enables connectivity between them through the Microsoft global network. This feature is specifically designed for scenarios where enterprises have multiple on-premises networks connected to different ExpressRoute circuits and wish to enable communication between these networks. By leveraging the Microsoft backbone, it ensures high availability and low latency. In this case, the company's requirement to link its European data centers with Azure regions in the US can be effectively met using ExpressRoute Global Reach, thus optimizing the connectivity across the global network.

Q267: You are the network architect for a financial services company that requires ultra-high-speed and dedicated connectivity to Azure for handling sensitive transactions. The company wants to ensure direct ownership of the physical infrastructure connecting to Azure. What ExpressRoute option should you recommend?

A) ExpressRoute Direct

B) ExpressRoute FastPath

C) ExpressRoute Premium

D) ExpressRoute Global Reach

E) VPN Gateway

F) Azure Load Balancer

Answer: A

Explanation: ExpressRoute Direct provides a dedicated and private connection to Azure services. It allows customers to connect directly to Microsoft's global network through a dedicated port pair at 10 Gbps or 100 Gbps. This is particularly useful for organizations that require high-speed, reliable connections with full control over the physical infrastructure, which is crucial for handling sensitive financial transactions. By availing ExpressRoute Direct, the company can ensure that it owns the physical layer of the connection to Azure, providing an additional layer of security and performance assurance.

Q268: For a company using ExpressRoute, enabling FastPath can improve the performance of data paths between on-premises networks and Azure Virtual Networks (VNets). True or False?

A) True

B) False

Answer: A

Explanation: FastPath is a feature of Azure ExpressRoute that optimizes the data path from on-premises networks to Azure Virtual Networks, bypassing the ExpressRoute gateway. By doing so, it reduces latency and improves performance for network traffic. When FastPath is enabled, data packets travel directly from the on-premises network to the Azure Virtual Network, eliminating the need to pass through the gateway. This results in a more efficient and faster connection, making it particularly beneficial for applications that require low-latency connectivity, such as real-time data processing or interactive applications.

Q269: A technology firm is designing its network architecture for a new Azure-based application. They need a solution that provides a reliable and high-performance pathway from their on-premises environment to Azure, while ensuring that data latency is minimized. Which ExpressRoute feature specifically enhances the data path from on-premises to Azure VNets, bypassing the ExpressRoute gateway?

A) ExpressRoute Direct

B) ExpressRoute Global Reach

C) ExpressRoute FastPath

D) ExpressRoute Premium

E) Azure Front Door

F) VNet-to-VNet Connectivity

Answer: C

Explanation: ExpressRoute FastPath is designed to improve the performance of data paths between on-premises networks and Azure VNets by allowing the data to bypass the ExpressRoute gateway. This direct pathway reduces latency and improves throughput by ensuring that the data takes the shortest possible route. FastPath is particularly beneficial for applications needing high performance, as it allows for more efficient data transfer and reduced delays, thereby optimizing the overall network experience.

Q270: A large retail enterprise operates multiple data centers globally and is planning to interconnect these data centers through Azure. They are looking for a solution that allows them to manage and monitor the data flow between these locations using Azure's backbone network while minimizing the complexity of setup and configuration. Which Azure feature should they implement?

A) ExpressRoute Metro Connectivity

B) Azure Virtual WAN

C) ExpressRoute Direct

D) ExpressRoute Global Reach

E) VPN Gateway

F) Azure Application Gateway

Answer: D

Explanation: ExpressRoute Global Reach is the ideal solution for interconnecting multiple data centers through Azure, as it leverages Microsoft's global backbone network to facilitate communication between on-premises networks connected to different ExpressRoute circuits. This feature simplifies the management and monitoring of data flows across global locations by using a single, cohesive network infrastructure. It minimizes the complexity typically associated with setting up multiple point-to-point connections, offering a streamlined and efficient way to connect disparate data centers under the same organizational umbrella.

Q271: Your company, Contoso Pharmaceuticals, operates globally with data centers in North America, Europe, and Asia. You are tasked with designing a network architecture that ensures low-latency connectivity between these data centers using Azure ExpressRoute. Furthermore, the solution must support cross-region connectivity for critical applications that require redundancy and disaster recovery. Contoso also has strict compliance requirements to maintain data sovereignty within each region. Which design consideration is most critical to meet these requirements?

A) Establishing local peering with Microsoft for each region separately.

B) Enabling ExpressRoute FastPath for improved performance.

C) Implementing Global Reach to connect on-premises networks across regions.

D) Using ExpressRoute Direct for direct connectivity.

E) Configuring VNet Peering across regions with ExpressRoute.

F) Utilizing VPN Gateway as a fallback option.

Answer: C

Explanation: Cross-region connectivity through Global Reach is essential in this scenario to ensure that on-premises networks in different parts of the world can communicate through ExpressRoute connections. Global Reach allows your on-premises networks connected to ExpressRoute to communicate with each other. This is particularly useful for global companies like Contoso Pharmaceuticals, which need low-latency and reliable connections between their data centers in different regions. Although enabling FastPath could improve performance, it is more relevant to the communication between Azure and on-premises networks rather than cross-region connectivity. ExpressRoute Direct and VNet Peering do not address cross-region requirements adequately, and using a VPN Gateway as a fallback does not provide the primary mechanism for meeting the cross-region requirement.

Q272: In a disaster recovery scenario, you need to ensure that your ExpressRoute circuit in the primary region can failover to a secondary region without manual intervention, maintaining continuous connectivity. Which Azure feature allows you to achieve this?

A) ExpressRoute Global Reach

B) ExpressRoute Failover Routing

C) ExpressRoute Primary/Secondary Circuit Pairing

D) ExpressRoute Circuit Redundancy

E) ExpressRoute Traffic Manager

F) ExpressRoute FastPath

Answer: C

Explanation: ExpressRoute Primary/Secondary Circuit Pairing is designed to provide automatic failover capabilities for ExpressRoute circuits. This feature ensures that if the primary circuit goes down, traffic can automatically be rerouted to a secondary circuit in a different region, providing seamless connectivity and minimizing downtime. This is crucial in disaster recovery scenarios where manual intervention is not feasible. This setup allows for a robust and resilient network architecture that can handle unexpected disruptions effectively. Global Reach, Traffic Manager, and other options do not specifically address the need for automatic failover between regions.

Q273: A multinational corporation requires an ExpressRoute setup that provides redundancy and high availability for its critical applications. The network must be designed to withstand the failure of a single ExpressRoute circuit without affecting connectivity. Which configuration would best meet these requirements?

A) Deploying two separate ExpressRoute circuits to different Azure regions.

B) Implementing ExpressRoute Premium with a single circuit.

C) Configuring a single ExpressRoute circuit with multiple peering locations.

D) Using ExpressRoute Direct with redundant routers.

E) Setting up dual ExpressRoute circuits in the same peering location.

F) Combining ExpressRoute with Azure VPN Gateway for backup.

Answer: E

Explanation: Setting up dual ExpressRoute circuits in the same peering location provides redundancy by ensuring there are two independent paths for connectivity. This setup is crucial for high availability and resilience. If one circuit experiences a failure, the other can take over, thus maintaining continuous network operations. While deploying circuits to different regions or using ExpressRoute Direct with redundant routers can provide redundancy, having dual circuits in the same location ensures immediate failover without the need for regional routing changes. Integrating VPN Gateway as a backup could be useful, but it typically doesn't provide the same level of performance and reliability as dual ExpressRoute circuits.

Q274: True/False: ExpressRoute Global Reach is a feature that allows Azure Virtual Networks across different regions to communicate directly with each other without passing through on-premises networks.

A) True

B) False

Answer: B

Explanation: ExpressRoute Global Reach is designed to enable connectivity between on-premises networks through the Azure backbone, rather than directly connecting Azure Virtual Networks across regions. It allows two on-premises networks connected to different ExpressRoute circuits to communicate as if they were on the same private network. This feature is particularly useful for enterprises with multiple on-premises sites that need to connect seamlessly through Azure. However, it does not facilitate direct VNet-to-VNet communication across regions; for that, VNet Peering or VPN connections would be needed.

Q275: You are tasked with implementing disaster recovery for an organization's Azure environment, which includes ensuring that the on-premises network can maintain connectivity to Azure services in the event of a regional failure. The organization uses ExpressRoute for primary connectivity. What additional configuration should you implement to ensure continuous connectivity in such scenarios?

A) Setting up an additional ExpressRoute circuit in a different Azure region.

B) Configuring ExpressRoute with Azure Traffic Manager.

C) Implementing ExpressRoute Premium features.

D) Utilizing Azure Site Recovery for network failover.

E) Creating a secondary ExpressRoute circuit in the same peering location.

F) Establishing a VPN Gateway connection as a backup.

Answer: F

Explanation: Establishing a VPN Gateway connection as a backup provides an alternative path for connectivity in case the primary ExpressRoute circuit fails due to a regional outage. This setup helps ensure that even if the primary connectivity path is disrupted, the on-premises network can still access Azure services through the VPN connection. While setting up an additional ExpressRoute circuit in a different region could also offer redundancy, it may not be immediately available in a disaster scenario without pre-configuration. Azure Site Recovery is more focused on application-level disaster recovery rather than network connectivity.

Q276: You are working as a network architect for a company that is migrating its on-premises infrastructure to Azure. The company has multiple Azure Virtual Networks (VNets) in different regions and wants to implement a custom routing solution to control the flow of traffic between VNets and on-premises networks. They have decided to use user-defined routes (UDRs) to manage this traffic. The company has specific requirements: traffic between VNets should be routed through a virtual network appliance for inspection, and traffic to on-premises should use an ExpressRoute connection. How should you configure the UDRs to meet these requirements?

A) Create UDRs in each subnet with a next hop type of Virtual Network Gateway for all traffic.

B) Configure UDRs with a next hop type of Internet for VNet-to-VNet traffic.

C) Use UDRs with a next hop type of Virtual Appliance for VNet-to-VNet traffic inspection.

D) Deploy UDRs in each subnet with a next hop type of None to use the default routing.

E) Set up UDRs with a next hop type of ExpressRoute for all traffic.

F) Apply UDRs in the gateway subnet with a next hop type of Virtual Network Gateway for VNet-to-VNet traffic.

Answer: C

Explanation: To fulfill the company's requirements, user-defined routes should be configured with a next hop type of Virtual Appliance for VNet-to-VNet traffic. This allows the traffic to be routed through a virtual network appliance, such as a firewall or other network device, for inspection. This is essential when you need to monitor, filter, or modify the traffic flow. For traffic to on-premises networks, the routing should be handled by the ExpressRoute connection, but that is not specified in the UDRs directly, since ExpressRoute is used automatically for traffic destined to on-premises IPs. The use of UDRs with next hop type Virtual Network Gateway is incorrect in this context as it is typically used for on-premises connectivity rather than VNet-to-VNet routing. Using Internet as a next hop would direct traffic out of Azure, which is not the desired behavior here.

Q277: You need to ensure that a specific Azure subnet routes all outbound traffic to a third-party network virtual appliance (NVA) for additional security filtering. Which next hop type should you specify in the user-defined route to achieve this configuration?

A) Internet

B) Virtual Network

C) Virtual Appliance

D) VNet Peering

E) Virtual Network Gateway

Answer: C

Explanation: In Azure, when you want a subnet to route its outbound traffic through a network virtual appliance (NVA), you need to set up a user-defined route with a next hop type of Virtual Appliance. This type of configuration is often used for scenarios where traffic needs to be inspected, filtered, or otherwise processed by a third-party application or system before reaching its destination. The Virtual Appliance next hop type allows Azure to forward traffic to the NVA's IP address that you specify in the UDR. This is particularly useful for implementing security appliances such as firewalls or intrusion detection systems.

Q278: Your organization has established multiple Azure VNets across different regions to support its global operations. A new compliance requirement mandates that all traffic between these VNets be logged for auditing purposes. Which Azure feature should you implement to ensure that all traffic between VNets is routed through a central logging appliance?

A) Azure Traffic Manager

B) Azure Application Gateway

C) User-Defined Routes with Virtual Appliance

D) Azure Route Server

E) Network Security Groups with Logging

F) Azure Firewall with Threat Intelligence

Answer: C

Explanation: To ensure that all traffic between VNets is logged for auditing purposes, you should implement user-defined routes with a next hop type of Virtual Appliance. This allows you to direct all traffic between VNets through a central logging appliance, where it can be monitored and logged. In this setup, the logging appliance acts as an intermediary that processes all inter-VNet traffic, capturing the necessary data for compliance audits. Azure Traffic Manager and Application Gateway are not suitable here as they handle traffic distribution and load balancing rather than routing. A Route Server is used for dynamic routing, and Network Security Groups focus on access control rather than routing and logging.

Q279: True or False: In Azure, user-defined routes (UDRs) can be used to override the default system routes for traffic destined to Azure-provided services like Azure Storage.

A) True

B) False

Answer: A

Explanation: In Azure, user-defined routes (UDRs) can indeed be used to override the default system routes, including those for traffic destined to Azure-provided services like Azure Storage. By using UDRs, you can direct traffic to specific next hops, such as virtual appliances, instead of letting it follow the default paths set by the Azure platform. This is particularly useful for scenarios where you need to route traffic through custom appliances for inspection or filtering before it reaches Azure services. However, it's important to note that careful planning is required to avoid unintended disruptions to service access.

Q280: You are tasked with designing a network architecture in Azure that requires specific traffic from one subnet to bypass the default route to the Internet and instead route through a secure tunnel to an on-premises data center. How can you achieve this using user-defined routes?

A) Set up UDRs with a next hop type of Virtual Network Gateway for the specific traffic.

B) Use UDRs with a next hop type of Internet for the traffic.

C) Implement UDRs with a next hop type of Virtual Appliance for the traffic.

D) Apply a forced tunneling configuration with a next hop type of None.

E) Deploy UDRs using a next hop type of VNet Peering.

F) Configure UDRs with a next hop type of ExpressRoute to the secure tunnel.

Answer: A

Explanation: To ensure that specific traffic from a subnet bypasses the default route to the Internet and routes through a secure tunnel to an on-premises data center, you should set up user-defined routes with a next hop type of Virtual Network Gateway. This configuration directs the specified traffic to the VPN gateway, which handles the secure tunneling to the on-premises data center. Forced tunneling generally refers to directing all internet-bound traffic to an on-premises network, typically used with a next hop type of Virtual Network Gateway, not None. Using ExpressRoute would be applicable if there is a dedicated ExpressRoute circuit, but in this scenario, the focus is on using a secure tunnel, which is typically achieved with a VPN connection facilitated by the Virtual Network Gateway.

Q281: A multinational corporation is planning to set up a high-availability site-to-site VPN connection using Azure. The company has multiple on-premises data centers located across different continents and wants to ensure minimal downtime in the event of a failure. They are considering using Azure's VPN Gateway for this purpose. In addition to the high availability requirement, the corporation needs to ensure that the VPN connection is secure and efficient, supporting dynamic routing and automatic failover. Which configuration should they implement to achieve high availability for their site-to-site VPN connection?

A) Deploy a single VPN Gateway in Azure and configure BGP for dynamic routing.

B) Deploy two VPN Gateways in the same Azure region and use Active-Active configuration.

C) Deploy a single VPN Gateway in Azure and enable Border Gateway Protocol (BGP).

D) Use ExpressRoute with dual circuits for redundancy.

E) Deploy two VPN Gateways in different Azure regions and configure them in an Active-Passive setup.

F) Configure a single VPN Gateway with static routing for simplicity and less overhead.

Answer: B

Explanation: To achieve high availability for a site-to-site VPN connection in Azure, deploying two VPN Gateways in the same region and configuring them in an Active-Active setup is an optimal solution. This configuration allows both gateways to actively handle traffic, providing redundancy and load balancing. If one gateway fails, the other can seamlessly take over, minimizing downtime. Active-Active also leverages BGP for dynamic routing, which enhances the efficiency and resilience of the VPN connection by automatically adjusting routes in response to network changes. While ExpressRoute offers redundancy, it is a different solution from a VPN and typically used for different requirements.

Q282: Select the correct statement about Azure VPN Gateway.

A) Azure VPN Gateway supports only static routing protocols.

B) To configure a site-to-site VPN, an Azure VPN Gateway must be in an Active-Passive configuration.

C) Azure VPN Gateway can be configured to support both IKEv1 and IKEv2 protocols.

D) Each Azure VPN Gateway requires a dedicated ExpressRoute circuit.

E) Azure VPN Gateway is only compatible with Azure Resource Manager (ARM) deployments.

F) You must manually failover connections in an Active-Active configuration to ensure high availability.

Answer: C

Explanation: Azure VPN Gateway supports both IKEv1 and IKEv2 protocols, providing flexibility for secure connection setups. IKEv1 and IKEv2 are used to establish secure, authenticated communications channels between VPN endpoints. The use of IKEv2 is recommended for its enhanced security features and support for mobility and multihoming. Azure VPN Gateway supports both static and dynamic routing protocols, and Active-Active configurations enable automatic failover, eliminating the need for manual intervention. It does not require an ExpressRoute circuit, as VPN and ExpressRoute are separate connection types.

Q283: A company with two on-premises data centers needs to establish a site-to-site VPN connection to their Azure Virtual Network. They want to ensure high availability and use dynamic routing for optimal performance. Which of the following steps should they take to configure this setup in Azure?

A) Use Azure Traffic Manager to route traffic between VPN connections.

B) Deploy a single VPN Gateway and configure BGP.

C) Set up two VPN Gateways in an Active-Passive configuration.

D) Deploy redundant VPN connections using Azure Load Balancer.

E) Configure Active-Active VPN Gateway and enable BGP.

F) Use a single VPN Gateway with dual tunnels.

Answer: E

Explanation: For high availability and dynamic routing, configuring an Active-Active VPN Gateway with BGP is the best approach. An Active-Active setup allows both VPN Gateway instances to handle traffic simultaneously, providing load balancing and redundancy. BGP facilitates dynamic routing, which automatically adjusts to network changes, ensuring efficient data transfer. Active-Active configurations are designed to provide seamless failover without manual intervention, enhancing the reliability of the VPN connection.

Q284: True or False: Azure VPN Gateway can be configured to support high availability using an Active-Active setup with dual VPN tunnels from the same on-premises network.

A) True

B) False

Answer: A

Explanation: True. Azure VPN Gateway can indeed be configured in an Active-Active setup to support high availability. This configuration involves setting up dual VPN tunnels from the same on-premises network to the two instances of the Azure VPN Gateway. Both tunnels can be active simultaneously, which not only provides redundancy in case one tunnel fails but also allows for load balancing of network traffic across the tunnels. This setup ensures that the network remains resilient and maintains connectivity during partial outages or maintenance events.

Q285: A financial services company is planning to migrate their infrastructure to Azure and needs to set up a secure, high-availability VPN connection between their on-premises data centers and Azure. They require a solution that supports dynamic routing and can handle large volumes of data traffic efficiently. The company also wants the VPN connection to automatically adapt in case of any link failure. Which Azure feature should they leverage to meet these requirements?

A) Static routing with a single Azure VPN Gateway

B) Active-Active VPN Gateway with BGP

C) Azure ExpressRoute with BGP

D) Multi-site VPN with dual Azure VPN Gateways

E) Point-to-Site VPN with a single Azure VPN Gateway

F) Active-Passive VPN Gateway with BGP

Answer: B

Explanation: The Active-Active VPN Gateway configuration with BGP is the most suitable solution for this scenario. It supports high availability and dynamic routing, which are critical for handling large volumes of data efficiently. BGP enables the VPN connection to automatically adjust routes in response to network changes or failures, ensuring continuous connectivity and optimal performance. The Active-Active setup allows both gateways to be active simultaneously, providing redundancy and load balancing, which is essential for maintaining high availability in a financial services environment where reliability and efficiency are paramount.

Q286: Designing a Multi-Region Virtual WAN for a Global Enterprise A global enterprise with headquarters in New York and branch offices in London, Singapore, and Sydney is looking to implement a Virtual WAN architecture to connect these offices efficiently. The primary goal is to ensure high availability and low latency for mission-critical applications that are hosted in Azure. The company plans to utilize Azure's global network to optimize connectivity. As the Azure Solutions Architect, you are tasked with designing this architecture. The solution should support site-to-site VPN, point-to-site VPN, and ExpressRoute connections while allowing for future scalability. Additionally, the company wants to integrate Azure Firewall for secure traffic management. Which design approach should you recommend for implementing a robust and scalable Azure Virtual WAN architecture?

A) Deploy a single Virtual WAN hub in the East US region and connect all branch offices to this hub.

B) Deploy separate Virtual WAN hubs in each region (East US, UK South, Southeast Asia, and Australia East) and connect each branch office to its local hub.

C) Implement a Virtual WAN hub in each region and use Azure Traffic Manager for traffic distribution.

D) Deploy a multi-region Virtual WAN with a central hub in East US and regional hubs in UK South and Southeast Asia, with Sydney using a site-to-site VPN to UK South.

E) Utilize a Virtual WAN hub in East US and use Azure Load Balancer for distributing traffic between regions.

F) Create a Virtual WAN hub in each region and leverage Azure Front Door for managing global traffic.

Answer: B

Explanation: Deploying separate Virtual WAN hubs in each region (East US, UK South, Southeast Asia, and Australia East) ensures that each branch office connects to its nearest hub, optimizing performance and reducing latency due to geographical proximity. This regional hub deployment allows for high availability, as each region's connectivity can be managed independently, and reduces the risk of a single point of failure. By leveraging Azure's global network, this design also supports site-to-site VPN, point-to-site VPN, and ExpressRoute connections seamlessly. Integrating Azure Firewall into each hub provides a unified and secure traffic management solution. This scalable architecture supports future expansions and additional connections as the enterprise grows.

Q287: Selecting an Appropriate Virtual WAN Type In Azure, when configuring a Virtual WAN architecture, it is important to choose the correct Virtual WAN type to match the organization's networking requirements. Which Virtual WAN type should be chosen if the organization needs to prioritize secure and private connectivity over the public internet, while utilizing ExpressRoute and VPN connections?

A) Basic Virtual WAN

B) Standard Virtual WAN

C) Secure Virtual WAN

D) Dedicated Virtual WAN

E) Hybrid Virtual WAN

F) Premium Virtual WAN

Answer: B

Explanation: The Standard Virtual WAN type in Azure supports both ExpressRoute and VPN connections, providing secure and private connectivity options that extend beyond the public internet. This type is ideal for organizations that require a mix of connection types and want to leverage Azure's advanced networking features, including the integration of security services such as Azure Firewall. The Standard Virtual WAN is designed for more complex network architectures, offering scalability and flexibility to meet diverse organizational needs.

Q288: True/False - Azure Virtual WAN and Traffic Manager Integration Azure Virtual WAN can natively integrate with Azure Traffic Manager to provide automatic load balancing and failover for global traffic.

A) True

B) False

Answer: B

Explanation: Azure Virtual WAN and Azure Traffic Manager serve different purposes and do not natively integrate for automatic load balancing and failover. Azure Virtual WAN focuses on providing a unified network architecture that connects different branches and regions through VPN and ExpressRoute connections, while Azure Traffic Manager is a DNS-based traffic load balancer that distributes traffic across various endpoints globally. These services can complement each other in a broader network solution, but they do not have direct integration capabilities.

Q289: Configuring Azure Virtual WAN for Optimal Security An organization requires a Virtual WAN setup that emphasizes security for its inter-regional traffic. They want to ensure that all traffic is inspected and filtered by a central security appliance before reaching its destination. Which Azure service should be integrated with Virtual WAN to achieve this level of security?

A) Azure DDoS Protection

B) Azure Network Watcher

C) Azure Firewall Manager

D) Azure Bastion

E) Azure Traffic Analytics

F) Azure Security Center

Answer: C

Explanation: Azure Firewall Manager is the appropriate service to integrate with Azure Virtual WAN for centralized security management. It allows organizations to configure and enforce security policies across multiple regions and connections within the Virtual WAN architecture. By integrating Azure Firewall through the Firewall Manager, all traffic can be inspected and filtered before reaching its destination, ensuring compliance with the organization's security requirements. This setup provides a unified approach to managing and enforcing security measures across the entire network infrastructure.

Q290: Scenario-Based Planning for Future Expansion A mid-sized company has just deployed a Virtual WAN architecture with a single hub in the East US region. They plan to expand their operations into Europe and Asia within the next year. The IT team wants to ensure that the current setup can be easily scaled to accommodate new branch offices and increased network traffic. What steps should be taken now to facilitate a smooth transition and expansion in the future?

A) Enable global VNet peering across all existing VNets.

B) Deploy additional hubs in strategic regions such as UK South and Southeast Asia preemptively.

C) Use a single large subnet in the current hub for all future connections.

D) Upgrade the existing hub to a Premium SKU to handle more connections.

E) Implement Azure Front Door to manage global traffic routing.

F) Configure Azure ExpressRoute now for anticipated future use.

Answer: B

Explanation: Deploying additional hubs in strategic regions such as UK South and Southeast Asia preemptively positions the company for a seamless transition when expanding operations into Europe and Asia. This proactive approach leverages Azure's global infrastructure capabilities, ensuring that new branch offices in these regions can connect to local hubs, thus reducing latency and improving performance. By setting up regional hubs in advance, the company can also distribute network traffic more efficiently and avoid potential bottlenecks in the future. Preemptive deployment facilitates quick integration of new connections and allows the IT team to implement and test security and network policies before the expansion occurs.

Q291: A multinational company operates a hybrid cloud environment using Azure. They have multiple VNets across different regions and require a robust name resolution strategy to ensure seamless connectivity and service discovery. The company is considering Azure DNS Private Resolver and wants to implement a solution that allows for name resolution across VNets without deploying individual DNS servers in each VNet. The solution should be scalable and require minimal management overhead. What is the most appropriate solution that the company should use to achieve cross-region name resolution in Azure? ---

A) Configure a DNS forwarder in each VNet.

B) Use Azure DNS Private Zones with auto-registration.

C) Deploy Azure DNS Private Resolver with inbound endpoints.

D) Implement Azure Traffic Manager for DNS resolution.

E) Use Azure Load Balancer with DNS proxy enabled.

F) Create a custom DNS server in a central VNet.

Answer: C

Explanation: Azure DNS Private Resolver allows you to resolve DNS queries across different VNets without needing to deploy and manage your own DNS servers. By configuring inbound endpoints, you can centralize DNS query handling, providing a scalable and low-maintenance solution for name resolution across regions. This approach reduces the complexity and overhead compared to deploying DNS forwarders or custom DNS servers in each VNet. The use of Azure Traffic Manager and Azure Load Balancer are not directly related to DNS resolution across VNets. Azure DNS Private Zones with auto-registration is useful for automatic handling of VM name records but does not inherently solve cross-region resolution without additional configuration.

Q292: An organization is planning to set up internal name resolution for their applications running in a single Azure VNet. They want to ensure that their Azure VMs can resolve names of other VMs within the same VNet without relying on external DNS configurations. Which Azure feature should they implement to achieve this requirement? ---

A) Azure Public DNS

B) Azure Traffic Manager

C) Azure Load Balancer

D) Azure DNS Private Zones

E) Azure NSG Flow Logs

F) Azure Virtual Network Peering

Answer: D

Explanation: Azure DNS Private Zones provide a secure and reliable way to manage and resolve domain names within a VNet. By using Azure DNS Private Zones, you can manage DNS records for your internal VMs without relying on external DNS services. This service is specifically designed to handle private DNS resolution, making it ideal for resolving VMs' names within a VNet. Public DNS and Azure Traffic Manager are used for internet-facing resources, while NSG Flow Logs and Virtual Network Peering do not address DNS resolution requirements.

Q293: A company has deployed multiple applications across different Azure VNets. They need an efficient name resolution strategy to ensure that applications in one VNet can resolve names of services hosted in another VNet. The solution should minimize latency and not require internet-based resolution paths. Which feature should they use to enable this connectivity? ---

A) Azure DNS Private Resolver

B) Azure Bastion

C) Azure Application Gateway

D) Azure ExpressRoute

E) Azure VNet Peering with custom DNS

F) Azure Virtual WAN

Answer: E

Explanation: Azure VNet Peering with custom DNS settings allows VNets to communicate with each other using private IP addresses, enabling applications in one VNet to resolve names of services in another VNet. By configuring custom DNS settings through peering, you ensure that DNS queries do not traverse the internet, thereby minimizing latency and maintaining a secure and efficient resolution path. Azure DNS Private Resolver and Azure Virtual WAN are not directly involved in DNS resolution between peered VNets. Azure Bastion, Application Gateway, and ExpressRoute do not provide the necessary DNS resolution capabilities for this scenario.

Q294: A financial services company is implementing a microservices architecture within a single Azure VNet. They require a robust name resolution strategy that ensures high availability and fault tolerance. Considering the need for automatic recovery and failover capabilities, what is the best Azure service or feature to ensure that their internal DNS resolution is resilient? ---

A) Azure DNS Private Zones with zone redundancy

B) Azure Load Balancer with custom DNS

C) Azure Traffic Manager with geo-redundancy

D) Azure DNS Private Resolver with failover endpoints

E) Azure Front Door with DNS routing

F) Azure Application Gateway with DNS failover

Answer: A

Explanation: Azure DNS Private Zones with zone redundancy provides high availability and fault tolerance for DNS records within an Azure environment. By leveraging Azure's global infrastructure, you can ensure that your DNS resolution remains resilient even in the event of a regional failure. This setup automatically handles failover and recovery, ensuring continuous name resolution for microservices within a VNet. Other options like Azure Traffic Manager, Front Door, and Application Gateway do not inherently provide the same level of DNS redundancy and are more suited for traffic management and routing tasks.

Q295: True/False In Azure, DNS resolution using Azure DNS Private Zones is limited to resolving names within a single VNet unless explicitly linked to other VNets.

A) True

B) False

Answer: A

Explanation: Azure DNS Private Zones are designed to provide DNS services within a specific VNet or a set of linked VNets. Without explicit links to other VNets, name resolution is confined to the VNet where the private zone is configured. This design ensures isolation and security of DNS records. To enable DNS resolution across multiple VNets, you need to establish links between the VNets and the private DNS zone, allowing them to share DNS records within the linked environments.

Q296: You are the lead network architect for a global e-commerce company. Your company has multiple Azure subscriptions and uses a complex network architecture that includes several virtual networks (VNets) across different regions. The network design requires internal domain name resolution for resources within VNets, and integration with on-premises DNS infrastructure. You need to design a private DNS solution that ensures high availability and efficient management while keeping DNS traffic secure. Which Azure feature should you implement to meet these requirements?

A) Azure DNS Private Zones with auto-registration

B) Azure Traffic Manager

C) Azure Front Door

D) Azure Application Gateway

E) Azure DNS Public Zones with conditional forwarding

F) Azure VPN Gateway with custom DNS servers

Answer: A

Explanation: Azure DNS Private Zones provide a scalable and secure way to manage and resolve domain names in a private network setup. By using Azure DNS Private Zones with auto-registration, you can automatically register virtual machines (VMs) in the DNS zone, simplifying management and ensuring that DNS records are up-to-date. This solution supports integration with on-premises DNS infrastructure via conditional forwarders, maintaining DNS traffic security. It also ensures high availability through Azure's global infrastructure, which is essential for a global e-commerce company. Other options, like public zones or traffic management services, do not offer the required internal network resolution and integration capabilities.

Q297: Select the most appropriate command to link an Azure Private DNS Zone to a virtual network using Azure PowerShell.

A) New-AzDnsZoneLink

B) Add-AzDnsVirtualNetworkLink

C) Add-AzPrivateDnsZoneVirtualNetworkLink

D) Set-AzDnsZoneLink

E) Link-AzPrivateDnsZone

F) Connect-AzDnsZoneToVNet

Answer: C

Explanation: The command Add-AzPrivateDnsZoneVirtualNetworkLink is specifically designed to create a link between an Azure Private DNS Zone and a virtual network. This command is part of the Azure PowerShell module and allows network resources within the linked virtual network to resolve DNS names from the private DNS zone. This is crucial for enabling domain name resolution within private networks, a common requirement for advanced network configurations in Azure.

Q298: You want to ensure that DNS queries originating from Azure VMs in your private network are resolved using Azure Private DNS Zones without exposing these queries to the public internet. Which aspect of Azure Private DNS Zone architecture inherently provides this capability?

A) Use of Azure Firewall

B) Built-in network isolation

C) Integration with Azure Key Vault

D) Role-Based Access Control (RBAC)

E) Conditional DNS forwarding

F) Use of custom DNS servers

Answer: B

Explanation: Azure Private DNS Zones are designed to provide built-in network isolation, which ensures that DNS queries stay within the Azure environment and do not traverse the public internet. This design inherently isolates DNS queries and responses to the private network, preventing exposure to the public domain. This is achieved by resolving DNS queries within the Azure infrastructure itself, making it a secure and efficient solution for private DNS management.

Q299: True or False: Azure Private DNS Zones can be directly used to resolve domain names for resources in on-premises networks without any additional configuration.

A) True

B) False

Answer: B

Explanation: Azure Private DNS Zones cannot directly resolve domain names for resources in on-premises networks without additional configuration. To enable DNS resolution between Azure and on-premises resources, you need to configure conditional forwarding or use a VPN/ExpressRoute connection with appropriate DNS forwarding rules. This setup allows on-premises DNS servers to forward DNS queries for specific domains to Azure Private DNS Zones, facilitating hybrid network scenarios.

Q300: Your organization is planning to use Azure Private DNS Zones to manage internal DNS resolution. However, you've observed that there are regularly occurring changes to the virtual machines that need to be reflected in the DNS records. What feature or configuration should you leverage to ensure these changes are automatically updated in the Private DNS Zone?

A) Manual DNS record management

B) Azure DNS Traffic Manager profiles

C) Autoscaling groups

D) Virtual network links

E) Automatic registration with Private DNS Zone

F) Azure Policy for DNS updates

Answer: E

Explanation: To ensure that changes to virtual machines are automatically updated in the Private DNS Zone, you should leverage the automatic registration feature of Azure Private DNS Zones. This feature allows VMs within a linked virtual network to automatically register their DNS records with the private zone. This automatic registration simplifies DNS management and ensures that DNS records are consistently updated as VMs are added, removed, or modified, thus eliminating the need for manual updates or complex configurations.

Q301: Contoso Ltd. is planning to migrate its on-premises DNS infrastructure to Azure for improved scalability and reliability. They have several domain names for different business units and want to manage them using Azure DNS. All public-facing services should be accessible via these domain names. Contoso needs to ensure DNS records are updated dynamically as services scale out or change. They also want to implement DNSSEC for enhanced security. Which solution best meets Contoso's requirements for managing public DNS zones in Azure? ---

A) Use Azure DNS to host the DNS zones and enable DNSSEC for security.

B) Host the DNS zones on a virtual machine running BIND in Azure and manage DNS records manually.

C) Use Azure Traffic Manager to manage DNS zones and enable automatic updates.

D) Implement Azure Private DNS Zones and enable DNS forwarding for public access.

E) Use Azure DNS with Azure AD integration to manage DNS records dynamically.

F) Implement a third-party DNS service that integrates with Azure and supports DNSSEC.

Answer: A

Explanation: Azure DNS is a scalable and reliable DNS service that allows you to host your domain in Azure. It supports hosting public DNS zones and can be configured to dynamically update DNS records as services scale out or change. Azure DNS also supports DNS Security Extensions (DNSSEC), which adds an additional layer of security to prevent DNS spoofing and other attacks. Using Azure DNS for public zones ensures that all public-facing services are accessible via the domain names, and DNSSEC can be enabled to enhance the security of these DNS zones. Hosting the DNS zones on a virtual machine or using Azure Traffic Manager would not meet the requirements for DNSSEC or dynamic updates as efficiently as Azure DNS.

Q302: A company wants to improve the security of its DNS infrastructure by using DNS Security Extensions (DNSSEC) in Azure DNS. Which of the following statements about DNSSEC in Azure DNS is true? ---

A) DNSSEC is automatically enabled for all DNS zones in Azure DNS.

B) DNSSEC can only be enabled for specific domain registrars that support it.

Answer: B

Explanation: DNSSEC in Azure DNS is not automatically enabled for all DNS zones; it must be enabled manually. Additionally, DNSSEC support depends on the domain registrar's capabilities. Some registrars may not support DNSSEC, so it is crucial to verify that the registrar in use can handle DNSSEC for the domain. DNSSEC provides an additional layer of security by using digital signatures to ensure the authenticity of DNS data, thus preventing certain types of attacks, such as DNS spoofing.

Q303: Which command would you use in Azure PowerShell to create a new public DNS zone named "example.com" in a resource group called "DNSResourceGroup"? ---

A) New-AzureRmDnsZone -Name "example.com" -ResourceGroupName "DNSResourceGroup"

B) New-AzDnsZone -Name "example.com" -ResourceGroupName "DNSResourceGroup"

C) az dns zone create --name "example.com" --resource-group "DNSResourceGroup"

D) New-AzDnsZone -ZoneName "example.com" -ResourceGroup "DNSResourceGroup"

E) az network dns zone create --name "example.com" --resource-group "DNSResourceGroup"

F) New-DnsZone -Name "example.com" -ResourceGroupName "DNSResourceGroup"

Answer: B

Explanation: The correct command to create a new public DNS zone in Azure using Azure PowerShell is New-AzDnsZone -Name "example.com" -ResourceGroupName "DNSResourceGroup". This command specifies the DNS zone's name and the resource group where it should be created. Azure PowerShell's Az module is the current module used to manage Azure resources, replacing the older AzureRm module. The New-AzDnsZone cmdlet is specifically used for creating DNS zones in Azure DNS.

Q304: You have set up a public DNS zone in Azure DNS for your company's domain. Your company has expanded its services to new regions, and you need to ensure that users are directed to the nearest regional endpoint. Which Azure service should you integrate with Azure DNS to achieve this? ---

A) Azure Traffic Manager

B) Azure Load Balancer

C) Azure Front Door

D) Azure Application Gateway

E) Azure Content Delivery Network (CDN)

F) Azure Firewall

Answer: A

Explanation: Azure Traffic Manager is the appropriate service to integrate with Azure DNS for directing users to the nearest regional endpoint. Traffic Manager uses DNS to direct client requests to the most appropriate endpoint based on the configured traffic-routing method, such as geographic or performance routing. This ensures that users are directed to the nearest available endpoint, improving response times and user experience. While other services like Azure Front Door also provide global routing capabilities, Traffic Manager is specifically designed to work with DNS for routing decisions.

Q305: To ensure high availability and fault tolerance for your public DNS zones, you plan to implement failover capabilities. Which strategy should you employ in Azure to achieve this?

A) Use Azure Traffic Manager with a failover routing method.

B) Create multiple Azure DNS zones in different Azure regions.

C) Deploy Azure DNS zones with automatic zone replication enabled.

D) Implement a third-party DNS service to manage failover.

E) Configure Azure Load Balancer for DNS zone redundancy.

F) Use Azure Application Gateway with active/passive configuration.

Answer: A

Explanation: Azure Traffic Manager with a failover routing method is the best strategy to implement high availability and fault tolerance for public DNS zones. By configuring Traffic Manager with the failover routing method, you can specify a primary endpoint, and additional endpoints to be used in case the primary becomes unavailable. Traffic Manager uses DNS to direct requests to the primary endpoint, and automatically switches to the secondary endpoints when a failure is detected. This approach ensures minimal downtime and maintains service availability, without needing to create multiple DNS zones or rely on third-party services.

Q306: A company named Contoso Ltd. is expanding its cloud Infrastructure to improve its application delivery mechanisms. They have multiple virtual networks (VNets) across several Azure regions and wish to optimize their network traffic flow by implementing service chaining. The goal is to centralize their network security resources and ensure that all inter-VNet traffic passes through a specific security appliance. They are considering using Azure Route Server and Azure Firewall to achieve this. Given these requirements, what is the most appropriate design choice to ensure efficient service chaining and gateway transit? ---

A) Deploy Azure Firewall in each VNet and use user-defined routes (UDRs) to route traffic.

B) Use VNet peering with remote gateways and configure service chaining through Azure Firewall in a central VNet.

C) Implement an Azure Load Balancer to distribute traffic across VNets.

D) Deploy a Virtual Network Gateway in each VNet and use Azure Traffic Manager for service chaining.

E) Utilize Azure Bastion to manage inter-VNet traffic and ensure security.

F) Set up a custom DNS to redirect traffic through a centralized security appliance.

Answer: B

Explanation: The most efficient way to centralize network security and ensure all inter-VNet traffic is processed by a specific security appliance is to use VNet peering with remote gateways. Configuring service chaining through Azure Firewall in a central VNet allows you to direct traffic through a centralized security solution. Azure Route Server can facilitate dynamic routing updates, ensuring that traffic is consistently routed through the security appliance. This design minimizes the need for multiple security appliances and leverages Azure's built-in capabilities to optimize network traffic flow. Deploying Azure Firewall in each VNet would be resource-intensive and complex to manage. Azure Traffic Manager and Load Balancer are more suited for traffic distribution rather than service chaining, and Azure Bastion and custom DNS do not provide the required service chaining functionality.

Q307: The implementation of gateway transit in Azure allows for efficient routing between peered VNets without the need for a separate VPN gateway in each VNet. ---

A) True

B) False

Answer: A

Explanation: Gateway transit in Azure is a feature that allows a virtual network to utilize a VPN gateway in a peered virtual network. This means that traffic can be routed through a single gateway, reducing the need for multiple gateways in each peered VNet. This capability is particularly useful for scenarios where multiple VNets need secure connectivity to on-premises resources or other VNets, as it simplifies architecture and reduces costs. By leveraging gateway transit, organizations can centralize gateway management and enhance network efficiency.

Q308: In a scenario where you have multiple VNets in different Azure regions, and you need to implement service chaining with Azure Application Gateway in a hub-and-spoke topology, which configuration option would best meet the requirement of centralized traffic inspection and routing? ---

A) Deploy an Application Gateway in each VNet and configure UDRs for routing.

B) Use Azure Traffic Manager to balance traffic between regional VNets.

C) Implement a centralized Application Gateway in the hub VNet and configure spoke VNets with gateway transit.

D) Set up a Virtual Network Gateway in each region and link them with VNet peering.

E) Use Azure Front Door for global routing and traffic management.

F) Configure Azure ExpressRoute for each VNet for secure connectivity.

Answer: C

Explanation: Implementing a centralized Application Gateway in the hub VNet with gateway transit configured in the spoke VNets is the optimal approach for centralized traffic inspection and routing in a hub-and-spoke topology. This approach allows all spoke VNets to route their traffic through the central hub for inspection and processing by the Application Gateway. Gateway transit ensures that the spokes can utilize the hub's resources without the need for duplicating them in each spoke VNet, thus optimizing resource usage and simplifying management. Azure Traffic Manager and Front Door are designed for global traffic distribution, not regional service chaining. Using a Virtual Network Gateway in each region would be unnecessary for this requirement, and ExpressRoute is primarily for secure on-premise connectivity.

Q309: A financial services company wants to ensure all their Azure-hosted applications' traffic passes through a security appliance before reaching the applications. They need a solution that integrates with Azure's existing services and provides scalability and resilience. What setup should they consider to achieve effective service chaining? ---

A) Deploy a Network Security Group (NSG) in every VNet.

B) Implement Azure Firewall with forced tunneling enabled.

C) Use Azure Traffic Manager for directing traffic through the security appliance.

D) Set up an Azure Load Balancer in front of the security appliance.

E) Integrate Azure Bastion with the security appliance for secure management.

F) Deploy Azure Application Gateway with Web Application Firewall (WAF) enabled.

Answer: B

Explanation: Implementing Azure Firewall with forced tunneling enabled is the most appropriate setup for ensuring that all application traffic passes through a security appliance before reaching the applications. Forced tunneling ensures that all traffic is sent to a specific endpoint, in this case, the security appliance, for inspection and processing. Azure Firewall provides a scalable and resilient security solution that integrates seamlessly with Azure's networking services. Network Security Groups are more focused on controlling inbound and outbound traffic at the subnet level, while Azure Traffic Manager and Load Balancer are not designed for service chaining purposes. Azure Bastion is primarily for secure management rather than traffic inspection, and while Application Gateway with WAF provides application-layer protection, it does not inherently support the specific requirement of directing all traffic through a security appliance.

Q310: When configuring service chaining in Azure using a central security appliance in a hub VNet, which command would you use to create a route table that directs all traffic to the appliance from a spoke VNet?

A) az network route-table create --name MyRouteTable --resource-group MyResourceGroup --location eastus

B) az network vnet peering create --name SpokeToHub --remote-vnet HubVNet --resource-group MyResourceGroup

C) az network route-table route create --resource-group MyResourceGroup --route-table-name MyRouteTable --name RouteToFirewall --address-prefix 0.0.0.0/0 --next-hop-type VirtualAppliance --next-hop-ip-address 10.0.0.4

D) az network vnet create --name MyVnet --resource-group MyResourceGroup --location eastus

E) az network nsg create --name MyNSG --resource-group MyResourceGroup --location eastus

F) az network firewall create --name MyFirewall --resource-group MyResourceGroup --location eastus

Answer: C

Explanation: To configure service chaining where a central security appliance in a hub VNet is used, you need to create a route in the route table of the spoke VNet that directs all traffic to the security appliance. Using the command to create a route with the next-hop type set to VirtualAppliance and specifying the IP address of the security appliance ensures that all traffic destined for external networks is routed through this appliance. The command effectively creates a user-defined route that dictates that all traffic (0.0.0.0/0) should be sent to the specified IP address of the security appliance. The other commands listed are relevant to different aspects of Azure network configuration, such as creating VNets, NSGs, or firewalls, but do not directly contribute to the route table setup needed for service chaining.

Q311: Contoso Ltd is experiencing intermittent connectivity issues with their Azure-hosted applications. The IT team suspects that the issues are related to Azure's Traffic Manager, which they use to route traffic globally. The Traffic Manager profile is configured with a priority routing method to ensure traffic is directed to the primary endpoint, with failover to secondary endpoints. However, users are reporting authentication errors and slow responses from different geographical locations. The team needs to diagnose and resolve these issues to ensure seamless connectivity and authentication. Which Azure tool or method should the team use to identify and resolve the routing and authentication issues? ---

A) Azure Network Watcher Connection Monitor

B) Azure Traffic Manager Diagnostics Logs

C) Azure Application Gateway Web Application Firewall (WAF) Logs

D) Azure Monitor Metrics for Traffic Manager

E) Azure Advisor Recommendations

F) Azure Network Performance Monitor

Answer: B

Explanation: Azure Traffic Manager Diagnostics Logs provide detailed insights into the traffic routing and endpoint health status. By analyzing these logs, the IT team can identify if the Traffic Manager is correctly prioritizing the endpoints and if any endpoint health checks are failing, which could lead to the reported authentication errors. Additionally, these logs can help in understanding the routing decisions made by Traffic Manager and whether any misconfigurations exist. While other tools like Network Watcher and Monitor Metrics provide valuable network insights, they do not specifically address Traffic Manager routing behavior and endpoint health status.

Q312: When diagnosing client-side connectivity issues in Azure, it is essential to understand the impact of DNS misconfigurations. You suspect that the DNS settings on a virtual network in Azure are incorrect, leading to authentication failures when clients attempt to reach services hosted on Azure VMs. What is the most effective way to verify and resolve DNS configuration issues for these virtual machines? ---

A) Use Azure DNS zones to verify DNS records

B) Run nslookup from the affected virtual machines

C) Check the DNS server settings in the virtual network properties

D) Use Azure Resource Health to check the DNS status

E) Verify the DNS settings in the Azure VM's network interface properties

F) Use Azure Traffic Analytics to analyze DNS traffic

Answer: C

Explanation: The DNS server settings for a virtual network in Azure are crucial for ensuring that DNS queries are correctly resolved. By checking the DNS server settings in the virtual network properties, you can verify if the correct DNS servers are specified. This is essential because any incorrect DNS configuration at the virtual network level can lead to authentication failures, as clients may not be able to resolve the domain names of authentication services. While tools like nslookup can diagnose DNS issues at the VM level, they do not provide a solution if the root cause lies in the virtual network's DNS settings.

Q313: A company is using Azure Active Directory (Azure AD) for authentication across multiple Azure services. They have implemented conditional access policies to enhance security. Recently, users have been unable to access specific services, and the issue seems to be related to these policies. Which Azure tool can provide insights into the application of conditional access policies and help diagnose the authentication issues? ---

A) Azure AD Sign-ins Logs

B) Azure Security Center Alerts

C) Azure Monitor Logs

D) Azure AD Conditional Access Policy Simulator

E) Azure AD Audit Logs

F) Azure Network Watcher

Answer: A

Explanation: Azure AD Sign-ins Logs are an essential tool for diagnosing authentication issues related to conditional access policies. These logs provide detailed information about user sign-in attempts, including whether a conditional access policy was applied and the result of that evaluation. By examining these logs, administrators can determine if the policies are causing access denials and identify any misconfigurations. While the Conditional Access Policy Simulator can model policy effects, it does not provide historical data on actual sign-in attempts.

Q314: True or False: Azure Network Performance Monitor can be used to diagnose authentication issues by monitoring network connectivity between Azure virtual machines and Azure AD. ---

A) True

B) False

Answer: B

Explanation: Azure Network Performance Monitor is designed to monitor network connectivity and performance between Azure resources and on-premises locations, focusing on network paths and latency. However, it does not specifically diagnose authentication issues related to Azure AD, as these are typically related to identity management and access policies rather than network performance. For authentication issues, tools like Azure AD Sign-ins Logs and Conditional Access insights are more appropriate.

Q315: A technical team is troubleshooting client-side connectivity problems in a hybrid environment where on-premises users access Azure-hosted applications. They suspect that authentication issues are caused by a misconfiguration in the VPN connection between the on-premises network and Azure. Which Azure service or feature should be primarily checked to ensure the VPN configuration supports seamless authentication?

A) Azure VPN Gateway Diagnostics

B) Azure Traffic Manager

C) Azure AD Connect Health

D) Azure ExpressRoute Monitor

E) Azure Network Security Group Logs

F) Azure Bastion Host

Answer: A

Explanation: Azure VPN Gateway Diagnostics is the most suitable feature to check when troubleshooting VPN-related issues. This service provides insights into the health and performance of the VPN connection, including connection status, bandwidth usage, and potential configuration errors. Ensuring the VPN connection is correctly configured is crucial for maintaining seamless authentication between on-premises users and Azure-hosted applications. While Azure AD Connect Health provides insights into directory synchronization health, it does not address VPN-specific connectivity issues.

Q316: Your company, Globex Corporation, has established an ExpressRoute circuit to connect their on-premises data center to Microsoft Azure. Recently, users have reported intermittent connectivity issues when accessing Azure resources. You have been tasked with diagnosing and resolving these connectivity issues. Upon reviewing the ExpressRoute configuration, you notice that the BGP sessions are flapping. You suspect that this might be due to incorrect MTU settings or suboptimal routing configuration on the on-premises router. Which Azure command will help you verify the MTU settings on the ExpressRoute circuit to isolate the issue? ---

A) az network express-route list

B) az network express-route show

C) az network express-route list-service-providers

D) az network express-route peering show

E) az network express-route get-stats

F) az network express-route show-usage

Answer: B

Explanation: To diagnose issues related to MTU settings on an ExpressRoute circuit, you need detailed information about the circuit's configuration. The command az network express-route show provides comprehensive details about the ExpressRoute circuit, including its current configuration such as the MTU settings. This command helps ascertain if the MTU settings are aligned with the on-premises configuration, which is crucial to avoid packet fragmentation and BGP session flapping. Ensuring consistent MTU settings across the network path is essential for maintaining stable BGP sessions and preventing connectivity issues.

Q317: You are troubleshooting a connectivity issue where your on-premises data center is unable to connect to Azure VMs over an ExpressRoute circuit. During your investigation, you find out that the ExpressRoute circuit is in a "Provisioned" state, and the peering status shows "Not Configured." What could be the primary reason for the lack of connectivity? ---

A) The ExpressRoute circuit is not linked to a virtual network.

B) There is a mismatch in the BGP ASN numbers.

C) The service key is incorrect.

D) The ExpressRoute gateway is not properly configured.

E) The route filters are misconfigured.

F) The BGP session is not established.

Answer: A

Explanation: The "Provisioned" state of an ExpressRoute circuit indicates that the circuit is ready for use, but if the peering status is "Not Configured," it suggests that the ExpressRoute circuit has not been associated with a virtual network. Without linking the circuit to a virtual network, there is no path for traffic between Azure and the on-premises data center. This step is crucial for establishing the required routing paths and enabling connectivity. Configuring peering and linking the ExpressRoute circuit to a virtual network ensures that Azure resources can communicate with on-premises resources over the private connection.

Q318: True/False: The ExpressRoute circuit is automatically monitored by Azure, and any BGP session failure is instantly reported to the network administrator via email notifications. ---

A) True

B) False

Answer: B

Explanation: While Azure provides monitoring tools and capabilities for ExpressRoute circuits, it does not automatically send email notifications of BGP session failures. Administrators need to set up Azure Monitor or Azure Network Watcher to track the health of their ExpressRoute circuits and create alert rules that trigger notifications via email or other channels. Proactive monitoring and alert configuration are essential practices for maintaining network reliability and quickly responding to issues such as BGP session failures.

Q319: Consider a scenario where your organization has multiple ExpressRoute circuits in different geographical locations but notices varying network performance in terms of latency and throughput. You suspect that the issue might be related to suboptimal routing paths chosen by BGP. Which of the following actions can help optimize routing and improve performance across these circuits? ---

A) Increase the MTU size on all circuits.

B) Enable FastPath on all ExpressRoute circuits.

C) Configure BGP communities to prefer certain routes.

D) Use QoS policies to prioritize traffic.

E) Adjust the bandwidth of the ExpressRoute circuits.

F) Use a single ASN for all BGP sessions.

Answer: C

Explanation: To address performance issues related to routing over multiple ExpressRoute circuits, configuring BGP communities can be an effective solution. BGP communities allow you to tag routes with specific attributes, which can influence the preference and selection of routes. By setting appropriate BGP community values, you can guide traffic to take the most efficient paths, minimizing latency and maximizing throughput. This is especially useful in multi-circuit deployments where routing decisions need to consider geographic and performance factors.

Q320: Your enterprise has deployed an ExpressRoute circuit connecting multiple Azure regions to your on-premises data centers. After a recent network change, you observe that traffic from Azure to on-premises is being dropped unexpectedly. Initial checks show that all ExpressRoute circuits are up, with BGP sessions active. Which Azure feature can you use to further diagnose the issue by capturing and analyzing the network traffic flowing through the ExpressRoute circuit?

A) Azure Traffic Manager

B) Azure Network Watcher Connection Monitor

C) Azure DDoS Protection

D) Azure Monitor

E) Azure Network Watcher Packet Capture

F) Azure Security Center

Answer: E

Explanation: Azure Network Watcher Packet Capture is a powerful diagnostic tool that allows you to capture and analyze network traffic on Azure resources. By using packet capture, you can inspect the actual data packets flowing through the ExpressRoute circuit, helping you identify issues such as packet drops, incorrect routing, or security rules blocking traffic. This level of analysis is crucial when initial diagnostics indicate that the circuit and BGP sessions are operating normally, allowing you to pinpoint the root cause of the traffic drop.

Q321: A multinational corporation has deployed a hub-and-spoke architecture on Azure to interconnect its regional offices spread across North America, Europe, and Asia. The company uses Azure Virtual Network Peering between the hub and the spokes. Recently, users in the European office reported intermittent connectivity issues when accessing resources in the Asia spoke. The network team suspects a routing issue but needs to diagnose and resolve it. They have already verified that all Virtual Network Peerings are in place and are correctly configured. As an Azure administrator, what would be your next step to diagnose the routing issue?

A) Check the effective routes for the network interface of a VM in the European office.

B) Verify the Network Security Group rules applied to the European spoke.

C) Use Azure Traffic Manager to monitor the health of the network endpoints.

D) Enable diagnostic logs on the Azure Firewall in the hub network.

E) Check for any misconfigured User Defined Routes in the European office's virtual network.

F) Use Azure Network Watcher to run a Connection Troubleshoot between the European and Asia spokes.

Answer: F

Explanation: In this scenario, the network team has already confirmed that Virtual Network Peering is correctly configured. To diagnose the routing issue, using Azure Network Watcher's Connection Troubleshoot tool is a practical approach. This tool allows you to test connectivity between two endpoints and provides insights into the network paths taken, helping identify any potential routing issues or packet losses. Checking effective routes or NSG rules might not directly reveal connectivity issues related to routing paths across regions. Azure Traffic Manager is not suitable for diagnosing internal Azure network connectivity, and enabling diagnostic logs, while useful, would not directly address the routing issue at hand.

Q322: Which Azure service allows you to analyze and troubleshoot network connectivity issues by providing a visual representation of network paths and metrics?

A) Azure Traffic Analytics

B) Azure Network Performance Monitor

C) Azure Monitor

D) Azure Network Security Group Analytics

E) Azure Network Watcher

F) Azure Connection Monitor

Answer: E

Explanation: Azure Network Watcher is an extensive service that offers tools to monitor, diagnose, and view network performance on Azure. It includes capabilities such as Connection Monitor, Packet Capture, and Next Hop, among others. The service provides visual representations of the network paths, helping administrators understand and troubleshoot connectivity issues effectively. While Azure Monitor and Network Performance Monitor provide valuable insights into general performance metrics and application performance, Network Watcher is specifically designed for deep network diagnostics and visualization.

Q323: A company is configuring User Defined Routes (UDRs) for a virtual network in Azure. They want to ensure that all traffic destined for a specific on-premises subnet is routed through their on-premises VPN gateway. Which property should be specifically configured to achieve this?

A) Next hop type

B) Address prefix

C) Route name

D) Priority

E) Virtual Network Gateway

F) Source IP range

Answer: A

Explanation: To route traffic through a specific gateway, the next hop type in the User Defined Route must be configured correctly. In this case, the next hop type should be set to "Virtual Network Gateway," which directs the traffic to the on-premises network via the VPN gateway. The address prefix defines the destination subnet, while other properties such as route name and priority are not directly responsible for routing decisions. Virtual Network Gateway is relevant, but the next hop type is the specific property that determines the routing path.

Q324: A new Azure subscription is being configured, and the network administrator is tasked with ensuring that only the necessary traffic routes through the Azure Firewall deployed in the hub network. The administrator uses User Defined Routes (UDRs) to customize the traffic flow. True or False: By default, System Routes will always take precedence over User Defined Routes in Azure.

A) True

B) False

Answer: B

Explanation: In Azure, User Defined Routes (UDRs) take precedence over System Routes when both are applicable to a network traffic scenario. This allows network administrators to customize routing paths to meet specific needs, such as directing traffic through an Azure Firewall or other network virtual appliances. System Routes serve as default routing paths provided by Azure, but they can be overridden by UDRs for specified address prefixes, enabling precise control over network traffic flow.

Q325: An organization uses Azure Virtual WAN to connect multiple Azure regions and on-premises locations. They are experiencing latency issues in one of the regions and suspect it's due to suboptimal routing. Which feature of Azure Virtual WAN can help them optimize the routing and reduce latency?

A) ExpressRoute Direct

B) Virtual Network Peering

C) Route Propagation

D) BGP Communities

E) Azure Front Door

F) Hub-to-Hub Connectivity

Answer: D

Explanation: BGP (Border Gateway Protocol) Communities in Azure Virtual WAN can be used to optimize routing by providing greater control over how routes are propagated across the network. This feature allows administrators to influence routing decisions and ensure that traffic takes the most efficient path, potentially reducing latency. ExpressRoute Direct and Virtual Network Peering are not directly relevant to optimizing routing within Azure Virtual WAN, while Route Propagation deals with route distribution rather than optimization. Hub-to-Hub Connectivity facilitates connectivity between hubs but does not directly optimize routing paths. Azure Front Door is focused on optimizing internet-facing applications and does not influence internal Azure network routing.

Q326: Your company, TechInnovators Ltd., has deployed a complex architecture in Azure, which includes several virtual networks distributed across different regions. Recently, the finance department has reported connectivity issues between the virtual networks in the East US and West Europe regions. The architecture uses a Virtual Network Gateway to facilitate this connectivity. As the lead Azure engineer, you've been tasked with diagnosing and resolving this issue. After reviewing the configurations, you suspect there might be a problem with the gateway configuration or the IPsec/IKE policy. You need to find and resolve the issue to restore connectivity swiftly.

A) Create a new Virtual Network Gateway in the West Europe region to replace the existing one.

B) Verify and update the IPsec/IKE policy to ensure it matches on both gateways.

C) Disable the VPN gateway and re-enable it to refresh the connection.

D) Increase the VPN gateway SKU to a higher capacity option.

E) Use Azure Traffic Manager to reroute traffic temporarily until the issue is resolved.

F) Check the network security group (NSG) rules associated with the subnet where the Virtual Network Gateway is deployed.

Answer: B

Explanation: When diagnosing connectivity issues between virtual networks that utilize a Virtual Network Gateway, it's essential to ensure that the IPsec/IKE policy is correctly configured and synchronized on both sides of the connection. Mismatched policies can lead to connection failures due to encryption mismatches or incorrect settings. Updating the IPsec/IKE policy to ensure both gateways have matching parameters (such as encryption algorithms, key strengths, and SA lifetimes) can resolve the issue without the need to replace or disable the gateway. Other options, such as creating a new gateway or increasing the SKU, might be unnecessary unless performance or capacity is the root cause. Network security groups and Traffic Manager are unrelated to IPsec/IKE policy mismatches.

Q327: The Azure Network Watcher provides a tool to diagnose Virtual Network Gateway issues. Which tool should you use to verify the connectivity between two virtual networks using the Virtual Network Gateway?

A) Connection Troubleshoot

B) Packet Capture

C) VPN Diagnostics

D) Next Hop

E) IP Flow Verify

F) Network Performance Monitor

Answer: A

Explanation: Azure Network Watcher's Connection Troubleshoot tool is specifically designed to verify the connectivity between two endpoints, such as virtual networks connected by a Virtual Network Gateway. It provides insights into the connection status, latency, and potential issues affecting connectivity. Packet Capture and IP Flow Verify are useful for examining data packets and checking traffic rules, respectively, but they do not directly diagnose gateway connectivity issues. VPN Diagnostics is not a specific tool in Network Watcher, and Network Performance Monitor is used for monitoring network performance rather than diagnosing connectivity.

Q328: You are tasked with resolving a connectivity issue in Azure where the virtual network gateway is not establishing a connection with the on-premises network. You suspect a mismatch in the IP address configuration. What should you verify first to ensure the IP configuration is correct?

A) Ensure the Local Network Gateway's IP address matches the on-premises VPN device.

B) Check the virtual network peerings for any misconfigurations.

C) Verify the DNS server settings in the virtual network.

D) Confirm that the BGP settings are correctly configured.

E) Ensure the gateway subnet size is adequate for the deployment.

F) Check the subscription limits for the number of VPN connections.

Answer: A

Explanation: When a virtual network gateway cannot establish a connection with an on-premises network, the first step is to verify that the Local Network Gateway's IP address is correctly configured to match the on-premises VPN device. This entry is critical for the gateway to route traffic correctly. Misconfigurations in this IP address can prevent the VPN tunnel from establishing. DNS server settings, BGP configuration, and gateway subnet sizes, while important, do not directly impact the initial establishment of the connection between the virtual network gateway and the on-premises network. Subscription limits are also unrelated to this specific issue.

Q329: True or False: If a Virtual Network Gateway connection is not established, adjusting the BGP ASN (Autonomous System Number) will resolve the issue.

A) True

B) False

Answer: B

Explanation: BGP ASN adjustments are only relevant if BGP is being used as part of the connection configuration. If BGP is not enabled or if the connection issue is unrelated to BGP, changing the ASN will not resolve the connectivity issue. Connectivity problems can arise from several factors, such as incorrect IPsec/IKE policies, mismatched IP addresses, or even network security group rules. BGP ASN changes are a specific solution for issues related to routing configurations when BGP is involved.

Q330: During a routine audit, your team discovers that a Virtual Network Gateway connection is dropping intermittently. Logs indicate that the issue might be related to the network latency or throughput. Which Azure feature should you use to gain more insights into the performance of the gateway connection?

A) Network Watcher Connection Monitor

B) Azure Monitor Logs

C) Traffic Analytics

D) ExpressRoute Monitor

E) Azure Policy

F) Application Insights

Answer: A

Explanation: The Network Watcher Connection Monitor feature is designed to provide detailed insights into the performance of connections, including latency, packet loss, and throughput. It allows you to monitor and diagnose network issues over time, making it a suitable tool for identifying issues with intermittent connection drops. Azure Monitor Logs can provide log data but lacks real-time performance metrics. Traffic Analytics is more suited for understanding traffic flow rather than performance diagnostics. ExpressRoute Monitor is specific to ExpressRoute connections, and Azure Policy and Application Insights are not directly related to network performance monitoring.

Q331: A multinational corporation, Contoso Ltd., has a complex Azure infrastructure spread across multiple regions. The company's IT security team has noticed an increase in unauthorized access attempts and is now using Microsoft Defender for Cloud to assess their network security posture. The Defender's Attack Path Analysis has identified potential vulnerabilities in their network architecture. To mitigate these vulnerabilities, the team is considering various network security recommendations, including the implementation of Network Security Groups (NSGs) and Azure Firewall. The team needs to ensure that only authorized traffic is allowed while minimizing disruption to legitimate operations. Which of the following actions would best enhance the security of Contoso Ltd.'s Azure network using Microsoft Defender for Cloud's recommendations?

A) Implement NSGs to restrict traffic between the application and database tiers.

B) Deploy Azure Firewall to enforce traffic rules at the perimeter of the virtual network.

C) Use Azure DDoS Protection Standard to mitigate external attacks.

D) Enable Just-In-Time VM Access to reduce exposure to management ports.

E) Configure Azure Policy to enforce secure configurations across all resources.

F) Set up Azure Bastion for secure RDP and SSH access to virtual machines.

Answer: A

Explanation: Implementing Network Security Groups (NSGs) to restrict traffic between the application and database tiers is a critical step in enhancing security. NSGs provide a way to filter network traffic to and from Azure resources in an Azure virtual network. By defining inbound and outbound security rules, NSGs can limit access to critical resources, such as databases, to only those application servers that require it. This approach reduces the risk of unauthorized access and potential lateral movement by attackers, which is a common vulnerability highlighted by Microsoft's Attack Path Analysis. While other measures like Azure Firewall and Just-In-Time VM Access are beneficial, the immediate and most targeted action to protect sensitive data flow between tiers is through NSGs.

Q332: You are tasked with analyzing the network security recommendations provided by Microsoft Defender for Cloud. One of the recommendations includes enabling network segmentation to improve security posture. Which service is most appropriate to configure segmentation of virtual networks in Azure?

A) Azure Application Gateway

B) Azure Load Balancer

C) Network Security Groups (NSGs)

D) Azure Virtual Network Peering

E) Azure Traffic Manager

F) Azure DDoS Protection

Answer: C

Explanation: Network Security Groups (NSGs) are the most appropriate Azure service for configuring network segmentation. NSGs allow for the creation of rules that define the inbound and outbound network traffic to and from network interfaces, subnets, or both, effectively segmenting the network. By using NSGs, you can enforce a layered security model, controlling traffic flow within and across different virtual networks. This segmentation helps isolate workloads and limit the reach of potential threats, aligning with Defender for Cloud's recommendation for enhanced security. Other services listed, such as Azure Load Balancer or Virtual Network Peering, do not specifically focus on traffic filtering and segmentation.

Q333: Evaluate the following statement: "Microsoft Defender for Cloud's Attack Path Analysis is primarily used for identifying external threats to the Azure environment."

A) True

B) False

Answer: B

Explanation: The statement is false. Microsoft Defender for Cloud's Attack Path Analysis is a feature designed to help identify potential attack paths within an organization's Azure environment, focusing on both internal and external threats. It analyzes the configuration of Azure resources and their interactions to discover potential vulnerabilities that could be exploited by attackers. This tool provides insights into how an attacker might move laterally within the network once they have gained initial access, emphasizing the importance of securing internal pathways between resources, not just external threats.

Q334: Which Azure service can be used to provide a comprehensive view of network traffic patterns and threats, thereby supporting the recommendations identified by Microsoft Defender for Cloud?

A) Azure Monitor

B) Azure Sentinel

C) Azure Security Center

D) Azure Traffic Manager

E) Azure Policy

F) Azure ExpressRoute

Answer: B

Explanation: Azure Sentinel is a cloud-native security information and event management (SIEM) solution that provides a comprehensive view of network traffic patterns and threats. It integrates with Microsoft Defender for Cloud to offer advanced threat detection and response capabilities. By analyzing data collected from different sources, Azure Sentinel can correlate security events and provide actionable insights to mitigate potential threats. This makes it an ideal tool for supporting the recommendations identified by Defender for Cloud, as it enhances visibility into network security and helps prioritize actions based on threat intelligence.

Q335: During a security audit, the IT team at Fabrikam Inc. is using Microsoft Defender for Cloud to analyze potential attack paths within their Azure infrastructure. The analysis suggests that management ports on several virtual machines are exposed to the internet, posing a risk of unauthorized access. As a security measure, which feature should the team enable to mitigate this specific risk?

A) Azure Bastion

B) Azure VPN Gateway

C) Just-In-Time VM Access

D) Azure Site Recovery

E) Azure Front Door

F) Azure Monitor

Answer: C

Explanation: Enabling Just-In-Time VM Access is the recommended feature to mitigate the risk of exposed management ports on virtual machines. This feature reduces exposure to management ports by allowing you to control when and for how long the ports are open. It requires users to request access to these ports, which is granted for a limited time period. By minimizing the time management ports are open, Just-In-Time VM Access significantly lowers the risk of unauthorized access and aligns with the security recommendations from Microsoft Defender for Cloud's Attack Path Analysis. Azure Bastion and VPN Gateway are also security features, but they do not specifically address the issue of controlling port exposure in this manner.

Q336: Your company, Contoso Ltd., has recently migrated its applications to Azure and is using several Azure resources for hosting and managing these applications. Microsoft Defender for Cloud has provided a secure score that includes recommendations for improving network security. You are tasked with evaluating these recommendations to enhance the security posture of your Azure environment. The current setup includes a Virtual Network (VNet) with multiple subnets, Network Security Groups (NSGs) associated with each subnet, and an Azure Firewall. One of the recommendations from the secure score indicates the need to restrict network access to certain critical resources. You need to prioritize actions that will immediately increase the secure score by addressing the highest impact recommendations.

A) Implement Just-In-Time VM Access for all virtual machines.

B) Enable Azure DDOS Protection on all VNets.

C) Deploy a Web Application Firewall (WAF) in front of the application gateway.

D) Configure NSG rules to deny inbound traffic from all sources except trusted IPs.

E) Enable diagnostic logs for all NSGs and analyze the traffic patterns.

F) Create an Azure Policy to automatically apply security recommendations.

Answer: A

Explanation: Just-In-Time (JIT) VM Access is a powerful feature that significantly improves security by reducing exposure to potential attacks. By configuring JIT, you restrict access to virtual machines to only the required times and IP addresses, reducing the attack surface. This is a high-impact recommendation from Microsoft Defender for Cloud Secure Score because it directly addresses potential vulnerabilities associated with open management ports on VMs. Enabling JIT can immediately improve the secure score by mitigating the risk of unauthorized access. Other options, such as enabling DDOS protection or deploying a WAF, are important but may not have as immediate a direct impact on the secure score as JIT does in protecting management ports.

Q337: In the context of network security recommendations provided by Microsoft Defender for Cloud, enabling network security group (NSG) flow logs is a critical task. What is the primary benefit of enabling NSG flow logs in an Azure environment?

A) They automatically block malicious IP addresses.

B) They provide detailed information on traffic flow for auditing and analysis.

C) They reduce latency in network communication.

D) They enhance encryption standards for data in transit.

E) They enable faster recovery of network resources during downtime.

F) They increase the speed of data transfer between VNets.

Answer: B

Explanation: Enabling NSG flow logs is crucial for gaining visibility into network traffic patterns. These logs provide detailed information about the traffic flowing in and out of resources governed by NSGs, which can be used for auditing, analyzing, and identifying unusual or malicious activities. This data is invaluable for security teams to assess potential threats and take appropriate actions. While flow logs themselves do not automatically block IP addresses or directly affect latency, encryption, or data transfer speeds, they help in understanding and securing the network by providing actionable insights into traffic behavior.

Q338: True or False: Microsoft Defender for Cloud Secure Score directly impacts the billing amount for Azure resources by increasing the cost when recommendations are not addressed.

A) True

B) False

Answer: B

Explanation: The Microsoft Defender for Cloud Secure Score is a tool designed to help organizations assess and improve their security posture in Azure. It provides recommendations based on best practices but does not directly impact the billing amount for Azure resources. The secure score serves as a guide to help prioritize security improvements but does not impose additional costs for non-compliance. However, addressing the recommendations could lead to additional resource usage or enablement of certain features, which might have associated costs.

Q339: When evaluating network security recommendations in Microsoft Defender for Cloud, one of the suggestions is to reduce the exposure of your virtual network resources. Which Azure feature can be configured to provide additional protection by segmenting the network at the application layer?

A) Azure Traffic Manager

B) Azure Front Door

C) Azure Application Gateway with Web Application Firewall (WAF)

D) Azure Load Balancer

E) Azure ExpressRoute

F) Virtual Network Peering

Answer: C

Explanation: Azure Application Gateway with the Web Application Firewall (WAF) provides application layer protection by inspecting traffic and filtering malicious requests before they reach backend resources. This feature is specifically designed to safeguard applications against common web vulnerabilities and attacks such as SQL injection and cross-site scripting. By segmenting the network at the application layer and providing a dedicated security layer, the Application Gateway with WAF enhances the overall network security posture in Azure. Other options like Traffic Manager and Front Door provide traffic routing and acceleration but do not offer the same level of security segmentation as WAF.

Q340: Your organization is reviewing the network security recommendations from Microsoft Defender for Cloud. One of the recommendations is to improve the security of your Azure Virtual Network. You have been asked to implement a solution that provides distributed denial-of-service (DDoS) protection and integrates seamlessly with existing Azure services without requiring any additional configuration. Which solution would meet this requirement?

A) Configure Azure Firewall to block all inbound traffic.

B) Enable DDoS Protection Standard on the VNet.

C) Deploy a Network Virtual Appliance (NVA) for DDoS protection.

D) Use Azure Security Center to monitor DDoS attacks.

E) Implement NSG rules to restrict inbound and outbound traffic.

F) Utilize Azure Bastion for secure VM management access.

Answer: B

Explanation: Enabling DDoS Protection Standard on a Virtual Network provides comprehensive protection against DDoS attacks. This service is fully integrated with Azure and does not require additional configuration or deployment of new services. It provides always-on traffic monitoring and real-time mitigation of network-level attacks, ensuring that resources remain available even during an attack. Unlike deploying NVAs or configuring NSG rules, which require manual setup and maintenance, DDoS Protection Standard is built into the Azure platform and automatically scales to protect against attacks, offering seamless integration with existing services.

Q341: An e-commerce company is planning to deploy its web application on Azure. The application requires secure and efficient load balancing, SSL offloading, URL-based routing, and Web Application Firewall (WAF) capabilities to protect against common web exploits. The company expects variable traffic loads and needs a scalable solution that can handle sudden spikes in demand. They also want to ensure that they can perform traffic analytics and monitoring to optimize application performance. Which Azure service should they implement to fulfill all these requirements? ---

A) Azure Load Balancer

B) Azure Traffic Manager

C) Azure Front Door

D) Azure Application Gateway

E) Azure CDN

F) Azure API Management

Answer: D

Explanation: Azure Application Gateway is the ideal solution for this scenario as it provides advanced features such as SSL offloading, URL-based routing, and integration with a Web Application Firewall (WAF) to protect against vulnerabilities like SQL injection and cross-site scripting. It supports autoscaling, which is essential for handling variable traffic loads and spikes. Additionally, it offers built-in traffic analytics and monitoring capabilities, allowing the company to optimize application performance. Unlike Azure Load Balancer, which operates at the transport layer, Azure Application Gateway works at the application layer, making it more suitable for the specified requirements. Azure Traffic Manager and Azure Front Door offer global traffic management but do not provide SSL termination or WAF capabilities directly. Azure CDN is primarily for delivering static content, and Azure API Management is used for managing APIs rather than general web application traffic.

Q342: A financial services firm is migrating its customer-facing applications to Azure. These applications require a high level of security and compliance, including protection against DDoS attacks, SSL termination, and the ability to handle session persistence. The firm also needs to ensure that their applications can perform efficiently under different geographical traffic loads. Which Azure solution should they choose to meet these requirements effectively? ---

A) Azure Load Balancer

B) Azure Application Gateway

C) Azure Traffic Manager

D) Azure Front Door

E) Azure DDoS Protection

F) Azure VPN Gateway

Answer: B

Explanation: Azure Application Gateway provides the necessary features for this financial services firm, including SSL termination, session persistence (affinity), and integration with Azure's Web Application Firewall (WAF) to protect against application-layer attacks. It is designed to handle application-layer traffic efficiently, making it suitable for web applications that require high security and compliance. While Azure DDoS Protection can handle DDoS attacks, it does not provide SSL termination or session persistence. Azure Load Balancer handles network-layer traffic but lacks application-layer features. Azure Front Door provides global traffic management but does not offer session persistence. Azure Traffic Manager also manages traffic globally but does not include built-in WAF or SSL termination features.

Q343: A multinational corporation is using Azure to host several web applications across different regions. They are looking to implement a solution that can distribute incoming network traffic based on the lowest response time for users, improve application availability, and provide SSL offloading capabilities. Which Azure service should they choose to achieve these objectives? ---

A) Azure Load Balancer

B) Azure Application Gateway

C) Azure Traffic Manager

D) Azure Front Door

E) Azure Virtual WAN

F) Azure Site Recovery

Answer: D

Explanation: Azure Front Door is designed to optimize the delivery of web applications by distributing traffic based on the lowest latency, which ensures users receive content from the closest and fastest endpoint. It also provides SSL offloading capabilities, which reduces the load on backend servers by terminating SSL connections at the edge. This service improves application availability by offering global failover and dynamic route optimization. Unlike Azure Traffic Manager, which is DNS-based and does not offer SSL offloading, Azure Front Door operates at the application layer and can provide additional capabilities such as caching and dynamic site acceleration. Azure Load Balancer and Virtual WAN are more suited for network traffic management rather than application delivery.

Q344: True or False: Azure Application Gateway can automatically scale based on traffic demand without any user intervention. ---

A) True

B) False

Answer: A

Explanation: Azure Application Gateway supports autoscaling, which means it can automatically adjust its capacity based on incoming traffic loads. This feature allows it to handle varying amounts of traffic without requiring manual scaling configurations. Autoscaling ensures that the Application Gateway can efficiently manage spikes in traffic demand while maintaining optimal performance and resource utilization. This capability is crucial for applications that experience fluctuating loads and require consistent performance without user intervention to adjust capacity manually.

Q345: A digital marketing agency needs to deploy a solution on Azure that allows them to perform SSL offloading, URL-based routing, and integrate with a Web Application Firewall to protect their client websites from common vulnerabilities. They also require the solution to provide detailed logging and diagnostics information to monitor application performance and security threats. Which Azure service should they select to fulfill these needs?

A) Azure CDN

B) Azure Traffic Manager

C) Azure Load Balancer

D) Azure Application Gateway

E) Azure Front Door

F) Azure API Management

Answer: D

Explanation: Azure Application Gateway is the most suitable choice for the digital marketing agency's requirements because it offers SSL offloading, URL-based routing, and integration with Azure's Web Application Firewall (WAF). These features are essential for protecting client websites from vulnerabilities like SQL injection and cross-site scripting. Additionally, Azure Application Gateway provides detailed logging and diagnostics through Azure Monitor, which allows the agency to gain insights into application performance and security threats. While Azure Front Door also offers SSL offloading and routing capabilities, it does not provide the same level of integration with a WAF as Azure Application Gateway. Azure Load Balancer and Traffic Manager lack application-layer security features, and Azure CDN and API Management do not offer the required routing and WAF capabilities.

Q346: A multinational e-commerce company is experiencing performance issues with its global website due to high traffic in certain regions. They want to ensure that users receive the best possible performance and availability regardless of their location. Additionally, they need to protect their application from potential security threats and manage failover scenarios efficiently. Which Azure service would be most appropriate for improving the performance and reliability of their web application while providing security features?

A) Azure Traffic Manager

B) Azure Application Gateway

C) Azure Load Balancer

D) Azure Front Door

E) Azure Content Delivery Network (CDN)

F) Azure Virtual Network

Answer: D

Explanation: Azure Front Door is designed to improve the performance and reliability of applications by routing users' traffic to the nearest available backend. It provides global load balancing and application acceleration through dynamic site acceleration. Furthermore, Azure Front Door offers built-in security features such as Web Application Firewall (WAF) to protect against DDoS attacks and other threats. This service is suitable for applications needing high availability, low latency, and robust security on a global scale. Unlike Azure Traffic Manager or CDN, which also address performance and routing but do not provide security, Azure Front Door integrates these functionalities into a single solution, making it ideal for the e-commerce company's requirements.

Q347: You are in charge of designing a high-availability architecture for a new online multimedia streaming service. The service requires real-time global content delivery with low latency. In addition, the architecture should support automatic failover and traffic management across multiple regions. What Azure service should you prioritize to meet these requirements?

A) Azure Traffic Manager

B) Azure Front Door

C) Azure Application Gateway

D) Azure Load Balancer

E) Azure Content Delivery Network (CDN)

F) Azure ExpressRoute

Answer: B

Explanation: Azure Front Door provides a global, scalable entry point for fast delivery of high-quality streaming media and other web applications. It combines global load balancing with dynamic site acceleration, which is crucial for minimizing latency in media streaming services. The automatic failover and traffic management across regions are managed efficiently by Azure Front Door, ensuring high availability and resilience. While Azure CDN also offers content delivery capabilities, it lacks the global load balancing and failover features that Azure Front Door provides, which are critical for this use case.

Q348: A financial services company is deploying a new web application that must comply with stringent security and compliance regulations. They need a solution that provides secure, high-performance routing for HTTPS traffic, along with detailed logging and analytics capabilities. Which Azure service should they use to fulfill these requirements?

A) Azure Application Gateway

B) Azure Firewall

C) Azure Front Door

D) Azure Security Center

E) Azure Traffic Manager

F) Azure Content Delivery Network (CDN)

Answer: C

Explanation: Azure Front Door is well-suited for the financial services company because it offers secure HTTPS traffic routing with built-in Web Application Firewall (WAF) capabilities. This ensures compliance with security standards by protecting against common web vulnerabilities. Azure Front Door also provides detailed logging and analytics, which are essential for tracking access patterns and detecting potential security breaches. Unlike Azure Application Gateway or Traffic Manager, Azure Front Door extends beyond regional load balancing to provide a comprehensive global solution that addresses both performance and security.

Q349: Consider the statement: "Azure Front Door can be used to implement session persistence for web applications."

A) True

B) False

Answer: A

Explanation: True. Azure Front Door supports session persistence, which is also known as "session affinity" or "sticky sessions". This feature allows Azure Front Door to route subsequent requests from the same user session to the same backend server. This is useful for web applications that maintain state information or require sessions to be persisted to a specific server. By using session affinity, Azure Front Door helps ensure a consistent user experience and reduces the complexity of managing state in distributed applications.

Q350: A retail company wants to optimize the delivery of static and dynamic content for their global customer base. Their goals include reducing latency, improving load times during peak holiday sales, and protecting against common web threats. Which Azure service best fits their needs for combined performance optimization and security?

A) Azure Traffic Manager

B) Azure Front Door

C) Azure Content Delivery Network (CDN)

D) Azure Application Gateway

E) Azure Load Balancer

F) Azure Policy

Answer: B

Explanation: Azure Front Door is the optimal choice for the retail company because it provides both global load balancing and dynamic content acceleration to reduce latency and improve load times. It is specifically designed to handle both static and dynamic content efficiently, which is crucial for maintaining performance during high-traffic periods like holiday sales. Furthermore, Azure Front Door includes a Web Application Firewall (WAF) to protect against web threats such as SQL injection and cross-site scripting, ensuring the security of the application. While Azure CDN focuses primarily on static content delivery, Azure Front Door offers a comprehensive solution that addresses both performance and security concerns, making it the ideal service for the company's needs.

Q351: Contoso Ltd. is a global e-commerce company that has deployed its web application on Azure. The traffic to the application is increasing, and they need to ensure high availability and resilience across multiple regions. They want to distribute incoming traffic to different virtual machines in multiple regions and need a solution that supports both HTTP and HTTPS protocols. Additionally, the solution should allow them to perform health checks on their backend resources. Which Azure service should Contoso Ltd. use to meet these requirements? ###

A) Azure Traffic Manager

B) Azure Application Gateway

C) Azure Load Balancer

D) Azure Front Door

E) Azure VPN Gateway

F) Azure ExpressRoute

Answer: D

Explanation: Azure Front Door is the most suitable option for Contoso Ltd. because it is a global, scalable entry point that uses Microsoft's global edge network to create fast, secure, and highly available web applications. It supports both HTTP and HTTPS protocols and provides URL-based routing, SSL offloading, and application-layer processing. Unlike Azure Load Balancer, which operates at the network layer (Layer 4), Azure Front Door works at the application layer (Layer 7), offering more advanced traffic management features. It also allows for health checks on backend resources to ensure traffic is directed only to healthy endpoints, making it ideal for a global e-commerce platform that requires high availability and resilience across multiple regions.

Q352: You are designing a network architecture for a new Azure-based application. The application requires internal load balancing across a set of virtual machines within the same virtual network. The traffic is non-HTTP and non-HTTPS, and you need to maintain client IP for auditing purposes. Which Azure service should you choose? ###

A) Azure Traffic Manager

B) Azure Application Gateway

C) Azure Load Balancer

D) Azure Front Door

E) Azure Kubernetes Service

F) Azure ExpressRoute

Answer: C

Explanation: Azure Load Balancer is the appropriate choice for internal load balancing when dealing with non-HTTP/HTTPS traffic within the same virtual network. It operates at the network layer (Layer 4) and is capable of distributing incoming network traffic across multiple virtual machines, ensuring high availability and reliability. Azure Load Balancer also preserves the client IP address, which is crucial for auditing purposes. Azure Application Gateway, Azure Traffic Manager, and Azure Front Door are designed for application-layer routing and are not suitable for non-HTTP/HTTPS protocols.

Q353: A company has deployed an Azure Load Balancer with several backend VMs. They noticed that traffic is not being equally distributed among the VMs. Upon further inspection, they found that one VM is receiving most of the traffic. Which configuration setting should be adjusted to achieve equal distribution? ###

A) Session persistence

B) Probe frequency

C) Idle timeout

D) Frontend IP configuration

E) Load balancing algorithm

F) Health probe protocol

Answer: E

Explanation: The load balancing algorithm setting is crucial for determining how incoming traffic is distributed among backend VMs in an Azure Load Balancer. If traffic is not equally distributed, it is likely that the load balancing algorithm is set to a mode that does not promote equal distribution, such as 'Source IP Affinity' (also known as session persistence). To achieve equal distribution, the algorithm should be set to 'Hash-based' which uses a five-tuple hash (source IP, source port, destination IP, destination port, protocol type) to distribute traffic evenly across the available VMs. Adjusting this setting will help achieve a more balanced traffic distribution.

Q354: True or False: Azure Load Balancer can be used to distribute incoming traffic based on the URL of the request.

A) True

B) False

Answer: B

Explanation: Azure Load Balancer operates at the network layer (Layer 4) and does not have the capability to make routing decisions based on the URL of the request. It simply distributes incoming network traffic based on a five-tuple hash, which includes source and destination IP addresses, source and destination ports, and the protocol type. For URL-based traffic distribution, Azure Application Gateway or Azure Front Door should be used, as they operate at the application layer (Layer 7) and provide advanced routing features based on URL paths.

Q355: A financial services company needs to implement a load balancing solution for their Azure-based application that supports SSL termination, URL-based routing, and Web Application Firewall (WAF) capabilities. What is the best Azure service for this requirement?

A) Azure Traffic Manager

B) Azure Application Gateway

C) Azure Load Balancer

D) Azure Front Door

E) Azure VPN Gateway

F) Azure Bastion

Answer: B

Explanation: Azure Application Gateway is specifically designed to provide advanced application-layer (Layer 7) routing features that include SSL termination, URL-based routing, and Web Application Firewall (WAF) capabilities. This makes it the ideal choice for applications that require these features. SSL termination offloads encryption/decryption work from the backend servers, improving performance. URL-based routing allows for intelligent request distribution based on the URL path. The built-in WAF provides protection against common web vulnerabilities, which is essential for a financial services company that handles sensitive data. Azure Load Balancer does not offer these application-layer features, while Azure Front Door provides similar capabilities but is more suited for global, multi-region scenarios.

Q356: A multinational corporation is deploying a series of web applications in Azure that will be consumed by users globally. The applications need to access external services on the internet, but for security and compliance reasons, all outbound traffic must appear to originate from a fixed range of public IP addresses. The company is considering different Azure services to facilitate this requirement. Additionally, the solution must support high availability and scalability to handle large volumes of traffic as the user base grows. Which Azure service should be deployed to meet these requirements?

A) Azure Load Balancer

B) Azure Traffic Manager

C) Azure Application Gateway

D) Azure NAT Gateway

E) Azure Firewall

F) Azure Bastion

Answer: D

Explanation: The Azure NAT Gateway is designed to provide a stable and secure outbound internet connection for VMs in a virtual network, using a specific range of public IP addresses. This service ensures that all outbound traffic from the VMs appears to originate from the same set of public IPs, which is crucial for maintaining compliance and security. The NAT Gateway also supports high availability and automatic scaling, making it ideal for large-scale applications needing consistent outbound connections. Other options like the Load Balancer or Traffic Manager do not offer the same outbound IP address management or scalability features specific to NAT Gateway.

Q357: A company is migrating its on-premises workloads to Azure. They want to ensure that their Azure VMs can make outbound connections to the internet without exposing their private IP addresses. Which of the following Azure services should the company use to meet this requirement?

A) Azure VPN Gateway

B) Azure NAT Gateway

C) Azure Application Gateway

D) Azure ExpressRoute

E) Azure Virtual Network Peering

F) Azure Bastion

Answer: B

Explanation: Azure NAT Gateway is specifically used to enable VMs within a virtual network to make outbound connections to the internet while ensuring that their private IP addresses are not exposed. By using NAT Gateway, all outbound internet traffic from the VMs will be routed through a set of public IP addresses, providing a level of abstraction and security. Other services such as VPN Gateway, ExpressRoute, and Bastion serve different purposes and do not provide the specific NAT functionality required here.

Q358: A company has multiple Azure subscriptions and wants to centralize the management of outbound internet traffic across different virtual networks in each subscription. They also want to minimize the number of public IP addresses used for this purpose. Which strategy would best achieve this goal?

A) Deploy a NAT Gateway in each virtual network

B) Use Azure ExpressRoute for all subscriptions

C) Implement a hub-and-spoke network topology with a central NAT Gateway

D) Configure a load balancer with NAT rules in each subscription

E) Use Azure Virtual Network Peering with a NAT Gateway in one subscription

F) Deploy Azure Bastion for secure remote access

Answer: C

Explanation: Implementing a hub-and-spoke network topology with a central NAT Gateway allows the company to centralize outbound internet traffic management across multiple subscriptions. By configuring a NAT Gateway in the hub network, all spoke networks can route their outbound traffic through the hub, minimizing the number of public IP addresses required. This setup is efficient and cost-effective, providing centralized control over outbound traffic. Other options like deploying NAT Gateways in each network or using load balancers do not achieve the centralization or public IP address minimization goals.

Q359: A retail business is setting up an Azure virtual network to host its backend services and needs to ensure that these services can connect to external APIs over the internet. However, the backend services must not accept any unsolicited inbound traffic from the internet. Which service configuration would best meet this requirement?

A) Use Azure Application Gateway

B) Deploy Azure Load Balancer with inbound NAT rules

C) Implement Azure Firewall with outbound rules

D) Configure Azure NAT Gateway for outbound connectivity

E) Set up Azure Traffic Manager for global routing

F) Enable Azure Bastion for secure access

Answer: D

Explanation: Azure NAT Gateway is specifically designed to enable secure outbound internet connectivity for virtual network resources without opening the network to unsolicited inbound traffic. It allows backend services to access external APIs while hiding their private IP addresses and ensuring that no inbound connections are accepted. This configuration is ideal for scenarios where secure, outbound-only internet connectivity is required. Other options like Application Gateway or Load Balancer are focused on managing inbound traffic and do not address the specific requirement of preventing inbound access.

Q360: True/False: Azure NAT Gateway can be used to manage both inbound and outbound traffic for virtual machines in an Azure virtual network.

A) True

B) False

Answer: B

Explanation: Azure NAT Gateway is designed specifically for managing outbound traffic from virtual machines in a virtual network. It provides a way for VMs to access the internet using a defined set of public IP addresses without allowing unsolicited inbound connections. For managing inbound traffic, other Azure services like Azure Load Balancer or Azure Application Gateway are used. Thus, Azure NAT Gateway is not suitable for handling inbound traffic, making the statement false.

Q361: Your company, Contoso Ltd., is in the process of migrating its on-premises data center to Microsoft Azure. As part of the migration, the IT team needs to ensure that all network resources are identified and secured using Microsoft Defender for Cloud Security Explorer. The team has deployed several virtual networks, network security groups, and application gateways across multiple regions. They have been tasked with ensuring that these resources are monitored and any security vulnerabilities are addressed promptly. How can the IT team effectively use Microsoft Defender for Cloud Security Explorer to achieve this?

A) Utilize Security Explorer to automatically tag resources with security vulnerabilities.

B) Use Security Explorer to generate a report of all network resources and their security status.

C) Manually scan each resource in the Azure portal for security vulnerabilities.

D) Deploy Azure Policy to automatically remediate vulnerabilities detected by Security Explorer.

E) Integrate Security Explorer with Azure Sentinel for enhanced threat detection.

F) Use Security Explorer's built-in AI to auto-heal detected vulnerabilities.

Answer: B

Explanation: Microsoft Defender for Cloud Security Explorer provides a centralized view of network resources and their security posture. By using Security Explorer, the IT team can generate comprehensive reports that detail the security status of all network resources. This allows them to identify which resources are not compliant with security best practices and take appropriate action. Unlike manual scanning, this feature provides a scalable and efficient way to monitor resource security across multiple regions. Additionally, while Azure Policy can be used for remediation, it does not replace the need for Security Explorer's reporting capabilities.

Q362: Microsoft Defender for Cloud Security Explorer is primarily used for which of the following purposes?

A) To provide a visual map of all Azure subscriptions.

B) To identify and assess network security vulnerabilities.

C) To automate the deployment of virtual machines.

D) To manage Azure Active Directory user accounts.

E) To create custom dashboards for Azure metrics.

F) To configure Azure Traffic Manager for load balancing.

Answer: B

Explanation: The primary purpose of Microsoft Defender for Cloud Security Explorer is to identify and assess security vulnerabilities within the Azure network resources. It provides insights into potential security risks, enabling organizations to enhance their security posture. This tool does not manage user accounts, automate VM deployment, or configure load balancing, which are functions of other Azure services. Security Explorer's main focus is on providing actionable insights into network security, which helps organizations maintain a robust security framework.

Q363: You are responsible for the security of a large-scale Azure deployment that includes hundreds of virtual machines, databases, and network resources. Your company has recently implemented Microsoft Defender for Cloud Security Explorer. What initial steps should you take to ensure that all network resources are identified and monitored effectively?

A) Configure Security Explorer to automatically resolve all detected vulnerabilities.

B) Set up alerts in Security Explorer for any changes in network configurations.

C) Use Security Explorer to create an inventory of all network resources.

D) Deploy custom machine learning models in Security Explorer for advanced threat detection.

E) Integrate Security Explorer with third-party security solutions for enhanced monitoring.

F) Schedule daily security assessment reports from Security Explorer.

Answer: C

Explanation: To ensure that all network resources are identified and monitored effectively, the initial step is to use Security Explorer to create a comprehensive inventory of all network resources. This inventory provides a foundational understanding of the existing network landscape, enabling you to monitor and assess the security posture of each resource. While setting up alerts and scheduling reports are important subsequent steps, the inventory creation is crucial for establishing a baseline for security monitoring. Integration with third-party solutions and machine learning are advanced steps that may follow after a clear understanding of the network environment is established.

Q364: True or False: Microsoft Defender for Cloud Security Explorer can be used to automatically remediate all security vulnerabilities in Azure network resources.

A) True

B) False

Answer: B

Explanation: Microsoft Defender for Cloud Security Explorer is designed to identify and assess security vulnerabilities in Azure network resources, but it does not automatically remediate all issues. While it provides critical insights and recommendations on how to address vulnerabilities, the remediation process often requires manual intervention or the use of additional tools like Azure Policy for automated remediation. Automatic remediation is not a function of Security Explorer itself, which focuses on detection and reporting rather than direct action.

Q365: During a security audit, you discovered several misconfigured network security groups (NSGs) in your Azure environment. To quickly identify similar issues in other network resources, you decide to leverage Microsoft Defender for Cloud Security Explorer. What is the most effective approach to accomplish this using Security Explorer?

A) Enable automatic remediation in Security Explorer to fix all NSG misconfigurations.

B) Use Security Explorer's search functionality to filter for resources with NSG configurations.

C) Create a custom policy in Security Explorer to flag misconfigured NSGs.

D) Analyze the Security Explorer's security recommendations dashboard for NSG issues.

E) Use Security Explorer to export a list of all NSGs to a CSV file for manual review.

F) Integrate Security Explorer with Microsoft Power BI for advanced data visualization of NSG configurations.

Answer: D

Explanation: The most effective approach to identify and address misconfigured network security groups using Microsoft Defender for Cloud Security Explorer is to analyze the security recommendations dashboard. This dashboard provides a centralized overview of potential security issues, including NSG misconfigurations. By reviewing these recommendations, you can quickly pinpoint and prioritize the misconfigurations that need to be addressed. While exporting data or filtering can be useful, the recommendations dashboard is specifically designed to highlight security concerns and provide guidance on how to remediate them efficiently.

Q366: A multinational corporation needs to establish a secure connection between its on-premises data center and its Azure VNet. The on-premises network team prefers using IPsec/IKE policy configurations to specify certain cryptographic algorithms for the VPN tunnel due to security compliance requirements. However, they also need to support dynamic routing protocols like BGP between the on-premises routers and Azure. The connection must accommodate these requirements. Which type of VPN should they use to achieve this?

A) Route-based VPN with custom IPsec policies

B) Policy-based VPN

C) Route-based VPN with Azure default policies

D) ExpressRoute with VPN failover

E) Site-to-Site VPN with static routing

F) Point-to-Site VPN

Answer: A

Explanation: In Azure, a policy-based VPN is limited to static routing and cannot support dynamic routing protocols like BGP. For dynamic routing and the ability to specify custom IPsec/IKE policies, a route-based VPN is necessary. Route-based VPNs in Azure can support BGP, which allows the corporation to establish dynamic routing between its on-premises network and Azure. Furthermore, route-based VPNs can be configured with custom IPsec policies to meet specific cryptographic requirements, making them suitable for the corporation's compliance needs.

Q367: When configuring a VPN connection in Azure that requires custom IPsec/IKE policies and needs to support dynamic routing protocols, which VPN type is appropriate?

A) Site-to-Site VPN

B) Point-to-Site VPN

C) Policy-based VPN

D) Route-based VPN

E) ExpressRoute

F) VNet-to-VNet VPN

Answer: D

Explanation: A route-based VPN in Azure is ideal for scenarios where custom IPsec/IKE policies are required along with support for dynamic routing protocols like BGP. Route-based VPNs use any-to-any (wildcard) traffic selectors, which allow them to handle dynamic routing protocols. Policy-based VPNs, on the other hand, are limited to static routing and specific traffic selectors, making them unsuitable for dynamic routing needs.

Q368: A company has a legacy on-premises system that uses static routes and does not support dynamic routing protocols. They want to connect this system to an Azure VNet. The security team insists on using specific IPsec policies for encryption. The company wants a simple setup with minimal changes to their existing network infrastructure. Which Azure VPN configuration should they select?

A) Policy-based VPN

B) Route-based VPN

C) VNet Peering

D) ExpressRoute with dynamic routing

E) Site-to-Site VPN with BGP

F) Point-to-Site VPN

Answer: A

Explanation: For a legacy system that relies on static routes and does not support dynamic routing protocols, a policy-based VPN is more suitable. Policy-based VPNs in Azure support specific IPsec policies and are designed for static routing. This setup requires minimal changes to the existing network infrastructure, aligning with the company's goal of a simple setup. However, they won't support dynamic routing protocols, which is consistent with the legacy system's limitations.

Q369: An organization is considering using a policy-based VPN to connect its on-premises network to Azure. The organization needs to implement advanced routing features and wants to dynamically exchange routes between the on-premises environment and Azure. True or False: A policy-based VPN will fulfill the organization's requirements.

A) True

B) False

Answer: B

Explanation: A policy-based VPN in Azure is not capable of supporting dynamic routing features such as BGP. Policy-based VPNs use static routing and do not support the dynamic exchange of routes. Therefore, if an organization requires advanced routing features and dynamic route exchange, a route-based VPN is necessary. Route-based VPNs in Azure allow for dynamic routing and can be configured to work with BGP to meet these requirements.

Q370: A regional healthcare provider must establish a secure connection between its main office and its Azure VNet. The connection should comply with specific security policies requiring custom encryption algorithms and utilize dynamic IP routing to accommodate future scalability. What is the most appropriate VPN solution for the provider to implement?

A) Policy-based VPN

B) Route-based VPN with custom IPsec/IKE policies

C) Azure VNet Peering

D) ExpressRoute with static routes

E) Point-to-Site VPN with policy-based routing

F) Site-to-Site VPN without BGP

Answer: B

Explanation: The healthcare provider's requirement for custom encryption algorithms and dynamic IP routing necessitates the use of a route-based VPN with custom IPsec/IKE policies. This VPN type in Azure supports dynamic routing through protocols like BGP, which allows for future scalability and flexibility in route management. Policy-based VPNs do not support dynamic routing and are limited to static configurations, making them unsuitable for the provider's needs. Azure VNet Peering and ExpressRoute are not VPN solutions and have different use cases.

Q371: A multinational corporation, Contoso Ltd, has expanded its operations to multiple regions across the globe. They have deployed several virtual networks in Azure to support their regional operations. Contoso Ltd wants to implement a centralized management solution to efficiently connect these virtual networks, ensuring seamless communication and maintaining security compliance. They are considering using Azure Virtual Network Manager for this task. Which step should be prioritized to ensure successful implementation and management of virtual network connectivity across multiple regions?

A) Define and apply network security groups to each virtual network.

B) Create a virtual network peering between each pair of virtual networks.

C) Deploy Azure Virtual Network Manager and define network groups.

D) Configure BGP (Border Gateway Protocol) across all virtual networks.

E) Implement Azure Traffic Manager to balance the traffic across regions.

F) Set up a dedicated VPN gateway for each virtual network.

Answer: C

Explanation: Azure Virtual Network Manager allows you to centrally manage network connectivity and security. The first step is to deploy the Azure Virtual Network Manager and define network groups that will include the specific virtual networks you intend to manage. By organizing virtual networks into groups, you can apply connectivity configurations and network security policies at scale, which is efficient for a large organization like Contoso Ltd. This approach aligns with Contoso's need to manage multiple virtual networks across regions while ensuring compliance and security. Configuring BGP or setting up VPN gateways are tasks typically performed after establishing the foundational management framework, which in this case, begins with deploying Azure Virtual Network Manager and defining network groups.

Q372: To ensure that your Azure Virtual Network Manager policies are being applied correctly, what command would you use to validate the effective connectivity configuration for a specific network group?

A) az network vnet list --output table

B) az network vnet show-effective-route-table

C) az network vnet-manager connectivity-configuration list-effective

D) az network vnet-manager validate-policy

E) az network watcher test-connectivity

F) az network vnet-manager connectivity-configuration show

Answer: C

Explanation: The command az network vnet-manager connectivity-configuration list-effective is used to retrieve and validate the effective connectivity configuration for a specified network group managed by Azure Virtual Network Manager. This command helps ensure that the intended policies and connectivity settings are correctly applied to the virtual networks within the group. It is crucial for administrators to verify these configurations to maintain the desired network topology and security compliance.

Q373: When utilizing Azure Virtual Network Manager for managing virtual network connectivity, which feature would allow you to control and manage the traffic flow between virtual networks within a network group?

A) Network Security Groups

B) User-Defined Routes

C) Network Connectivity Policies

D) Azure Firewall Policies

E) Application Security Groups

F) Virtual Network Peering

Answer: C

Explanation: Network Connectivity Policies within Azure Virtual Network Manager provide a way to control and manage traffic flow between virtual networks in a network group. These policies allow you to define which virtual networks can communicate with each other, effectively managing the network topology. This feature is particularly useful for organizations that need to enforce specific communication rules across a diverse set of virtual networks. While Network Security Groups and Azure Firewall Policies can control traffic at a more granular level, Network Connectivity Policies are designed specifically for managing connectivity between networks.

Q374: You are tasked with ensuring that a newly created virtual network in the East US region is automatically configured according to your organization's predefined network security and connectivity policies using Azure Virtual Network Manager. What is the correct approach to achieve this?

A) Manually configure each new virtual network to match existing policies.

B) Use Azure Policy to enforce configurations on all virtual networks.

C) Integrate the new virtual network into an existing network group.

D) Deploy a new instance of Azure Virtual Network Manager for the East US region.

E) Create a custom ARM template to apply configurations upon deployment.

F) Set up Azure Automation to apply configurations periodically.

Answer: C

Explanation: To ensure that a newly created virtual network automatically adheres to your organization's predefined policies, you should integrate it into an existing network group managed by Azure Virtual Network Manager. By doing so, the virtual network will inherit the network security and connectivity policies applied to the group. This approach streamlines the process and minimizes the need for manual configuration, ensuring consistency and compliance across your organization's virtual networks. While Azure Policy can enforce configurations, integrating with Azure Virtual Network Manager provides a more centralized and efficient management capability.

Q375: Azure Virtual Network Manager can automatically manage and enforce connectivity and security policies across multiple virtual networks.

A) True

B) False

Answer: A

Explanation: True. Azure Virtual Network Manager is designed to automate the management and enforcement of connectivity and security policies across multiple virtual networks. It allows administrators to define network groups and apply connectivity configurations and security policies uniformly across these groups. This capability ensures that all virtual networks within a group adhere to the organization's network policy requirements, reducing the risk of misconfiguration and improving overall security posture. The automation provided by Azure Virtual Network Manager simplifies network management, especially in environments with numerous virtual networks spread across different regions.

Q376: A large retail company, RetailCo, operates across multiple regions and has recently adopted Azure services to improve its global network reach. They have set up their primary infrastructure in the East US region and want to extend their on-premises network to Azure without changing their existing IP address scheme. RetailCo is considering the use of Azure Extended Network to achieve this goal. They need a solution that allows seamless extension of their on-premises subnets to Azure virtual networks to ensure low latency and high availability for their critical applications. Which component is crucial for implementing Azure Extended Network in this scenario?

A) Azure Virtual WAN

B) Azure ExpressRoute

C) Azure VPN Gateway

D) Azure Load Balancer

E) Azure Network Adapter

F) Azure Bastion

Answer: E

Explanation: Azure Extended Network allows on-premises subnets to be extended into Azure without changing IP addressing schemes, thus providing a seamless hybrid networking experience. The Azure Network Adapter is a key component in this setup, enabling the extension of on-premises networks to Azure virtual networks. This adapter is designed specifically to address the challenge of maintaining consistent IP schemes when extending networks, ensuring that applications can operate without any reconfiguration. Other options like VPN Gateway or ExpressRoute are useful for connectivity and bandwidth requirements but do not address the specific need to maintain IP addresses across the network extension.

Q377: You have been tasked with configuring Azure Extended Network for your organization. One of the requirements is to ensure that extended networks can support multicast traffic between on-premises and Azure. Which Azure feature should you enable to meet this requirement?

A) Azure Traffic Manager

B) VNet Peering

C) Azure Route Server

D) Network Security Groups

E) UDR (User-Defined Routing)

F) IP Forwarding

Answer: F

Explanation: For Azure Extended Network to support multicast or broadcast traffic, IP forwarding must be enabled on the network interfaces involved in the extended network. This feature allows the virtual machines to forward packets not originally destined for them, which is crucial for handling multicast or broadcast traffic. Other options like Route Server or UDR focus on routing control but do not inherently support multicast traffic. VNet Peering connects virtual networks but does not handle broadcast traffic either.

Q378: True or False: Azure Extended Network allows an organization to seamlessly extend their on-premises subnets into Azure without the need to change IP address schemes, but It does not support layer-2 network connectivity.

A) True

B) False

Answer: B

Explanation: Azure Extended Network indeed allows the extension of on-premises subnets into Azure while maintaining the existing IP address scheme. Contrary to the statement, Azure Extended Network does support layer-2 network connectivity, which is critical for maintaining IP address continuity and enables functionalities like multicast traffic. This capability distinguishes it from typical layer-3 solutions that do not allow such seamless integration.

Q379: A global enterprise, TechGlobal, is aiming to improve its disaster recovery strategy by leveraging Azure Extended Network. They plan to extend their on-premises networks to the Azure West Europe region. The network team needs to ensure that the Azure infrastructure is prepared for this integration. Which of the following steps should be taken first to prepare for Azure Extended Network deployment?

A) Set up an Azure Application Gateway

B) Deploy a Virtual Network in Azure

C) Create a Site-to-Site VPN connection

D) Enable Azure Traffic Analytics

E) Configure an Azure Firewall

F) Implement Azure Front Door

Answer: B

Explanation: The first step in preparing for Azure Extended Network deployment is to deploy a Virtual Network within the Azure region where the network extension is planned. This virtual network will serve as the foundation for extending the on-premises subnets and is necessary before other configurations like VPN connections or additional security components can be configured. Creating the virtual network ensures that the infrastructure is in place for further steps in the extended network setup.

Q380: An organization is in the process of setting up Azure Extended Network and wants to ensure that the solution is optimized for minimal latency and high availability. Which Azure service should they integrate into their design to achieve these objectives?

A) Azure ExpressRoute Direct

B) Azure Traffic Manager

C) Azure Load Balancer

D) Azure Bastion

E) Azure Virtual Network NAT

F) Azure Monitor

Answer: B

Explanation: Azure Traffic Manager is a DNS-based traffic load balancer that enables organizations to distribute traffic optimally to services across global Azure regions. By integrating Traffic Manager into the Azure Extended Network design, the organization can optimize for minimal latency by routing client requests to the nearest Azure endpoint. Additionally, it provides high availability by automatically directing traffic to alternative endpoints in the event of a failure. This ensures that the network extension is robust and performance-optimized. Other options like ExpressRoute or Load Balancer offer connectivity and distribution features but are not primarily focused on latency optimization across regions.

Q381: A global e-commerce company wants to improve the availability and performance of its website hosted in multiple Azure regions. They need to route users to the nearest available endpoint based on their geographic location to ensure low latency. The company is considering using Azure Traffic Manager to achieve this goal. Additionally, they want to ensure that if any endpoint goes down, traffic is redirected to the next best available endpoint without manual intervention. The solution should also provide metrics and logging for monitoring purposes. What Traffic Manager routing method should the company implement to meet these requirements?

A) Priority

B) Weighted

C) Performance

D) Geographic

E) MultiValue

F) Subnet

Answer: C

Explanation: The Performance routing method in Azure Traffic Manager is designed for scenarios where users need to be directed to the closest endpoint with the lowest latency. This method uses the network performance statistics to determine the best endpoint for a user based on their geographic location. In this case, it aligns perfectly with the company's requirement to route users to the nearest endpoint to minimize latency. Additionally, Azure Traffic Manager automatically provides failover capabilities, redirecting users to the next best endpoint if one goes down. Metrics and logging are integrated into Azure Traffic Manager, allowing the company to monitor traffic and endpoint performance effectively.

Q382: You are tasked with setting up Azure Traffic Manager for a multinational corporation with offices in various regions. The corporation wants each office to access specific applications hosted in Azure based on their geographical location, ensuring compliance with local data residency regulations. The corporation also needs to ensure that if a specific endpoint fails, the traffic is redirected to a predefined backup endpoint. Which Azure Traffic Manager routing method is the most appropriate for this use case?

A) Performance

B) Geographic

C) Weighted

D) MultiValue

E) Subnet

F) Priority

Answer: B

Explanation: The Geographic routing method in Azure Traffic Manager is tailored for scenarios where traffic needs to be directed based on the geographic location of the users. This is particularly useful for ensuring compliance with local data residency regulations, as it allows organizations to direct users from specific regions to region-specific endpoints. In the event of an endpoint failure, Azure Traffic Manager can be configured with a backup endpoint, ensuring continuity of service. This method is ideal for multinational corporations needing to manage traffic according to geographic boundaries and regulatory requirements.

Q383: A company has implemented Azure Traffic Manager with the Priority routing method to manage traffic across its global endpoints. They have configured the primary endpoint for North America and a secondary endpoint in Europe. Recently, they've noticed that traffic is not failing over to the secondary endpoint when the primary endpoint is down. Which configuration change is most likely needed to resolve this issue?

A) Increase the TTL (Time-to-Live) value.

B) Enable health probes and ensure they are configured correctly.

C) Change the routing method to Performance.

D) Add more endpoints to the Traffic Manager profile.

E) Configure endpoint monitoring to use TCP instead of HTTP.

F) Decrease the priority of the secondary endpoint.

Answer: B

Explanation: For Azure Traffic Manager to perform failover correctly using the Priority routing method, health probes must be enabled and correctly configured. Health probes are responsible for determining the availability of an endpoint. If a primary endpoint fails a health probe, Traffic Manager will redirect traffic to the next available endpoint in the priority list. In this scenario, it's likely that health probes are either not enabled or misconfigured, leading to the failure in detecting the downtime of the primary endpoint. Ensuring that health probes are set up correctly to monitor endpoint health is crucial for the failover mechanism to function as expected.

Q384: True or False: Azure Traffic Manager can be used for internal (intra-Azure) load balancing of resources within the same Azure region.

A) True

B) False

Answer: B

Explanation: Azure Traffic Manager is a DNS-based traffic load balancer that is primarily used for distributing traffic to different Azure regions or external endpoints. It is designed for global load balancing and not for internal (intra-Azure) load balancing within the same Azure region. For internal load balancing within a single region, Azure Load Balancer or Application Gateway should be used. These services provide layer-4 and layer-7 load balancing capabilities, respectively, for resources within the same Azure region.

Q385: Your organization is deploying a new application across multiple Azure regions to ensure high availability and low latency access for users worldwide. They intend to use Azure Traffic Manager to manage the distribution of user traffic. However, the organization wants to maintain control over how much traffic is routed to each endpoint, irrespective of the user's location. Which Azure Traffic Manager routing method should be implemented?

A) Priority

B) Performance

C) Geographic

D) Weighted

E) MultiValue

F) Subnet

Answer: D

Explanation: The Weighted routing method in Azure Traffic Manager allows for manual control over the distribution of traffic to different endpoints by assigning weights. This method is useful when an organization wants to specify exactly how much traffic each endpoint should receive, irrespective of the user's geographic location or performance considerations. This can be beneficial for load testing scenarios, gradual deployments, or when balancing load between different regions or datacenters. By using weights, administrators can fine-tune traffic distribution according to their specific needs and business requirements.

Q386: A multinational retail company is migrating its on-premises applications to Azure. They are deploying a web application that requires high availability and resilience across multiple regions. To ensure optimal performance, the IT team decides to implement a gateway load balancer in front of their application gateway. This setup needs to support traffic distribution across multiple back-end instances and manage sudden spikes in traffic efficiently. What is the most appropriate step to implement a gateway load balancer in this scenario?

A) Configure a standard load balancer with a public IP and associate it with the application gateway.

B) Deploy an Azure Traffic Manager profile and configure it for geographic traffic distribution.

C) Utilize an internal load balancer with a private IP and integrate it with the application gateway.

D) Set up a gateway load balancer with a backend pool of virtual machines and configure health probes.

E) Implement a virtual network gateway and establish VPN connections for secure traffic routing.

F) Deploy Azure Front Door for global load balancing and integrate with the application gateway.

Answer: D

Explanation: To implement a gateway load balancer in Azure, you must configure it to distribute traffic across multiple back-end instances effectively. A gateway load balancer is specifically designed to work with virtual network appliances and can efficiently manage traffic spikes by routing requests based on health probes. By setting up a backend pool of virtual machines, the load balancer can distribute incoming traffic, ensuring high availability. Options like Traffic Manager or Front Door are not primarily designed for internal traffic balancing, and using an internal load balancer or virtual network gateway would not directly address the need for a gateway load balancer.

Q387: When configuring a gateway load balancer in Azure, it is necessary to define backend pools that determine how network traffic is distributed to instances. True or False?

A) True

B) False

Answer: A

Explanation: A gateway load balancer in Azure requires backend pools to distribute traffic effectively. These pools consist of the virtual machines or virtual machine scale sets that will receive the network traffic. Configuring backend pools is crucial for load balancing because they determine how incoming requests are allocated across different instances, ensuring that the load is evenly distributed and that resources are used efficiently. This setup also allows for scaling and redundancy, which are essential for maintaining application availability.

Q388: What is a key benefit of using a gateway load balancer in conjunction with network virtual appliances (NVAs) within an Azure virtual network?

A) It allows for automatic SSL termination at the load balancer.

B) The gateway load balancer supports multi-region failover natively.

C) Provides a unified interface for managing all network traffic.

D) Supports high-performance data caching at the network perimeter.

E) Facilitates seamless scaling of NVAs without downtime.

F) Automatically integrates with Azure AD for enhanced security.

Answer: E

Explanation: A gateway load balancer in Azure provides the ability to seamlessly scale network virtual appliances (NVAs) without experiencing downtime. This is critical for maintaining high availability and performance as the demand on the network increases. The gateway load balancer can distribute traffic across multiple NVAs, ensuring that the load is balanced and that additional instances can be added or removed as needed. This capability is essential for dynamic environments where network demands can fluctuate, and NVAs need to scale accordingly.

Q389: You are tasked with configuring a gateway load balancer to manage incoming traffic to a set of application servers hosted in Azure. Which Azure CLI command would you use to create a new gateway load balancer frontend configuration?

A) az network lb frontend-ip create

B) az network application-gateway frontend-ip create

C) az network lb create

D) az network traffic-manager profile create

E) az network vnet-gateway create

F) az network public-ip create

Answer: A

Explanation: To create a new frontend configuration for a gateway load balancer in Azure, you would use the Azure CLI command az network lb frontend-ip create. This command is specifically designed for configuring the frontend IP address of a load balancer, which is critical for directing incoming traffic to the appropriate backend resources. The frontend configuration defines how traffic is received by the load balancer before it is distributed across the backend pool. Other options, like application gateways or traffic manager profiles, are not suitable for this specific task.

Q390: A company is using Azure to host its online services and wants to ensure that a gateway load balancer is correctly handling specific traffic flows. They need to ensure that the health of their backend instances is constantly monitored. What configuration should they apply to achieve this?

A) Enable diagnostic logs on the load balancer and set up alerts.

B) Configure health probes for each backend pool to monitor instance availability.

C) Integrate Azure Monitor to track performance metrics of the load balancer.

D) Use Azure Bastion to regularly test connectivity to backend instances.

E) Implement Azure Security Center recommendations for the load balancer.

F) Establish a VPN tunnel to monitor traffic flow and instance health.

Answer: B

Explanation: Configuring health probes for each backend pool is the most direct and effective way to monitor the availability and health of backend instances in a gateway load balancer setup. Health probes are used to check the status of each instance, ensuring that only healthy instances receive traffic. This configuration helps maintain high availability and performance by dynamically adjusting traffic distribution based on the health status of individual instances. Although diagnostic logs and Azure Monitor can provide additional insights, health probes are specifically designed for real-time health monitoring in a load balancing context.

Q391: You are a network engineer at a company that has recently migrated its applications to Azure. The company's architecture includes a web application running on a series of Azure virtual machines (VMs) that need to efficiently distribute incoming HTTP traffic. To ensure high availability and reliability, you are tasked with implementing a load balancing rule using Azure Load Balancer. The solution must maintain session persistence and support HTTPS traffic, while also minimizing latency and ensuring efficient resource utilization. What configuration should you apply to the load balancing rule?

A) Use a Basic Load Balancer with a TCP probe for the health check.

B) Configure a Load Balancer with a round-robin distribution method and enable floating IP.

C) Implement an Application Gateway with a path-based routing rule.

D) Set up a Standard Load Balancer with session persistence set to Client IP and Protocol.

E) Use a Standard Load Balancer with a custom probe and enable direct server return.

F) Deploy a Traffic Manager with priority routing and SSL termination.

Answer: D

Explanation: To achieve the desired configuration for HTTPS traffic with session persistence, a Standard Load Balancer should be used with the session persistence set to Client IP and Protocol. This configuration ensures that traffic from the same client IP is directed to the same backend instance, maintaining session persistence. The Standard Load Balancer is preferred over the Basic Load Balancer because it provides more advanced features, including the ability to handle HTTPS traffic efficiently. Floating IP is not necessary for maintaining session persistence, and while Traffic Manager and Application Gateway offer routing capabilities, they serve different purposes, such as global traffic management and web traffic routing, respectively. Direct server return is not typically used for HTTPS traffic as it can complicate the network flow.

Q392: When configuring a load balancing rule in Azure, which parameter determines the number of consecutive probing failures before a backend is considered unhealthy and removed from the load balancing rotation?

A) Backend Pool Configuration

B) Load Balancer SKU

C) Health Probe Interval

D) Idle Timeout

E) Health Probe Unhealthy Threshold

F) Frontend IP Configuration

Answer: E

Explanation: The Health Probe Unhealthy Threshold is the parameter that determines the number of consecutive probing failures required before a backend instance is considered unhealthy and subsequently removed from the load balancing rotation. This threshold is crucial for maintaining high availability and reliability of the applications by preventing traffic from being sent to an unresponsive or faulty backend. Configuring an appropriate unhealthy threshold ensures that transient issues do not cause unnecessary removal of healthy instances, while persistent issues are promptly addressed by removing problematic backends from the rotation.

Q393: In a scenario where you need to distribute incoming traffic to multiple virtual machines in different availability zones within the same region, which Azure load balancing solution should you choose to best achieve zone redundancy?

A) Basic Load Balancer

B) Azure Traffic Manager

C) Application Gateway with WAF

D) Standard Load Balancer

E) Azure Front Door

F) VPN Gateway

Answer: D

Explanation: To achieve zone redundancy when distributing traffic to multiple virtual machines across different availability zones within the same region, the Standard Load Balancer is the appropriate solution. The Standard Load Balancer supports zone redundancy, which means it can span multiple availability zones, providing enhanced availability and resilience against zone failures. Unlike the Basic Load Balancer, which does not support zone redundancy, the Standard Load Balancer ensures that traffic can be distributed across resources in different zones, maintaining service continuity even if a zone becomes unavailable. Traffic Manager and Front Door are for global distribution and routing, and Application Gateway is more suited for web application scenarios with additional features like WAF.

Q394: True or False: The Azure Load Balancer supports both inbound and outbound traffic load balancing for virtual machines within a virtual network.

A) True

B) False

Answer: A

Explanation: The Azure Load Balancer indeed supports both inbound and outbound traffic load balancing. For inbound traffic, it distributes incoming client requests to the backend pool instances based on configured load balancing rules and health probes. For outbound traffic, the Load Balancer can provide outbound NAT (Network Address Translation) for virtual machines within a virtual network, allowing them to communicate with external resources while maintaining a consistent public IP address. This dual capability of handling both inbound and outbound traffic makes Azure Load Balancer a versatile tool for managing application traffic efficiently.

Q395: Your organization has deployed a multi-tier application in Azure that consists of a front-end web tier, a middle-tier for business logic, and a back-end database tier. The front-end and middle-tier need to communicate securely with minimal latency. You are tasked with implementing a load balancer solution that ensures secure communication between these tiers while maintaining efficient resource utilization. Which Azure feature would you leverage to achieve this?

A) Application Gateway with SSL offload

B) Standard Load Balancer with internal load balancing

C) Basic Load Balancer with TCP health probes

D) Azure Front Door with caching enabled

E) Traffic Manager with performance routing

F) VPN Gateway with site-to-site connection

Answer: B

Explanation: For secure and efficient communication between the front-end and middle-tier of a multi-tier application, the Standard Load Balancer with an internal load balancing configuration is ideal. Internal load balancing allows you to distribute network traffic across resources that are only accessible within a virtual network, ensuring secure communication without exposing the traffic to the internet. The Standard Load Balancer provides advanced features and better performance compared to the Basic Load Balancer, making it suitable for scenarios requiring minimal latency and high resource utilization. Using internal load balancing helps maintain security by keeping inter-tier communication private and within the Azure network. Application Gateway and Front Door are more suited for web traffic scenarios, while Traffic Manager and VPN Gateway address different networking needs.

Q396: Your company, Contoso Ltd., has recently deployed a set of web applications in Azure Virtual Network (VNet). These applications need to access external resources on the internet, but for security reasons, you want to prevent any inbound internet traffic to these applications. You decide to implement a NAT gateway to manage outbound traffic and assign static public IP addresses for tracking and compliance. Which step is necessary to ensure that the NAT gateway can be used by the web applications?

A) Associate the NAT gateway with the application subnet.

B) Configure a user-defined route to direct traffic through the NAT gateway.

C) Enable NAT gateway in the Network Security Group (NSG) rules.

D) Attach the NAT gateway to the virtual network directly.

E) Install the NAT gateway extension on the application VMs.

F) Enable public IP addresses on each VM in the application subnet.

Answer: A

Explanation: To use a NAT gateway for managing outbound internet traffic, it must be associated with the subnet where the resources reside. This configuration allows all outbound traffic from the subnet to be routed through the NAT gateway, providing a static public IP for egress traffic without requiring public IPs on individual VMs. The NAT gateway itself must be connected to the subnet, not directly to a virtual network or through NSG or VM extensions. User-defined routes are not needed for NAT gateway configurations as they automatically manage routing for outbound traffic.

Q397: You are tasked with configuring a NAT gateway to ensure reliable outbound connectivity for a large-scale application distributed across multiple Azure regions. Each region has its own Virtual Network (VNet) with multiple subnets. What is a critical step to ensure that your NAT gateway setup provides reliable connectivity?

A) Deploy a NAT gateway in each subnet within the VNet.

B) Use a single NAT gateway shared across all VNets in different regions.

C) Ensure each VNet has its own NAT gateway associated with at least one subnet.

D) Set up a global load balancer to distribute outbound traffic across NAT gateways.

E) Configure a single NAT gateway with multiple public IP addresses for redundancy.

F) Connect all regional VNets via VNet peering and use a central NAT gateway.

Answer: C

Explanation: To provide reliable outbound connectivity, each VNet should have its own NAT gateway associated with at least one of its subnets. This setup ensures that the traffic originating from resources within that VNet will have a consistent outbound path through the NAT gateway. A single NAT gateway cannot be shared across different VNets, particularly those in different regions, due to the isolation of network resources. Deploying a NAT gateway per subnet or using global load balancers is unnecessary for basic NAT gateway requirements. While multiple public IPs can enhance redundancy, they do not replace the necessity of having a NAT gateway per VNet.

Q398: True or False: A NAT gateway allows inbound connectivity to Azure resources by default.

A) True

B) False

Answer: B

Explanation: A NAT gateway is specifically designed to manage outbound connectivity for Azure resources. It does not allow or facilitate inbound connectivity. By providing a static public IP for outbound traffic, it ensures that resources within a VNet can communicate with external services without exposing themselves to unsolicited inbound traffic. For inbound traffic control, other Azure services like Azure Load Balancer or Application Gateway should be used.

Q399: When configuring a NAT gateway, you decide to use multiple public IP addresses. What is the primary benefit of this configuration?

A) Increased security for outbound traffic.

B) Load balancing of outbound traffic across multiple IP addresses.

C) Reduced configuration complexity for the NAT gateway.

D) Enhanced redundancy and scalability for outbound traffic.

E) Simplified DNS management for outbound connections.

F) Faster setup and deployment of the NAT gateway.

Answer: D

Explanation: Using multiple public IP addresses with a NAT gateway provides enhanced redundancy and scalability for outbound traffic. This configuration ensures that if one public IP encounters issues, traffic can still be routed through the remaining available IPs, minimizing downtime. While this setup does not inherently increase security or simplify DNS management, it does allow for a more robust and scalable outbound traffic management, essential for high-availability scenarios.

Q400: An organization plans to migrate its on-premises data center to Azure. They need a consistent public IP for outbound operations from multiple Azure VNets that are interconnected via VNet peering. Which Azure component should be employed to achieve this requirement?

A) Azure ExpressRoute

B) Azure VPN Gateway

C) Azure Application Gateway

D) Azure Load Balancer

E) Azure Front Door

F) Azure NAT Gateway

Answer: F

Explanation: Azure NAT Gateway is the correct choice for providing a consistent public IP for outbound traffic from Azure VNets. When VNets are interconnected via VNet peering, each VNet should have its own NAT gateway to manage and maintain a consistent public IP for outbound connections. This setup ensures that resources in peered VNets can access external services using a static public IP address, which is necessary for tracking, compliance, and avoiding IP address changes that can occur with other services like Application Gateway or Load Balancer. ExpressRoute and VPN Gateway are more suited for secure connectivity between Azure and on-premises environments rather than managing outbound internet traffic.

Q401: Contoso Ltd., a global manufacturing company, has its main data center in New York and an additional data center in London. They are planning to implement a site-to-site VPN connection between these two locations using Azure. The New York data center is already connected to Azure via an ExpressRoute circuit and the London data center uses a standard internet connection. Their requirement is to ensure secure, reliable connectivity with minimal latency between the two data centers, leveraging their existing infrastructure as much as possible. For the VPN setup, they need to configure the appropriate gateway type on Azure. Which gateway type should Contoso Ltd. choose to meet their requirements effectively?

A) Policy-based VPN

B) Route-based VPN

C) ExpressRoute Gateway

D) VNet Peering

E) Point-to-Site VPN

F) Azure Bastion

Answer: B

Explanation: To implement a site-to-site VPN connection between the two data centers, Contoso Ltd. should use a route-based VPN gateway. Route-based VPNs are capable of handling dynamic routing protocols and support multiple sites, making them suitable for complex network configurations like the one described. Policy-based VPNs are limited to static routing, which may not be flexible enough for Contoso's requirements. The ExpressRoute Gateway is not applicable here because it is used for dedicated private connections, not internet-based VPNs. VNet Peering is used for connecting virtual networks within Azure, not for site-to-site connectivity. Point-to-Site VPN is for individual client connections rather than site-to-site. Azure Bastion is unrelated to VPNs and is used for secure RDP/SSH access to VMs without needing a public IP. Therefore, the route-based VPN option best meets the needs for secure, reliable, and flexible connectivity between the two data centers.

Q402: When configuring a site-to-site VPN connection in Microsoft Azure, which of the following authentication methods is NOT supported directly for Azure VPN Gateway?

A) RADIUS

B) Kerberos

C) Pre-shared key

D) Azure AD

E) Certificate-based

F) LDAP

Answer: A

Explanation: nan

Q403: A company is setting up a site-to-site VPN between their on-premises network and Azure. They want to ensure high availability and redundancy of the VPN connection by using multiple VPN tunnels. Which configuration should they implement on the Azure side to achieve this?

A) Configure an Active-Active VPN Gateway

B) Set up multiple VNet-to-VNet connections

C) Use a single VPN Gateway with multiple IPs

D) Implement a Point-to-Site VPN as a backup

E) Deploy Azure Traffic Manager for VPN routing

F) Utilize Network Security Groups for redundancy

Answer: A

Explanation: To achieve high availability and redundancy in a site-to-site VPN configuration, the company should configure an Active-Active VPN Gateway on Azure. This setup allows for multiple VPN tunnels to be established, providing redundancy and load balancing between the tunnels. Active-Active configurations can handle multiple connections and failover scenarios more efficiently than a single tunnel setup. VNet-to-VNet connections are used for connecting virtual networks within Azure rather than external site-to-site connections. A single VPN Gateway with multiple IPs or a Point-to-Site VPN does not provide the required redundancy for site-to-site scenarios. Azure Traffic Manager is used for directing traffic to different endpoints but is not applicable for VPN configurations. Network Security Groups are used for filtering traffic within Azure and do not provide VPN redundancy.

Q404: True or False: To successfully implement a site-to-site VPN connection between an on-premises network and Azure, the on-premises VPN device must support IPsec/IKE protocols.

A) True

B) False

Answer: A

Explanation: For a site-to-site VPN connection to be established between an on-premises network and Azure, the on-premises VPN device must indeed support Internet Protocol Security (IPsec) and Internet Key Exchange (IKE) protocols. These protocols are essential for securing the VPN connection by enabling encryption and authentication between the two endpoints. IPsec is used for encrypting the data packets, while IKE is responsible for negotiating the encryption keys and establishing the secure tunnel. Without support for these protocols, the VPN connection would not be able to maintain the necessary level of security, and the connection establishment would fail. Therefore, the statement is true.

Q405: You are tasked with setting up a site-to-site VPN connection in Azure using PowerShell. Which PowerShell cmdlet should you use to create a new VPN connection between an Azure virtual network and your on-premises network?

A) New-AzVirtualNetwork

B) New-AzVpnClientConfiguration

C) New-AzVirtualNetworkGatewayConnection

D) Add-AzVirtualNetworkPeering

E) Set-AzVpnGatewayConfiguration

F) Invoke-AzVpnConnection

Answer: C

Explanation: The correct PowerShell cmdlet to create a new VPN connection between an Azure virtual network and an on-premises network is New-AzVirtualNetworkGatewayConnection. This cmdlet establishes the connection between the Azure Virtual Network Gateway and the on-premises VPN device, specifying the necessary parameters such as the connection type, shared key, and the local network gateway details. New-AzVirtualNetwork is used to create a new virtual network, not a VPN connection. New-AzVpnClientConfiguration pertains to point-to-site VPN client configurations. Add-AzVirtualNetworkPeering is used for VNet peering within Azure, not for site-to-site connections. Set-AzVpnGatewayConfiguration and Invoke-AzVpnConnection do not directly create a site-to-site VPN connection. Therefore, New-AzVirtualNetworkGatewayConnection is the appropriate cmdlet for this task.

Q406: A company named Contoso Ltd. has expanded its operations globally and requires secure connectivity for its remote employees to access resources in their Azure Virtual Network. The IT department is tasked with implementing a VPN client configuration using Azure VPN Gateway. The goal is to ensure that the VPN client configuration file is automatically updated whenever there are changes in the VPN gateway settings. Their current setup includes a Policy-based VPN gateway. What should the IT department do first to achieve this goal?

A) Switch the VPN gateway to a Route-based configuration.

B) Enable BGP on the existing Policy-based VPN gateway.

C) Use Azure AD for automatic client configuration updates.

D) Implement Azure Automation to update the configuration file.

E) Manually distribute updated configuration files to users.

F) Use a third-party VPN solution to manage updates.

Answer: A

Explanation: To ensure that the VPN client configuration file is automatically updated, the IT department must first switch from a Policy-based VPN gateway to a Route-based VPN gateway. Route-based VPN gateways in Azure support Point-to-Site (P2S) VPN, which allows for automatic updates to the client configuration file when changes are made to the VPN gateway, such as IP address changes or VPN type alterations. Policy-based VPNs do not support these automatic updates, as they are static and do not allow for dynamic routing or auto-configuration adjustments. Route-based VPNs use IP routing, enabling more flexibility and the ability to work with Azure's built-in mechanisms for updating client configurations.

Q407: When configuring a VPN client for Azure VPN Gateway, which file format is used for importing the configuration into a client device?

A) .ovpn

B) .xml

C) .json

D) .ovf

E) .cfg

F) .txt

Answer: A

Explanation: The .ovpn file format is used for configuring OpenVPN clients, which is commonly supported by Azure VPN Gateway for Point-to-Site (P2S) VPN connections. This file format is critical for importing VPN client configurations into devices, allowing users to establish secure connections to Azure Virtual Networks. The .ovpn file includes necessary parameters such as server addresses, authentication details, and encryption settings. Azure provides these files for download once the VPN gateway configuration is complete, ensuring that remote clients can easily import and set up their VPN connections with the correct settings.

Q408: True/False: Azure VPN Gateway allows for automatic distribution of VPN client configuration files to end-users.

A) True

B) False

Answer: B

Explanation: Azure VPN Gateway does not automatically distribute VPN client configuration files to end-users. While it generates the necessary configuration files, such as the .ovpn file for OpenVPN clients, these files must be manually distributed to users by the IT department or through an internal distribution mechanism. This process ensures that each client device receives the correct configuration to establish a secure connection to the Azure Virtual Network. Azure does not have a built-in service for direct client file distribution, emphasizing the importance of proper internal distribution practices.

Q409: A financial services company needs to implement a secure, scalable VPN solution that allows their clients to connect to multiple Azure regions seamlessly. The IT team is considering using Azure VPN Gateway and requires a VPN client configuration that supports multiple profile connections. Which of the following should they use?

A) Split tunneling configuration

B) Multiple P2S VPN configurations

C) IKEv2 with BGP

D) N-tier architecture

E) Azure Traffic Manager

F) Azure Load Balancer

Answer: B

Explanation: To support multiple profile connections for clients across different Azure regions, the IT team should use Multiple Point-to-Site (P2S) VPN configurations. This setup allows a single Azure VPN Gateway to support more than one configuration profile, enabling clients to connect to multiple Azure regions without needing separate VPN gateways for each one. By setting up multiple P2S configurations, the company can manage connections to different regions more efficiently, providing seamless access and ensuring high availability across their global Azure deployments. This method is particularly useful for organizations that have a presence in multiple geographical locations and need to maintain secure connectivity.

Q410: An e-commerce company is implementing Azure VPN Gateway for their remote employees and needs the VPN client configuration file to include specific DNS settings to resolve internal domain names. Which component must be configured in the Azure VPN Gateway to achieve this requirement?

A) Custom DNS server settings in the VNet

B) DNS forwarding in the local network

C) DNS resolver in the client devices

D) Ingress and egress rules in network security groups

E) Azure DNS Zone integration

F) DNS Proxy in the VPN Gateway settings

Answer: A

Explanation: To include specific DNS settings in the VPN client configuration file, the company must configure custom DNS server settings in the Virtual Network (VNet) associated with the Azure VPN Gateway. By specifying custom DNS servers, the VPN client configuration file will automatically include these DNS settings, allowing remote employees to resolve internal domain names correctly. This setup ensures that DNS queries from client devices are directed to the specified DNS servers, providing seamless integration with the company's existing internal network infrastructure. DNS settings are critical for maintaining network resource accessibility and ensuring that internal applications and services are reachable through domain names.

Q411: Your organization has a hybrid cloud architecture with multiple Azure Virtual Networks (VNets) connected through Azure VPN Gateway to an on-premises data center. The network experiences occasional connectivity issues, and you suspect that one of the links is intermittently down, leading to slow failover times. To improve the network's resilience and minimize failover time, you plan to implement Bidirectional Forwarding Detection (BFD) on your Azure VPN Gateway. Which of the following steps must you take to successfully enable BFD on your Azure VPN Gateway?

A) Ensure your on-premises VPN device supports BFD and configure it accordingly.

B) Upgrade the Azure VPN Gateway to a minimum of SKU VpnGw3 or higher.

C) Enable BFD on each local network gateway associated with the VPN connection.

D) Configure BFD settings through the Azure CLI using the "az network vnet-gateway update" command.

E) Implement BFD on the Azure VNet peering connections.

F) Modify the IPsec policy to include a BFD interval and multiplier.

Answer: A

Explanation: To enable BFD on an Azure VPN Gateway, it is crucial to ensure that the on-premises VPN device supports BFD. BFD is a network protocol used to detect faults in the path between two forwarding engines, including interfaces, data links, and even forwarding planes. It's essential that both ends of the VPN connection support and are configured to use BFD for it to function correctly. Azure VPN Gateway supports BFD for VPN connections to enable faster failover times by detecting path failures rapidly. While the Azure VPN Gateway itself does not require a specific SKU for BFD, the on-premises equipment must explicitly support and be configured for BFD. Therefore, the first step is to verify and configure the on-premises device for BFD support.

Q412: In Azure, Bidirectional Forwarding Detection (BFD) can help improve the resilience of VPN connections. BFD is primarily used to detect faults in the path between two forwarding engines, including interfaces, data links, and forwarding planes. Which of the following statements about implementing BFD in Azure is correct?

A) BFD can be directly applied to Azure VNet-to-VNet connections without any additional configuration.

B) BFD requires Azure ExpressRoute circuits to be in place for enhanced connectivity.

C) BFD is automatically enabled on all new Azure VPN Gateway connections.

D) BFD can be used with both policy-based and route-based VPN gateways in Azure.

E) BFD requires manual configuration on both Azure and on-premises devices to function.

F) BFD is only supported on Azure VPN Gateways with zone redundancy enabled.

Answer: E

Explanation: Bidirectional Forwarding Detection (BFD) is a network protocol used to detect faults quickly in the path between two forwarding engines. In Azure, BFD is not automatically enabled and requires manual configuration on both Azure VPN Gateway and the on-premises VPN device for it to function correctly. It is used specifically for route-based VPN gateways, and there is no requirement for Azure ExpressRoute circuits in order to implement BFD. Moreover, BFD is not automatically applied to VNet-to-VNet connections, nor is it exclusive to zone-redundant VPN gateways. The manual configuration ensures that both ends of the connection can detect failures quickly, thus improving the resilience and reliability of the VPN setup.

Q413: Your company, a global manufacturing firm, is experiencing network disruptions affecting critical applications hosted in Azure. The IT department has identified that the disruptions are caused by delays in route convergence during network failures. You have been tasked to implement a solution to reduce the failover time for your Azure VPN connections. After evaluating various options, you decide to use Bidirectional Forwarding Detection (BFD) to address this issue. What is a necessary consideration when implementing BFD in your Azure environment?

A) BFD is only supported on Azure VPN Gateway SKUs that offer high availability.

B) You must configure BFD on the Azure side only, as the Azure network automatically detects failures.

C) BFD is compatible with both IPv4 and IPv6 addresses without additional configuration.

D) The BFD session interval and multiplier must match on both Azure and on-premises devices.

E) BFD requires a special Azure subscription tier to be enabled.

F) BFD can only be enabled on VPN connections with specific encryption protocols.

Answer: D

Explanation: When implementing Bidirectional Forwarding Detection (BFD) in Azure, it is vital to ensure that the BFD session interval and multiplier are configured consistently on both the Azure VPN Gateway and the on-premises VPN device. BFD relies on these parameters to determine the frequency of control packet transmission and the number of missed packets required to declare a failure. Consistency between the two ends ensures that both devices have a synchronized understanding of the failure conditions, which enables rapid detection and failover. BFD does not require a special Azure subscription tier, nor is it limited by specific encryption protocols or high availability options offered by the VPN Gateway SKU. Additionally, while BFD can improve failover times for both IPv4 and IPv6, the configuration must be explicitly set on both endpoints.

Q414: True or False: In Azure, Bidirectional Forwarding Detection (BFD) is automatically enabled for all virtual network gateways as soon as they are created.

A) True

B) False

Answer: B

Explanation: Bidirectional Forwarding Detection (BFD) is not automatically enabled for all virtual network gateways in Azure upon their creation. BFD must be explicitly configured and enabled on both the Azure VPN Gateway and the corresponding on-premises equipment. This manual configuration step is necessary because BFD requires specific settings, such as session intervals and detection multipliers, to be aligned on both sides of the connection. Automatic enablement of BFD is not feasible due to the need for compatibility and configuration synchronization with the customer's on-premises equipment. Therefore, the statement is false, as BFD requires deliberate setup and coordination between Azure and on-premises devices.

Q415: You are tasked with enhancing the reliability of a critical Azure site-to-site VPN connection for a financial services company. The connection frequently experiences disruptions due to slow detection of path failures. To address this, you intend to implement Bidirectional Forwarding Detection (BFD). During the planning phase, which step is most critical to ensure the successful deployment of BFD?

A) Increase the bandwidth of the VPN connection to accommodate BFD traffic.

B) Configure Azure Traffic Manager to work with BFD for improved routing.

C) Validate that the on-premises VPN device is compatible with BFD and properly configured.

D) Deploy additional Azure VPN Gateways to support BFD functionality.

E) Integrate Azure Monitor to provide alerts for BFD session status.

F) Utilize Azure Load Balancer to distribute BFD traffic across multiple paths.

Answer: C

Explanation: The most critical step in successfully deploying Bidirectional Forwarding Detection (BFD) is to validate that the on-premises VPN device is compatible with BFD and is properly configured. BFD is a protocol that requires cooperation between both sides of the connection – in this case, the Azure VPN Gateway and the on-premises VPN device. Compatibility and proper configuration are essential to ensure that BFD can establish sessions and correctly perform its function of rapid fault detection. Without a compatible and correctly configured on-premises device, BFD cannot operate, and the expected improvements in failover times will not be realized. The other options, such as increasing bandwidth or using Traffic Manager, do not directly address the requirements for implementing BFD.

Q416: A multinational retail company is leveraging Azure Application Gateway to manage traffic to their web applications hosted across multiple regions. The company recently faced challenges with SEO due to non-canonical URLs and duplicate content issues. To resolve this, they aim to implement URL redirection to enforce canonical URLs and ensure that all non-secure HTTP traffic is redirected to HTTPS. The team is considering using the URL Rewrite feature for this purpose. Which of the following configurations should be implemented to achieve this goal using Azure Application Gateway?

A) Create a URL rewrite rule to redirect HTTP to HTTPS with a 301 status code.

B) Enable URL rewrite to append a query string for canonical URLs.

C) Set up a custom probe to check for canonical URLs.

D) Implement a listener with a wildcard host name for URL redirection.

E) Configure a URL redirect rule with a 302 status code for HTTP to HTTPS redirection.

F) Use Azure Front Door to handle URL redirections for canonical URLs.

Answer: A

Explanation: Implementing URL redirection from HTTP to HTTPS using a 301 status code is a best practice for SEO and security. A 301 redirect is a permanent redirect which tells search engines that the page has permanently moved to a new location, and it transfers full link equity to the new URL. Azure Application Gateway supports URL redirection rules that can be configured to redirect HTTP traffic to HTTPS. The URL rewrite feature in Azure Application Gateway can be used to create a rule that matches all HTTP requests and redirects them to the equivalent HTTPS URL. This ensures that all traffic is served securely, and canonical URLs are enforced, addressing SEO concerns. Options like appending query strings or using a 302 status code would not fully address the need for permanent redirection to secure URLs.

Q417: In Azure Application Gateway, URL rewrite and redirect rules can be applied to influence incoming traffic routing. When configuring a URL rewrite rule in the Azure portal, which of the following components must be specified?

A) Listener name and backend target

B) Host name and path pattern

C) Source pattern and destination pattern

D) Protocol and HTTP settings

E) Priority and timeout setting

F) Backend pool and health probe

Answer: C

Explanation: To configure a URL rewrite rule in Azure Application Gateway, you must specify a source pattern and a destination pattern. The source pattern defines the incoming

URL pattern that you want to match, while the destination pattern specifies the URL to which the incoming request should be rewritten. This allows you to modify the URL path or host name, enabling you to redirect users to different pages or services based on the incoming request. Other components such as listener name, backend target, or priority are not directly involved in defining rewrite rules.

Q418: A financial services company is using Azure's Application Gateway for their online portal. They want to configure URL redirection to improve security by ensuring all users access the portal over HTTPS. Additionally, they want the rule to be applied only if the incoming request does not already use HTTPS. Which of the following steps should the company follow to configure this in Azure's Application Gateway?

A) Add a new listener for HTTPS and associate it with a default backend pool.

B) Use a rewrite rule to add a secure header to HTTP requests.

C) Set up a routing rule with conditions to redirect HTTP requests to HTTPS.

D) Enable HTTP to HTTPS redirection globally in the Application Gateway settings.

E) Create a custom health probe to check HTTP responses.

F) Implement a custom domain certificate for HTTPS traffic.

Answer: C

Explanation: To ensure that all users access the portal over HTTPS, the company needs to configure a routing rule with conditions in Azure Application Gateway that specifically targets HTTP requests. This rule should redirect these requests to the HTTPS version of the URL. The Application Gateway allows you to create routing rules that can define conditions, such as matching the HTTP protocol, and then specify an action, like redirection to HTTPS. This ensures that users accessing the site over HTTP are seamlessly redirected to the secure version, improving security and user experience. Global settings or health probes would not provide the necessary conditional redirection required for this scenario.

Q419: True or False: In Azure Application Gateway, a URL rewrite rule can be used to change the host name of a request before it is forwarded to the backend pool.

A) True

B) False

Answer: A

Explanation: It is true that a URL rewrite rule in Azure Application Gateway can modify the host name of a request before forwarding it to the backend pool. This feature is particularly useful in scenarios where you need to forward requests to different backend pools based on the host name or to standardize host names for backend services. The URL rewrite capability allows you to match incoming requests based on specified patterns and then rewrite various components of the URL, including the host name, path, and query string. This flexibility is crucial for advanced routing and traffic management scenarios in complex application environments.

Q420: An e-commerce company is using Azure Application Gateway to manage traffic for their web applications. They have introduced a new promotion and want to ensure that all requests to the old promotions page are permanently redirected to the new promotions page. Which of the following actions should they take to achieve this using URL redirection in Azure Application Gateway?

A) Set up a health probe that checks for the old page and redirects to the new page.

B) Use a URL path-based rule to change requests to the old page to the new page.

C) Configure a URL redirect rule with a 301 status code from the old page to the new page.

D) Implement a listener that listens for the old page and directs traffic to the new page.

E) Use Azure Traffic Manager to distribute requests to the new page.

F) Deploy an additional Application Gateway instance for handling redirections.

Answer: C

Explanation: To permanently redirect requests from the old promotions page to the new promotions page, the e-commerce company should configure a URL redirect rule with a 301 status code in Azure Application Gateway. A 301 status code indicates a permanent redirect, informing browsers and search engines that the resource has been moved permanently to a new URL. This ensures that search engines update their indexes and users are automatically redirected to the updated page, preserving SEO rankings and providing a seamless user experience. URL path-based rules or health probes are not designed specifically for handling permanent redirections.

Q421: A multinational corporation has two Azure Virtual Networks (VNets) in different regions: VNet1 in the East US region and VNet2 in the West Europe region. The company wants these VNets to communicate seamlessly for their distributed application. However, the organization is concerned about potential latency and bandwidth limitations. They also need to ensure that the traffic between these VNets does not pass through the public internet. Which solution can meet these requirements without using Azure ExpressRoute or a VPN gateway?

A) Configure VNet peering between VNet1 and VNet2.

B) Use Azure Site-to-Site VPN to connect VNet1 and VNet2.

C) Implement an Application Gateway in each VNet for routing.

D) Set up a Virtual Network Gateway in both VNets for direct communication.

E) Deploy a load balancer to manage the traffic between VNet1 and VNet2.

F) Utilize Azure Traffic Manager for directing traffic between the VNets.

Answer: A

Explanation: VNet peering is a direct, private IP-only connection between two VNets, allowing seamless communication without using the public internet. This method ensures low latency and high bandwidth connections as it leverages the Azure backbone network. Unlike VPNs, VNet peering does not require a public IP or a VPN gateway, thus eliminating the complexity and potential latency associated with encryption and decryption of traffic.

Additionally, it supports communication between VNets in different regions, which aligns perfectly with the given scenario.

Q422: You need to implement VNet peering between two VNets in the same region. Which of the following must you ensure before configuring the peering?

A) Both VNets must be in the same Azure subscription.

B) Each VNet must have a different address space.

C) The VNets must be in different resource groups.

D) You must assign a public IP address to each VNet.

E) Network Security Groups (NSGs) must be removed from both VNets.

F) Both VNets must have a configured VPN gateway.

Answer: B

Explanation: When configuring VNet peering, it is essential to ensure that the VNets have non-overlapping IP address spaces. This is a fundamental requirement because overlapping address spaces can result in routing conflicts, making it impossible for Azure to determine the correct path for network traffic. The VNets do not need to be in the same subscription or resource group, and there is no requirement to assign a public IP or remove NSGs. A VPN gateway is also not necessary for VNet peering.

Q423: True/False: VNet peering allows transitive peering, enabling a VNet peered with another VNet to automatically connect to VNets that are peered with it.

A) True

B) False

Answer: B

Explanation: VNet peering does not support transitive peering by default. This means a VNet peered with another VNet cannot automatically communicate with a third VNet that is peered with the second VNet unless explicitly configured through additional peering connections. Each VNet involved must be directly peered with each other to enable communication among all of them. This non-transitive nature is a critical consideration when designing complex network topologies in Azure.

Q424: You have two VNets, VNetA and VNetB, peered together. VNetA is in the West US region, and VNetB is in the East US region. After setting up the peering, you notice that communication between Virtual Machines (VMs) across these VNets is failing. Which of the following could be the reason for this issue?

A) The VMs are in different Azure regions.

B) The peering status is in a "Disconnected" state.

C) Network Security Groups (NSGs) are blocking the traffic.

D) The address spaces of the VNets are overlapping.

E) The peering is not enabled for remote gateway usage.

F) The DNS settings are incorrectly configured.

Answer: C

Explanation: One of the common causes for communication failure between VNets after peering is misconfigured Network Security Groups (NSGs). NSGs act as a firewall for controlling inbound and outbound traffic to network interfaces, VMs, or subnets. If NSG rules are too restrictive or incorrectly set up, they can block traffic between the peered VNets, leading to connectivity issues. It's crucial to review and adjust NSG rules to ensure they allow the necessary traffic between the VNets.

Q425: You are tasked with enabling VNet peering between VNet1 and VNet2. However, VNet1 is in a subscription that is managed by a different Azure Active Directory tenant than VNet2. Which configuration step is necessary to successfully create this peering?

A) Assign the Global Administrator role to the user configuring the peering.

B) Create a service principal with the necessary permissions across both tenants.

C) Ensure the peering is initiated from a single tenant only.

D) Use PowerShell to configure the peering since the Azure portal does not support it.

E) Establish a bidirectional peering by setting up peering from each VNet.

F) Configure peering using Azure CLI with cross-tenant permissions.

Answer: E

Explanation: When dealing with VNet peering across different Azure Active Directory tenants, it's crucial to establish a bidirectional peering. This means configuring the peering from VNet1 to VNet2 and also from VNet2 to VNet1. Each side of the peering must be explicitly set up to allow traffic to flow in both directions. Additionally, the user configuring the peering needs to have the necessary network contributor permissions in each subscription. Cross-tenant peering requires careful coordination between administrators of both tenants, but it can be set up using the Azure portal, PowerShell, or Azure CLI.

Q426: A multinational corporation has multiple on-premises data centers in Europe and Asia. They are planning to integrate Azure Private Link services to securely connect their on-premises applications with Azure-hosted services without exposing them to the public internet. Their primary goal is to ensure low latency and high throughput between their on-premises clients and Azure services. They want to utilize Azure ExpressRoute for a private connection and need to configure a Private Link service that can be accessed from both the European and Asian data centers. What should be considered when configuring the Private Link service to meet these requirements?

A) Use a single Private Link service and configure it with global VNet peering to connect on-premises clients.

B) Deploy separate Private Link services for each region and connect them using Azure Traffic Manager.

C) Configure an ExpressRoute circuit for each data center and use BGP to advertise the Private Link service IPs.

D) Utilize Azure Front Door to route on-premises traffic to the Private Link service.

E) Implement a hub-spoke network topology and create a Private Link service in the hub.

F) Deploy Private Link services in each region's Azure Virtual Network and use IPsec tunnels for on-premises connectivity.

Answer: C

Explanation: When integrating a Private Link service with on-premises clients, especially in multiple regions, using ExpressRoute is crucial for achieving private connectivity with low latency and high throughput. By configuring an ExpressRoute circuit for each data center, you ensure that each regional data center has a dedicated private connection to Azure. Using BGP (Border Gateway Protocol) to advertise the Private Link service IP addresses allows the on-premises network to be aware of the private IPs of the Azure services, ensuring seamless connectivity without routing traffic over the public internet. This setup avoids the latency and potential security issues associated with public internet connections and provides a scalable solution for multinational operations.

Q427: In Azure, Private Link provides private connectivity to Azure services. True or False: Private Link can only be used for services within the same Azure region.

A) True

B) False

Answer: B

Explanation: Azure Private Link is designed to provide private connectivity to Azure services across different regions. It allows on-premises clients to securely connect to Azure services in any region by extending the private IP address space of the on-premises network into Azure. This capability is crucial for organizations that operate in multiple geographic locations and want to centralize their Azure services while maintaining private connectivity from various on-premises locations. Hence, Private Link is not limited to the same Azure region and can be used across different regions.

Q428: An enterprise wants to use Azure Private Link to connect its on-premises network to an Azure-hosted database service. Which of the following steps is NOT necessary to configure this setup?

A) Create a Private Link service in the Azure subscription.

B) Configure a private endpoint in the Azure Virtual Network.

C) Establish an ExpressRoute or VPN connection for private connectivity.

D) Set up a DNS zone to resolve the private endpoint's IP address.

E) Register the Azure service with a Private DNS Zone.

F) Configure a Network Security Group to allow inbound traffic from on-premises IPs.

Answer: A

Explanation: To connect an on-premises network to an Azure-hosted database service using Private Link, it is not necessary to create a Private Link service in the Azure subscription. Instead, you need to configure a private endpoint in the Azure Virtual Network, which acts as the interface for the Private Link. This setup involves establishing either an ExpressRoute or VPN connection for private connectivity and setting up DNS to resolve the private endpoint's IP address. Registering the Azure service with a Private DNS Zone is also crucial for resolving private DNS queries. Network Security Groups (NSGs) should be configured to allow traffic from on-premises IPs. Creating a Private Link service is typically used when you want to offer your own service over Private Link to your customers, rather than consuming an existing Azure service.

Q429: When configuring a Private Link service to allow on-premises clients to access an Azure-hosted web application, which DNS configuration is required to ensure proper name resolution?

A) Use Azure Traffic Manager to manage DNS resolution for the Private Link.

B) Configure custom DNS servers on Azure VNet to forward queries to on-premises DNS.

C) Set up Azure-provided DNS to resolve private endpoint IPs.

D) Use a Private DNS Zone and link it to the VNet hosting the private endpoint.

E) Implement a DNS forwarder in Azure to resolve all internal queries.

F) Create a public DNS record pointing to the private endpoint.

Answer: D

Explanation: To ensure proper DNS resolution for on-premises clients accessing an Azure-hosted web application via Private Link, it is essential to set up a Private DNS Zone. This DNS zone should contain records that map the Azure service's private endpoint IP to its fully qualified domain name (FQDN). By linking this Private DNS Zone to the Virtual Network hosting the private endpoint, Azure ensures that DNS queries for the service's FQDN resolve to the private IP address rather than the public IP, effectively directing traffic through the secure, private link. This configuration avoids exposure to the public internet and maintains the privacy and security of the connection.

Q430: A company wants to integrate Azure Private Link services with its on-premises environment using an existing ExpressRoute circuit. They need to ensure that on-premises DNS queries for Azure service FQDNs resolve to private IPs. What is the best approach to achieve this?

A) Modify the ExpressRoute circuit to include a DNS record for each Azure service.

B) Set up an Azure Application Gateway to handle DNS resolution.

C) Configure DNS conditional forwarding on on-premises DNS servers to the Private DNS Zone in Azure.

D) Use Azure Bastion to securely route DNS queries from on-premises to Azure.

E) Deploy an Azure Traffic Manager profile for DNS resolution.

F) Add host file entries on each on-premises client pointing to the private IPs.

Answer: C

Explanation: To integrate Azure Private Link services with an on-premises environment and ensure that DNS queries for Azure service FQDNs resolve to private IPs, configuring DNS conditional forwarding on on-premises DNS servers to the Private DNS Zone in Azure is the best approach. This setup allows on-premises DNS servers to forward specific queries for Azure service domains to the Private DNS Zone, where they can be resolved to the private endpoint IPs. This method ensures seamless integration and proper name resolution without requiring host file modifications or additional infrastructure like Azure Application Gateway or Traffic Manager. It provides a scalable solution that leverages existing DNS capabilities while maintaining secure, private connectivity.

Q431: A global enterprise, Contoso Ltd., is leveraging Microsoft Azure's Virtual WAN to streamline its cloud-based operations across multiple regions. As part of the network architecture, the company wants to integrate a third-party network virtual appliance (NVA) into their Virtual WAN hub to enhance security and optimize traffic management. The NVA must handle traffic inspection and enforce security policies for all traffic passing through the Virtual WAN. Contoso's IT team needs to ensure that the NVA can scale effectively to meet increasing traffic demands and that the solution remains cost-efficient. What is the best approach to achieve these requirements?

A) Deploy the NVA in a separate virtual network and use Azure ExpressRoute to connect it to the Virtual WAN hub.

B) Integrate the NVA directly into the Virtual WAN hub by enabling the NVA in the hub configuration.

C) Use Azure Firewall in conjunction with the NVA for enhanced security and scaling.

D) Deploy the NVA in a peered virtual network and route traffic through it using Virtual Network Peering.

E) Implement the NVA as a chained appliance in the Virtual WAN hub with manual route configuration.

F) Utilize Azure Load Balancer to distribute traffic to multiple instances of the NVA in the Virtual WAN hub.

Answer: E

Explanation: Integrating a third-party NVA with Azure's Virtual WAN hub involves deploying the NVA as a chained appliance in the hub. This setup allows for traffic inspection and policy enforcement at the hub level. By configuring the NVA as a chained appliance, traffic is automatically routed through the NVA, providing a centralized point for managing security and optimizing traffic flows. Additionally, this approach supports scaling as traffic demands increase, ensuring that the NVA can handle the load effectively. Manual route configuration is necessary to ensure that traffic is directed through the NVA, providing the required control over network traffic. This method is cost-efficient as it avoids additional infrastructure like ExpressRoute and leverages Azure's built-in capabilities for efficient scaling and traffic management.

Q432: Which command would you use in Azure CLI to associate a Network Virtual Appliance (NVA) with a Virtual WAN Hub to ensure all outgoing traffic is routed through the NVA?

A) az network vwan nva create --name NVAName --hub-name HubName --resource-group RGName

B) az network vwan hub update --name HubName --resource-group RGName --nva-route-table NvaRouteTable

C) az network vwan hub nva create --name NVAName --hub-name HubName --resource-group RGName

D) az network vwan nva update --name NVAName --hub-name HubName --resource-group RGName --route-table NvaRouteTable

E) az network vwan hub update --name HubName --resource-group RGName --add nva-routes NvaRouteTable

F) az network vwan nva associate --name NVAName --hub-name HubName --resource-group RGName --route-table NvaRouteTable

Answer: C

Explanation: To associate a Network Virtual Appliance (NVA) with a Virtual WAN hub, you need to create the NVA within the hub using the Azure CLI. The command az network vwan hub nva create is specifically designed for this purpose. It allows you to specify the name of the NVA, the hub, and the resource group where the hub is located. By creating the NVA within the hub, you ensure that the NVA can be configured to route all outgoing traffic through it. This setup is critical for applications that require network traffic inspection or security policy enforcement. Other commands might seem relevant but do not perform the exact task of creating and associating the NVA with a Virtual WAN hub for traffic routing.

Q433: True or False: Integrating a third-party Network Virtual Appliance (NVA) with Azure Virtual WAN requires the use of Azure Load Balancer to distribute traffic across multiple NVA instances.

A) True

B) False

Answer: B

Explanation: Integrating a third-party Network Virtual Appliance (NVA) with Azure Virtual WAN does not inherently require the use of Azure Load Balancer. Within the Virtual WAN architecture, NVAs can be deployed as chained appliances directly in the hub, which automatically manages the routing of traffic through these appliances. This setup provides a streamlined method for traffic inspection and security policy enforcement without needing additional load balancing infrastructure. While Azure Load Balancer can be used for distributing traffic across multiple instances of NVAs in other configurations, it is not a requirement when the NVAs are integrated into the Virtual WAN hub as chained appliances.

Q434: To ensure optimal performance and cost management, which feature should be enabled when integrating a third-party NVA with an Azure Virtual WAN hub?

A) Enable Azure Traffic Manager to route traffic to the NVA.

B) Use Azure Monitor to track performance metrics of the NVA.

C) Enable BGP propagation on the Virtual WAN hub.

D) Configure dynamic routing on the NVA using Azure Route Server.

E) Implement Azure Policy to restrict traffic not routed through the NVA.

F) Use Azure Bastion for secure access to the NVA management interface.

Answer: B

Explanation: When integrating a third-party Network Virtual Appliance (NVA) with an Azure Virtual WAN hub, enabling Azure Monitor is crucial for ensuring optimal performance and cost management. Azure Monitor provides comprehensive monitoring tools that can track the performance metrics of the NVA, allowing you to identify bottlenecks, assess resource utilization, and manage capacity effectively. By having detailed insights into the NVA's performance, you can make informed decisions about scaling and configuration adjustments to maintain cost efficiency and performance. Other options, such as enabling BGP or dynamic routing, do not provide the direct monitoring capabilities needed to manage performance and costs effectively.

Q435: When configuring an NVA in an Azure Virtual WAN hub, which routing strategy should be used to ensure all incoming traffic from on-premises networks is processed by the NVA first?

A) Implement user-defined routes (UDRs) in the hub with the NVA as the next hop.

B) Use Azure Route Server to dynamically advertise NVA routes to on-premises networks.

C) Enable forced tunneling to direct all traffic via the NVA.

D) Configure split tunneling to separate NVA traffic from other traffic.

E) Use a Virtual Network Gateway with BGP to propagate routes to the NVA.

F) Implement service chaining to route traffic through the NVA.

Answer: F

Explanation: Service chaining is the appropriate routing strategy when configuring an NVA in an Azure Virtual WAN hub to ensure all incoming traffic from on-premises networks is processed by the NVA first. Service chaining allows for the creation of a sequence in which traffic is routed through specific network services, such as NVAs, before reaching its final destination. This method ensures that all traffic is subject to inspection and policy enforcement by the NVA, providing a centralized point of control for security and traffic management. User-defined routes and other options may help route traffic, but service chaining provides a more integrated and automated approach within the Azure Virtual WAN architecture.

Q436: A multinational corporation is migrating its on-premises applications to Azure and wants to ensure secure communication between its Azure-hosted applications and on-premises resources. They are using Azure Private Link to connect to various PaaS services. The company has a complex DNS infrastructure and needs to ensure that DNS resolution for Private Endpoints is handled correctly. They have several business units, each with its own Azure subscription and virtual network. How should the company set up DNS to ensure reliable name resolution for the Private Endpoints across all subscriptions and virtual networks?

A) Use Azure DNS Private Zones and configure conditional forwarding on on-premises DNS servers.

B) Set up a custom DNS server in Azure and forward requests to Azure's recursive resolvers.

C) Deploy an Azure DNS Private Resolver in each virtual network.

D) Use Azure's default DNS service and rely on automatic DNS resolution.

E) Configure a DNS forwarding rule in the Azure Firewall.

F) Set up a DNS server in each virtual network and manually manage DNS records.

Answer: A

Explanation: Azure Private Link provides a secure connection to Azure services by mapping them to Private Endpoints. To resolve the private IP addresses assigned to these endpoints, Azure DNS Private Zones can be used effectively. By configuring conditional forwarding on on-premises DNS servers, requests for specific domains can be directed to Azure DNS Private Zones, ensuring seamless and secure DNS resolution across different environments and subscriptions. This approach centralizes DNS management and reduces the complexity associated with maintaining multiple DNS servers and records.

Q437: When integrating Azure Private Link with DNS, it's crucial to understand the role of Azure Private DNS Zones. Which of the following best describes the primary function of Azure Private DNS Zones in this context?

A) They provide an automatic failover mechanism for DNS queries.

B) They allow for the encryption of DNS queries over the internet.

C) They facilitate the resolution of private IP addresses for Azure resources.

D) They enable DNS caching to reduce query latency.

E) They integrate with Azure Traffic Manager for load balancing.

F) They provide a public DNS entry point for private endpoints.

Answer: C

Explanation: Azure Private DNS Zones are designed to handle the DNS resolution of private IP addresses associated with Azure Private Endpoints. By creating a DNS zone that is private, organizations can manage DNS records for Azure services that are connected via Private Link, ensuring that these services are resolved to their private IPs instead of the public IPs. This is essential for maintaining security and ensuring that traffic remains within the Azure network.

Q438: True or False: When using Private Link, DNS queries for the private endpoint are automatically resolved using Azure's public DNS servers.

A) True

B) False

Answer: B

Explanation: When using Azure Private Link, DNS queries for private endpoints are not automatically resolved using Azure's public DNS servers. Instead, Azure requires the use of Azure Private DNS Zones or custom DNS solutions to resolve the DNS queries to the private IP addresses assigned to the Private Endpoints. This setup ensures that traffic intended for the Private Endpoint remains within the Azure network and does not traverse the public internet, enhancing security and performance.

Q439: Fill-in-the-Gap: A company wants to ensure that DNS traffic for their Azure Private Endpoints is handled securely and remains within Azure. They decide to implement a custom DNS solution. Which Azure service should they deploy to manage DNS traffic without leaving Azure?

A) Azure Traffic Manager

B) Azure DNS Private Resolver

C) Azure Front Door

D) Azure Load Balancer

E) Azure Application Gateway

F) Azure Virtual WAN

Answer: B

Explanation: The Azure DNS Private Resolver is a service that allows for the resolution of DNS queries for private endpoints directly within Azure, without the need for the queries to leave the Azure network. This service helps to maintain a secure and efficient resolution process by ensuring that DNS traffic for Private Endpoints is handled internally, which is crucial for maintaining both performance and security within the Azure environment.

Q440: A financial services company uses multiple Azure services and has deployed Private Endpoints for SQL Database, Blob Storage, and Web App in separate virtual networks. They need to ensure that DNS resolution for these services is consistent across all virtual networks without duplicating DNS configuration efforts. Which strategy should they employ for DNS management?

A) Configure a Virtual Network Link for each service to a central Azure DNS Private Zone.

B) Use Azure Traffic Manager to route DNS requests between virtual networks.

C) Set up individual Azure DNS Private Zones in each virtual network.

D) Deploy an on-premises DNS server and connect it via VPN to Azure.

E) Use Azure ExpressRoute to handle DNS traffic between virtual networks.

F) Configure a load balancer to distribute DNS queries across virtual networks.

Answer: A

Explanation: By configuring a Virtual Network Link for each service to a central Azure DNS Private Zone, the company can centralize DNS management across multiple virtual networks. This approach allows them to manage DNS records for their Private Endpoints in a single location, ensuring consistency and reducing administrative overhead. Azure DNS Private Zones with Virtual Network Links provide a seamless method for sharing DNS zones across different virtual networks, facilitating a scalable and efficient DNS infrastructure.

Q441: An international retail company, Contoso Ltd, is expanding its Azure footprint to support its growing e-commerce platform. They have multiple Azure regions with VNets deployed in each. To enhance DNS resolution capabilities and minimize latency, they plan to use Azure Private DNS Zones. The goal is to link a private DNS zone to a VNet in their primary region, ensuring seamless name resolution for internal services. The team needs to ensure that the private DNS zone is correctly linked to the VNet and that DNS resolution is configured to support cross-region name resolution for future expansions. What is the most efficient way to link the private DNS zone to the VNet and ensure it works as intended?

A) Use Azure CLI to link the private DNS zone to the VNet using the az network private-dns link vnet create command with proper parameters.

B) Manually configure the DNS settings in the VNet properties to point to the private DNS zone.

C) Use the Azure Portal to create a DNS zone and then link it to the VNet through the VNet settings.

D) Use PowerShell to link the private DNS zone to the VNet using the New-AzPrivateDnsVirtualNetworkLink command.

E) Create an Azure Function that automatically links any new VNets to the private DNS zone.

F) Configure a cross-region VNet peering and manually update the DNS settings on each VNet.

Answer: A

Explanation: The most efficient way to link a private DNS zone to a VNet is by using the Azure CLI command az network private-dns link vnet create. This command allows you to specify the DNS zone and the VNet you want to link, ensuring that DNS queries within the VNet are resolved using the specified private DNS zone. This method is both efficient and scalable, as it can be easily scripted to automate the linking process in complex environments. Manually configuring DNS settings or using the Azure Portal is less efficient, especially when managing multiple VNets across regions. The Azure CLI offers precise control and automation capabilities, making it the best choice for advanced network configurations in Azure.

Q442: When linking a private DNS zone to a VNet, it is important to ensure that the DNS resolution settings are properly configured. This can impact the ability of resources within the VNet to resolve names using the private DNS zone. Which command would you use in Azure PowerShell to establish this link?

A) New-AzDnsZone

B) New-AzNetworkInterface

C) New-AzPrivateDnsVirtualNetworkLink

D) New-AzResourceGroup

E) Set-AzPrivateDnsRecordSet

F) New-AzDnsZoneLink

Answer: C

Explanation: The New-AzPrivateDnsVirtualNetworkLink command in Azure PowerShell is specifically designed to create a link between a private DNS zone and a virtual network. This command ensures that resources within the VNet can resolve DNS queries using the private DNS zone. It involves specifying the DNS zone, the VNet, and optional parameters such as registration options. This integration is crucial for internal DNS resolution, allowing resources within the VNet to communicate using domain names rather than IP addresses. Other commands like New-AzDnsZone and New-AzResourceGroup serve different purposes, such as creating DNS zones or resource groups, and do not establish the necessary link for DNS resolution.

Q443: You are a network engineer tasked with linking a private DNS zone to a VNet in a production environment. The goal is to ensure that DNS queries from the VNet can be resolved by the private DNS zone and that any new resources added to the VNet automatically register their DNS names in the zone. What setting must you enable during the linking process to achieve this automatic registration?

A) Enable virtual network DNS forwarding.

B) Enable automatic DNS zone propagation.

C) Enable registration of the virtual network.

D) Enable DNS zone replication.

E) Enable DNS record auto-creation.

F) Enable name resolution for external domains.

Answer: C

Explanation: When linking a private DNS zone to a VNet, enabling the registration of the virtual network ensures that any new resources added to the VNet automatically register their DNS names in the zone. This setting is crucial for environments where dynamic scaling occurs, such as autoscaling applications or adding new services. By enabling this feature, you ensure that all resources within the VNet are seamlessly integrated into the private DNS zone without manual intervention. This automatic registration is a core feature of Azure Private DNS, facilitating efficient and dynamic name resolution within the virtual network.

Q444: True or False: When a private DNS zone is linked to multiple VNets, DNS queries from any of these VNets will automatically resolve using the private DNS zone without additional configuration.

A) True

B) False

Answer: A

Explanation: When a private DNS zone is linked to multiple VNets in Azure, DNS queries from any of these VNets are automatically resolved using the private DNS zone. This is because the linking process establishes a direct relationship between the DNS zone and the VNets, allowing resources within the VNets to utilize the DNS zone for name resolution. This automatic resolution is a key benefit of using Azure Private DNS zones, as it simplifies the management of DNS configurations across multiple VNets and enables seamless communication between resources located in different VNets.

Q445: In a multi-region deployment, you want to ensure that DNS queries from VNets in different Azure regions can resolve names using a single private DNS zone. Which Azure service or feature can you leverage to achieve this cross-region name resolution without deploying separate DNS zones in each region?

A) Azure Traffic Manager

B) Azure DNS Forwarder

C) VNet Peering

D) Azure Bastion

E) ExpressRoute

F) Azure Application Gateway

Answer: C

Explanation: VNet Peering can be leveraged to achieve cross-region name resolution using a single private DNS zone. By establishing VNet peering connections between VNets in different regions, you create a network topology where VNets can communicate with each other over the Azure backbone. Once the VNets are peered, and the private DNS zone is linked to one or more of these VNets, DNS queries can be resolved across the peered VNets. This setup eliminates the need to deploy separate DNS zones in each region, simplifying DNS management and ensuring consistent name resolution across the entire Azure environment. Other options like Azure Traffic Manager and Azure Bastion serve different purposes and do not facilitate cross-region DNS resolution.

Q446: Your organization has a web application hosted on Azure that experiences heavy traffic during specific hours. To manage this traffic effectively, you need a solution that can distribute the incoming requests evenly across multiple instances of your web application. Additionally, you need to ensure that users have a seamless experience, even in the case of failover. The requirement also includes SSL offloading to enhance performance. Which feature should you implement to meet these requirements within Azure Application Gateway?

A) URL-based routing

B) Web Application Firewall (WAF)

C) Autoscaling

D) SSL termination

E) Connection draining

F) Priority-based routing

Answer: D

Explanation: Azure Application Gateway's SSL termination feature allows it to decrypt SSL traffic and pass it on to the backend servers in plain text. This offloads the SSL processing from the backend servers, reducing their load and improving performance. Additionally, the Application Gateway can distribute traffic effectively across multiple instances, ensuring availability and reliability. SSL termination also supports seamless failover by maintaining session persistence, which is crucial for user experience during peak traffic hours.

Q447: A retail company is planning to deploy an Azure Application Gateway to manage its online store traffic. The requirement is to ensure that requests from specific geographical locations are routed to a particular set of backend servers optimized for those regions. Which feature of Azure Application Gateway should be configured to meet this requirement?

A) URL-based routing

B) Priority-based routing

C) Path-based routing

D) Geo-filtering rules

E) Multi-site routing

F) IP-based routing

Answer: E

Explanation: Multi-site routing in Azure Application Gateway allows you to route traffic to different backend pools based on the incoming request's host header. This feature can effectively direct requests to specific backend servers based on geographical or regional requirements, as different domains or subdomains can be used for different regions. While geo-filtering rules are not directly available in Azure Application Gateway, multi-site routing can achieve similar outcomes by organizing backend pools.

Q448: A global enterprise requires a solution that automatically adjusts to varying traffic loads to optimize resource usage and costs. They are using Azure Application Gateway for their web services. What feature should be configured in the Application Gateway to achieve automatic scaling based on traffic demands?

A) Static IP configuration

B) Diagnostic logging

C) Autoscaling

D) URL-based routing

E) Connection draining

F) Static routing

Answer: C

Explanation: The autoscaling feature of Azure Application Gateway automatically adjusts the number of instances in response to the traffic load. This feature ensures that the Application Gateway can handle varying amounts of traffic efficiently, optimizing resource usage and reducing costs as it scales out during peak times and scales in when demand is low. Autoscaling is particularly useful for global enterprises with fluctuating traffic patterns, as it ensures continuous availability and performance without manual intervention.

Q449: Your company has implemented an Azure Application Gateway to secure its web applications. The company is particularly concerned about protecting its applications from common web vulnerabilities like SQL injection and cross-site scripting. What feature of Azure Application Gateway should be enabled to provide this protection?

A) SSL termination

B) URL-based routing

C) Multi-site routing

D) Web Application Firewall (WAF)

E) Connection draining

F) Static content caching

Answer: D

Explanation: The Web Application Firewall (WAF) feature within Azure Application Gateway is designed to protect web applications from common vulnerabilities such as SQL injection, cross-site scripting (XSS), and other OWASP top 10 threats. WAF provides centralized protection against these threats and can be configured to meet specific security policies. By enabling WAF, organizations can enhance the security posture of their web applications without making changes to the backend services.

Q450: Azure Application Gateway can be used to implement path-based routing to direct traffic to backend pools. True or False?

A) True

B) False

Answer: A

Explanation: Azure Application Gateway supports path-based routing, which allows traffic to be directed to different backend pools based on URL paths. This feature is particularly useful for applications that host multiple services or microservices under a single domain. By configuring path-based routing, administrators can ensure that requests for specific paths are routed to the appropriate backend servers, optimizing both performance and resource allocation. This capability is crucial for modern application architectures that rely on microservices.

Q451: A global e-commerce company is preparing for a massive global sales event and anticipates a significant surge in web traffic from multiple geographic locations. They currently have a web application hosted in three different Azure regions: East US, West Europe, and Southeast Asia. The company wants to ensure optimal performance, low latency, and high availability for users irrespective of their location. They also require the ability to quickly route traffic to the healthiest endpoints in the event of a regional failure. Which configuration in Azure Front Door best meets these requirements? ---

A) Implement a single Azure Front Door instance with priority-based traffic routing.

B) Configure multiple Azure Front Door instances, each serving a specific region.

C) Use Azure Traffic Manager with performance-based routing.

D) Deploy Azure Front Door with latency-based routing across all three regions.

E) Set up Azure Front Door with weighted traffic routing.

F) Use Azure Load Balancer with geo-proximity routing.

Answer: D

Explanation: To address the requirement of optimizing performance and ensuring low latency, Azure Front Door provides latency-based routing, which directs user requests to the region with the lowest latency. This ensures that users connect to the nearest and most responsive endpoint, improving response times. The global distribution of the application across multiple Azure regions aligns well with Azure Front Door's ability to manage traffic intelligently. Additionally, Azure Front Door supports automatic failover to route traffic to the healthiest endpoint if a regional failure occurs, maintaining high availability. This configuration is ideal for a global e-commerce platform anticipating high traffic volumes and requiring seamless performance across geographic locations.

Q452: Azure Front Door supports various TLS versions for securing communications between users and the Front Door service. An organization needs to ensure compliance with strict security standards that mandate the use of TLS 1.2 as the minimum protocol version. Which step should be taken to enforce this requirement? ---

A) Update Azure Front Door's backend pool settings to only allow TLS 1.2.

B) Configure the Azure Front Door's custom domain to enforce TLS 1.2.

C) Enable Azure Front Door's security policy to disable older TLS versions.

D) Set the Azure Front Door's front-end configuration to allow only TLS 1.2 or higher.

E) Apply a Web Application Firewall policy to restrict TLS protocols.

F) Modify the Azure Front Door's routing rules to support TLS 1.2 only.

Answer: D

Explanation: Securing communications through Azure Front Door involves setting the minimum TLS version for front-end connections, which are the connections between clients and the Azure Front Door service. By configuring the front-end settings, you can enforce the use of TLS 1.2 or higher, ensuring compliance with security standards that require more secure protocols. This setting is crucial for meeting organizational compliance and security policies by preventing the use of older, less secure TLS versions.

Q453: An enterprise needs to implement URL-based routing to distribute user traffic to different backend services based on the URL path. They have various services hosted on Azure, including a web application, a media service, and a REST API, each requiring separate handling. How can Azure Front Door be configured to achieve this? ---

A) Use Azure Front Door's URL path-based routing feature to direct traffic accordingly.

B) Implement Azure API Management to handle the routing based on URL paths.

C) Set up Azure Application Gateway with URL path-based routing.

D) Utilize Azure Traffic Manager with endpoint-specific routing.

E) Deploy multiple Azure Load Balancers to separate traffic by service.

F) Configure Azure Front Door with custom domains for each service.

Answer: A

Explanation: Azure Front Door's URL path-based routing feature is designed to route incoming requests to different backend pools based on the URL path specified in the request. This allows organizations to direct traffic to specific services like web applications, media services, or REST APIs, based on the structure of the URL. This configuration is particularly beneficial when different parts of an application or service require separate handling or processing, ensuring that requests are efficiently routed to the correct backend service for optimal performance and management.

Q454: True or False: Azure Front Door can be used to terminate SSL connections, which means that the SSL handshake is handled at the Front Door, and traffic between Front Door and the back-end service can optionally remain encrypted. ---

A) True

B) False

Answer: A

Explanation: Azure Front Door is capable of terminating SSL connections, which allows it to handle the SSL handshake process on behalf of the backend services. This means that the decryption of the data happens at the edge of the network, which can reduce the load on backend services. After the SSL termination, traffic between Azure Front Door and the backend service can remain encrypted if required, using HTTPS for backend pool settings. Terminating SSL at the edge can improve performance, provide centralized SSL management, and allow for inspection or modification of the traffic if necessary.

Q455: A multinational corporation is using Azure Front Door for their global application delivery. They have custom domains configured for their applications and require seamless redirection from HTTP to HTTPS to ensure secure connections. What is the correct way to configure Azure Front Door to handle this HTTP to HTTPS redirection?

A) Implement a custom redirect rule in Azure Front Door's routing rules.

B) Utilize Azure Traffic Manager to manage HTTP to HTTPS redirection.

C) Apply a Web Application Firewall policy to enforce HTTPS.

D) Configure a redirect HTTP setting in Azure Front Door's backend pool.

E) Enable HTTPS only in Azure Front Door's custom domain settings and let it handle the redirects automatically.

F) Set up Azure Application Gateway to manage the HTTP to HTTPS redirection.

Answer: A

Explanation: To ensure that all incoming HTTP requests are redirected to HTTPS, Azure Front Door supports custom redirect rules within its routing rules configuration. By setting up a custom rule, you can specify that any request received on HTTP should be redirected to the equivalent HTTPS URL. This ensures that users are automatically redirected to a secure connection, enhancing data security and meeting compliance requirements for secure communications. Azure Front Door's ability to handle these redirects natively helps streamline the configuration and management of secure web traffic.

Q456: Your company, a global e-commerce platform, is planning to enhance its infrastructure to handle high traffic during peak shopping seasons. Currently, the application is deployed in the East US Azure region using basic VMs. Your team is responsible for ensuring that the application can scale efficiently and provide high availability. You are tasked with configuring an Azure Load Balancer to distribute traffic across multiple VMs. The solution must meet the following requirements: handle up to 100,000 concurrent connections, support automatic failover, and provide health probes to ensure traffic is only sent to healthy VMs. Which Azure Load Balancer SKU should you choose to meet these requirements?

A) Basic Load Balancer

B) Standard Load Balancer

C) Traffic Manager

D) Application Gateway

E) Network Security Group

F) Azure Front Door

Answer: B

Explanation: The Standard Load Balancer supports up to millions of flows, which includes TCP and UDP, and is ideal for handling large volumes of concurrent connections. It also offers a higher level of availability and can be used for both public and internal scenarios. Additionally, it supports advanced features like zone redundancy, which is critical for automatic failover, and has configurable health probes to ensure traffic is routed only to healthy VMs. The Basic Load Balancer does not support the scale and features required, while other services like Traffic Manager and Application Gateway serve different purposes.

Q457: True or False: The Basic Azure Load Balancer supports availability zones for increased resilience.

A) True

B) False

Answer: B

Explanation: The Basic Azure Load Balancer does not support zone redundancy or availability zones. This capability is only available with the Standard Load Balancer, which is designed to provide high availability and resilience by distributing resources across multiple zones. The lack of availability zone support in the Basic Load Balancer makes it less suitable for critical applications requiring high availability and fault tolerance.

Q458: Which feature of the Azure Load Balancer allows it to direct traffic to the most appropriate virtual machine based on predefined rules and health status?

A) Session persistence

B) Health probes

C) Network Security Group

D) DNS-based routing

E) SSL termination

F) Auto-scaling

Answer: B

Explanation: Health probes are used by the Azure Load Balancer to monitor the health of the backend VMs. By periodically sending requests to the VM, the Load Balancer can determine whether the VM is healthy and capable of handling requests. If a VM fails to respond to the health probes, it is considered unhealthy, and the Load Balancer will stop directing traffic to it. This ensures that only healthy VMs receive traffic, thereby improving the application's overall reliability and performance.

Q459: Your organization is migrating a legacy application to Azure. The application requires session persistence to ensure that requests from a user session are consistently directed to the same backend virtual machine. Which configuration setting should you implement in the Azure Load Balancer to satisfy this requirement?

A) Source IP affinity

B) Round Robin

C) Least Connections

D) Geo-Distribution

E) Custom Probes

F) SSL Offloading

Answer: A

Explanation: Source IP affinity, also known as session persistence or sticky sessions, is a feature that ensures requests from the same client are consistently directed to the same backend server. This is achieved by using a hash of the source IP address to map the client to a specific VM. This configuration is critical for applications that necessitate session consistency, such as those that maintain stateful information about the user's session. Without this, user sessions could be distributed across multiple VMs, potentially leading to inconsistent application behavior.

Q460: A financial services company needs to ensure connections to their Azure-based trading application are not interrupted during maintenance or failures. They require a load balancing solution that supports automatic failover between different Azure regions. Which Azure service or feature should they implement to meet this requirement?

A) Azure Traffic Manager

B) Azure ExpressRoute

C) Azure Application Gateway

D) Basic Load Balancer

E) Azure VPN Gateway

F) Azure Site Recovery

Answer: A

Explanation: Azure Traffic Manager is designed to distribute traffic across multiple Azure regions, providing automatic failover by using DNS-based routing. It can direct client requests to the most appropriate endpoint based on routing methods like performance, priority, or geographic location. This capability ensures that if one region becomes unavailable, Traffic Manager can redirect traffic to another healthy region, maintaining application availability and minimizing disruption. This is particularly important for applications with stringent uptime requirements, such as financial trading platforms.

Q461: Contoso Ltd. has deployed a complex, multi-region network infrastructure on Azure to support its global operations. Recently, users from the Asia-Pacific region reported intermittent connectivity issues to a critical application hosted in the East US region. The application uses Azure Front Door for traffic distribution, and Azure Traffic Manager for DNS-based load balancing. To diagnose these issues, the network team needs to monitor and analyze traffic patterns and latency between regions. They have decided to leverage Azure Monitor Network Insights for this task. What is the most appropriate feature of Azure Monitor Network Insights for collecting and analyzing the necessary data to troubleshoot this issue? ---

A) Network Watcher Connection Monitor

B) Azure Monitor Logs

C) Azure Front Door Diagnostics

D) Traffic Manager Profiles

E) Network Performance Monitor

F) Activity Logs

Answer: E

Explanation: Azure Monitor Network Insights provides a comprehensive view of network health and performance. Network Performance Monitor (NPM), a feature of Network Insights, is particularly useful for monitoring network latency and providing insights into network traffic patterns. It allows for the creation of synthetic transactions that simulate user traffic between regions, helping to identify latency issues and packet loss. In this scenario, using NPM can help Contoso Ltd. analyze and diagnose the connectivity issues reported by users in the Asia-Pacific region by providing visibility into the performance metrics across their Azure network infrastructure. This is especially beneficial for scenarios involving complex, multi-region architectures where traditional monitoring might not provide sufficient granularity or insight.

Q462: A company has deployed multiple Azure Virtual Network (VNet) resources across different subscriptions within the same Azure Active Directory (AAD) tenant. They want to ensure consistent network monitoring and diagnostics are applied across all these VNets using Azure Monitor Network Insights. Which approach should they take to implement this monitoring strategy effectively? ---

A) Use Azure Policy to enforce network monitoring configurations across subscriptions.

B) Manually configure Network Watcher in each subscription.

C) Utilize Azure Blueprints to set up a unified configuration for all VNets.

D) Deploy a single Log Analytics workspace and connect all VNets to it.

E) Enable Azure Security Center for network monitoring.

F) Use Azure Resource Manager templates to deploy network diagnostics settings.

Answer: A

Explanation: Azure Policy is a powerful tool for enforcing organizational standards and assessing compliance at scale. By using Azure Policy, the company can ensure that all Azure

Virtual Networks across multiple subscriptions adhere to a consistent monitoring and diagnostic configuration. This approach allows for automated deployment and management of Azure Monitor Network Insights settings, reducing the need for manual configuration and ensuring that all resources are continuously monitored according to the organization's standards. Azure Policy can automate the enabling of Network Watcher and configuration of diagnostics settings, making it an effective solution for large-scale, multi-subscription environments.

Q463: True/False: Azure Monitor Network Insights can automatically create alerts based on predefined thresholds for network performance metrics without user intervention. ---

A) True

B) False

Answer: B

Explanation: While Azure Monitor Network Insights provides extensive capabilities for monitoring network performance metrics, it does not automatically create alerts based on predefined thresholds without user intervention. Users must configure alerts manually by defining specific conditions and thresholds for the metrics they wish to monitor. This allows for customization based on the unique requirements of each organization's network environment. Azure Monitor's alerting system is flexible, enabling users to specify criteria for when an alert should be triggered, who should be notified, and what actions should be taken in response.

Q464: An organization is using Azure Monitor Network Insights to track down a recurring issue with packet drops in one of their network segments. They need to visualize the network topology to identify potential bottlenecks or misconfigurations. Which feature of Azure Monitor Network Insights should they leverage to achieve this visualization? ---

A) Network Security Group Flow Logs

B) Topology Map

C) Connection Monitor

D) Azure Traffic Analytics

E) Azure Network Watcher Diagnostic Tools

F) ExpressRoute Monitor

Answer: B

Explanation: The Topology Map feature in Azure Monitor Network Insights provides a visual representation of the network architecture, allowing the organization to see how resources are connected and interact with each other. This visualization is crucial for identifying potential bottlenecks or misconfigurations that could be contributing to packet drops. By using the Topology Map, network administrators can visually trace paths, understand the flow of traffic, and pinpoint areas where issues may be occurring. It provides a high-level overview that simplifies the process of diagnosing complex network problems by offering an intuitive, graphical interface.

Q465: Your organization has recently migrated several on-premises applications to Azure. You are tasked with ensuring network performance aligns with service level agreements (SLAs). You plan to use Azure Monitor Network Insights. Which specific monitoring capability should you focus on to gather data on packet loss, latency, and jitter for these applications?

A) Network Security Group (NSG) Diagnostics

B) Azure Traffic Manager Metrics

C) Network Watcher Diagnostic Logs

D) Connection Monitor

E) Virtual Network Peering Metrics

F) Azure Front Door Analytics

Answer: D

Explanation: Connection Monitor, a feature within Azure Monitor Network Insights, is designed to provide insights into connectivity, network latency, packet loss, and jitter. It enables continuous monitoring of network connections and can be configured to simulate traffic between Azure resources and on-premises environments. This capability is essential for organizations needing to ensure their network performance aligns with SLAs, particularly after migrating applications to Azure. Connection Monitor allows for detailed analysis of network performance metrics, providing the data necessary to optimize and troubleshoot connectivity issues, thus ensuring reliable and efficient application performance.

Q466: Contoso Ltd., a global e-commerce company, has deployed a series of web applications across multiple Azure regions to ensure high availability and low latency for their customers worldwide. They've recently noticed intermittent connectivity issues between their virtual networks in the East US and West Europe regions. The network team suspects that the issues may be related to the performance of their cross-region VNet peering connections. To effectively diagnose and troubleshoot these issues, they need to monitor latency, packet loss, and jitter across their VNets. Which Azure Network Watcher feature should they use to gain insights into these metrics between their virtual networks?

A) Connection Monitor

B) IP Flow Verify

C) NSG Flow Logs

D) VPN Troubleshoot

E) Next Hop

F) Traffic Analytics

Answer: A

Explanation: Connection Monitor is a feature within Azure Network Watcher that allows users to monitor connectivity between Azure resources, including across virtual networks, by measuring critical metrics such as latency, packet loss, and jitter. This makes it an ideal tool for diagnosing network performance issues in scenarios involving cross-region VNet peering. By setting up Connection Monitor, Contoso Ltd.'s network team can gain real-time insights into the network health between their East US and West Europe regions, enabling them to pinpoint and address any connectivity problems efficiently. IP Flow Verify and NSG Flow Logs are more focused on validation of security rules and logging, respectively, while VPN Troubleshoot and Next Hop are not applicable for VNet peering scenarios. Traffic Analytics provides a broader view of network traffic but does not offer the detailed metrics required for this specific use case.

Q467: The Azure Network Watcher service can be used to diagnose and resolve network issues. When using Network Watcher to monitor the flow of traffic in your network, which feature will allow you to capture and analyze packets to understand the specific data being transferred?

A) Packet Capture

B) NSG Flow Logs

C) Connection Troubleshoot

D) IP Flow Verify

E) Traffic Analytics

F) Diagnostic Logs

Answer: A

Explanation: Packet Capture in Azure Network Watcher is used to capture traffic to and from a virtual machine in Azure. This feature is essential for deep analysis of network traffic, enabling users to diagnose issues by inspecting the actual packets being transferred. Packet Capture can be extremely useful for troubleshooting complex networking issues, as it provides visibility into the exact data being transmitted over the network. NSG Flow Logs, while useful for monitoring network security group rule applications, do not capture packet contents. Connection Troubleshoot and IP Flow Verify are more about connectivity testing and rule verification, respectively. Traffic Analytics and Diagnostic Logs provide insights at different levels and are not designed for packet analysis.

Q468: A company has implemented Azure Network Watcher to oversee their network infrastructure. They are particularly concerned with the security rules applied to their virtual machines and need to verify if a specific rule is allowing traffic as expected. Which Network Watcher tool should they use to determine if traffic is allowed or denied by the network security group rules?

A) Connection Monitor

B) IP Flow Verify

C) Packet Capture

D) Connection Troubleshoot

E) Next Hop

F) Traffic Analytics

Answer: B

Explanation: IP Flow Verify is a tool within Azure Network Watcher designed to check if a packet is allowed or denied by the configured security rules in a Network Security Group (NSG). This tool simulates the packet flow and determines the effect of NSG rules on the traffic, providing a clear answer on whether a specific rule permits or blocks the traffic. This makes it invaluable for security rule validation and troubleshooting. Connection Monitor and Connection Troubleshoot are more focused on connectivity and performance, while Packet Capture, Next Hop, and Traffic Analytics serve different purposes related to packet analysis, routing, and traffic insights, respectively.

Q469: In Azure Network Watcher, which feature enables the visualization and analysis of traffic patterns and trends across an Azure environment, allowing the identification of potential network bottlenecks and unusual traffic behavior?

A) Packet Capture

B) NSG Flow Logs

C) Connection Monitor

D) Traffic Analytics

E) IP Flow Verify

F) Diagnostic Logs

Answer: D

Explanation: Traffic Analytics is an advanced feature in Azure Network Watcher that provides rich insights into network traffic patterns and trends across an Azure environment. It leverages NSG Flow Logs to offer a comprehensive view of traffic flows, highlighting potential bottlenecks, security threats, and unusual traffic behavior. This capability is crucial for network administrators looking to optimize performance and ensure network security. Packet Capture and Diagnostic Logs do not provide the same level of traffic pattern analytics. NSG Flow Logs and IP Flow Verify serve different purposes related to logging and rule verification, while Connection Monitor focuses on connectivity monitoring rather than traffic analysis.

Q470: Azure Network Watcher provides tools to diagnose and solve network issues. Connection Troubleshoot is a feature that assists with identifying connectivity problems. True or False: Connection Troubleshoot can provide insights into the exact reason a connection failed, such as DNS resolution or firewall blocking.

A) True

B) False

Answer: A

Explanation: Connection Troubleshoot is a diagnostic tool within Azure Network Watcher that helps identify connectivity issues by testing the connection between a source and a destination. It provides detailed information on the path a packet takes and the point of failure if the connection is unsuccessful. This includes insights into issues such as DNS resolution failures, firewall rules blocking traffic, or other network misconfigurations. By giving specific reasons for connectivity failures, Connection Troubleshoot allows network administrators to quickly pinpoint and resolve the root cause of problems, ensuring network reliability and performance.

Q471: Contoso Ltd. is planning to migrate its on-premises applications to Azure. They require high availability and resilience for their e-commerce platform. The infrastructure team has decided to use Azure Virtual Network (VNet) with multiple subnets to segregate web, application, and database layers. The team wants to ensure that the database subnet is only accessible from the application subnet and not from the internet or the web subnet. They plan to use Network Security Groups (NSGs) and Route Tables to achieve this configuration. Which of the following steps should be part of their configuration?

A) Deploy an NSG to the database subnet and allow inbound traffic only from the application subnet.

B) Add a route table to the database subnet with a route to the internet via a public IP.

C) Add a UDR (User Defined Route) to the web subnet to block traffic to the database subnet.

D) Deploy an NSG to the web subnet to block outbound traffic to the database subnet.

E) Enable service endpoints for the database subnet to allow access from the application subnet.

F) Configure a VPN gateway to restrict traffic between the web and database subnets.

Answer: A

Explanation: To ensure that the database subnet is only accessible from the application subnet, deploying an NSG to the database subnet with an inbound rule allowing traffic only from the application subnet is the correct approach. This NSG should have rules that deny all inbound traffic from other sources, including the internet and the web subnet. Adding a route to the internet in the database subnet is not advisable as it contradicts the requirement of restricting internet access. User Defined Routes (UDR) are not required for this specific configuration as NSGs are sufficient to control traffic between subnets. Service endpoints and VPN gateways are not needed in this scenario as they serve different purposes, such as enabling more secure access to Azure services or connecting on-premises networks, respectively.

Q472: For a VNet that hosts both production and development environments, which is a best practice to prevent unnecessary exposure of development resources to production resources?

A) Use separate VNets for production and development environments.

B) Deploy Azure Bastion to manage development resources.

C) Apply the same NSG rules to both environments for consistency.

D) Implement Azure Firewall to control traffic between the environments.

E) Configure shared subnets for both environments to optimize resource usage.

F) Use VNet Peering with specific route filters to limit traffic.

Answer: A

Explanation: The best practice to prevent unnecessary exposure of development resources to production resources is to use separate VNets for each environment. This separation ensures that any security configurations, such as NSGs and route tables, can be applied independently, reducing the risk of accidental exposure or configuration drift. Azure Bastion is primarily used for secure access to VMs, not for isolating environments. Applying the same NSG rules to both environments could lead to security issues as development environments often require more open access for testing purposes. Azure Firewall could be part of a broader strategy but is not specific to the isolation of environments. Shared subnets would increase the risk of exposure rather than decrease it. VNet Peering with route filters could be used but would be more complex and resource-intensive than simply using separate VNets.

Q473: You are designing a network for a global company that requires low latency and high bandwidth connectivity between their Azure regions in North America and Europe. The company wants to ensure that their network traffic is not exposed to the public internet. Which Azure service should you recommend?

A) Azure VPN Gateway

B) ExpressRoute with Global Reach

C) Azure VNet Peering

D) Azure Front Door

E) Azure Traffic Manager

F) Azure Load Balancer

Answer: B

Explanation: For low latency and high bandwidth connectivity between Azure regions in different continents, with the requirement that traffic is not exposed to the public internet, ExpressRoute with Global Reach is the appropriate choice. ExpressRoute provides a private connection between Azure datacenters and on-premises infrastructure, and with the Global Reach feature, it allows the extension of connectivity across regions. VPN Gateway is not suitable as it involves internet-based connections. VNet Peering is confined to the same region or within a single geography and would not meet the requirement for global connectivity. Azure Front Door, Traffic Manager, and Load Balancer are primarily used for traffic management and distribution rather than secure, private connectivity between regions.

Q474: True/False: Azure Network Security Groups (NSGs) can be used to control traffic flow between subnets within the same virtual network.

A) True

B) False

Answer: A

Explanation: Azure Network Security Groups (NSGs) are designed to filter network traffic to and from Azure resources within an Azure Virtual Network. NSGs can be associated with subnets and individual network interfaces, allowing administrators to define security rules that control inbound and outbound traffic. This capability includes traffic flow between subnets within the same VNet, making NSGs an effective tool for managing internal network security policies. By applying NSGs to subnets, administrators can isolate traffic between different application tiers and ensure that only authorized communication occurs, thereby enhancing the overall security posture of the deployment.

Q475: Your organization has a multi-tier web application hosted on Azure. The application consists of a web frontend, an application middleware, and a backend database. The requirement is to configure the network in such a way that the web frontend can only directly communicate with the application middleware, and the middleware can only communicate with the backend database. Which of the following actions should be taken to achieve this?

A) Apply NSGs at each subnet level, allowing specific traffic flow between tiers.

B) Use Azure Firewall to block all traffic between the tiers.

C) Deploy an Azure Load Balancer to manage traffic between subnets.

D) Configure VNet Peering to isolate each tier.

E) Use service endpoints to facilitate communication between the tiers.

F) Enable DDoS protection to secure traffic between the tiers.

Answer: A

Explanation: The requirement to restrict communication such that each tier can only communicate with its adjacent tier should be accomplished by configuring NSGs at each subnet level. By applying specific NSG rules, you can allow or deny traffic based on source and destination IP address ranges and ports, ensuring that the web frontend can only communicate with the application middleware, and the middleware can only communicate with the backend database. Azure Firewall is more suited for centralized network security across multiple VNets rather than managing traffic between specific tiers. Load Balancers are used for distributing incoming network traffic, not for restricting traffic between tiers. VNet Peering is used to connect VNets, not for isolating communication within a single VNet. Service endpoints provide secure access to Azure services, not for tier isolation, while DDoS protection is used to mitigate distributed denial-of-service attacks, not for controlling internal traffic flow.

Q476: A multinational corporation is expanding its cloud infrastructure to accommodate increased demand across different geographic regions. The company plans to deploy a highly available web application in Azure, which will be accessible globally. They intend to use Azure Application Gateway for load balancing and require enhanced security with Azure Firewall. The architecture involves virtual network peering between VNets in different regions and the use of service endpoints to connect to Azure SQL Database. The company also plans to integrate Azure Bastion for secure and seamless RDP/SSH access to their VMs. Which subnet configuration strategy should they implement to ensure optimal performance, security, and cost-efficiency?

A) Deploy all services in a single large subnet and manage access using Network Security Groups (NSGs).

B) Allocate separate subnets for the application gateway, firewall, and VMs, with a shared subnet for service endpoints and Bastion.

C) Create individual subnets for each component: application gateway, firewall, VMs, Bastion, and service endpoints, and use NSGs for access control.

D) Use a single VNet with a large subnet for all services and utilize Azure Policy for security management.

E) Configure dedicated subnets for the application gateway and firewall, while grouping VMs and Bastion in a shared subnet.

F) Implement a flat network topology with no subnet segregation and rely on Azure's built-in security features.

Answer: C

Explanation: To ensure optimal performance and security, separating services into individual subnets is crucial. This approach allows for granular control over traffic flow and security policies via NSGs, reducing the risk of lateral movement in case of a security breach. By dedicating subnets for each service, like application gateway, firewall, VMs, Bastion, and service endpoints, you can efficiently manage and monitor network traffic, apply specific security rules, and optimize routing. This configuration also aids in achieving compliance and audits, as it provides clear segmentation of duties within the network. Grouping all services into a single subnet or using a flat network increases the risk surface and could lead to performance bottlenecks, as well as more complex troubleshooting and management.

Q477: When configuring a virtual network gateway in Azure, which subnet is required specifically for the gateway deployment?

A) Subnet with a minimum of /29 CIDR for exclusive gateway use.

B) Shared subnet with existing VMs to optimize IP usage.

C) A dedicated subnet named 'GatewaySubnet' with a minimum /27 CIDR.

D) A subnet with service endpoints enabled for Azure resources.

E) A large subnet shared between the application gateway and virtual network gateway.

F) A subnet with reserved IPs for future scaling.

Answer: C

Explanation: Azure requires a dedicated subnet named 'GatewaySubnet' for deploying a virtual network gateway. This subnet must have a minimum CIDR of /27 to accommodate the IP addresses needed by the gateway and associated services. The dedicated subnet ensures isolation from other resources in the virtual network, enhancing security and performance. Using a shared subnet could lead to conflicts and resource constraints, while a /29 CIDR does not provide sufficient IP addresses for gateway services and potential scaling. Service endpoints or reserved IPs are not specific requirements for the GatewaySubnet.

Q478: A company is implementing Azure Bastion to provide secure access to their virtual machines. They want to ensure the service is both secure and cost-effective. Which configuration is necessary for deploying Azure Bastion within their VNet?

A) Deploy Azure Bastion in the same subnet as the VMs to minimize latency.

B) Use a dedicated subnet named 'AzureBastionSubnet' with a /24 CIDR.

C) Integrate Azure Bastion with the application gateway for simplified access control.

D) Configure Bastion to use a shared subnet with the application gateway for cost savings.

E) Implement Bastion in a separate VNet and use VNet peering for access.

F) Deploy Bastion within a hub VNet and share it across spoke VNets using VNet peering.

Answer: B

Explanation: Azure Bastion requires a dedicated subnet named 'AzureBastionSubnet' for its deployment, which must have a /26 CIDR. This subnet ensures that Bastion can operate independently without interference from other services, providing secure and seamless RDP/SSH access to VMs. Deploying it in the same subnet as VMs or sharing subnets with other services, like an application gateway, violates best practices for isolation and security. While using VNet peering can extend access, Bastion itself must reside in the same VNet as the VMs it manages, not in a separate VNet.

Q479: True or False: Service endpoints can be used to extend private connectivity to Azure services across all subnets within a virtual network without any additional configuration.

A) True

B) False

Answer: B

Explanation: Service endpoints require explicit configuration to extend to Azure services and are not automatically applied across all subnets within a virtual network. Each subnet must be individually configured to enable service endpoints, specifying which Azure services should be accessible. This approach provides control over which subnets can access specific services, enhancing security and reducing potential exposure. Service endpoints also rely on the correct configuration of Network Security Groups to allow or deny traffic as required.

Q480: A company is planning to implement an Azure Virtual Network with integrated platform services. They want to leverage private endpoints to secure their connections. Which action must they take to ensure that Azure resources are accessible only through private IP addresses within the VNet?

A) Enable service endpoints on the VNet for all required Azure services.

B) Configure an Azure Application Gateway in the same subnet as the private endpoints.

C) Deploy a Network Virtual Appliance to route traffic through private endpoints.

D) Set up private DNS zones and link them to the VNet for name resolution.

E) Use Azure Traffic Manager to direct traffic through private endpoints.

F) Implement a custom DNS server with conditional forwarding to Azure services.

Answer: D

Explanation: To ensure Azure resources are accessible only through private IP addresses using private endpoints, it's essential to set up private DNS zones. These zones allow for the resolution of Azure service FQDNs to private IP addresses, ensuring that traffic remains within the VNet and does not traverse the public network. Linking these private DNS zones to the VNet ensures that all resources within the VNet can resolve the private IP addresses of services. Simply enabling service endpoints or deploying a network virtual appliance does not provide the necessary name resolution for private endpoints. Traffic Manager is not applicable, as it deals with global routing rather than private connectivity.

Q481: A global retail company is migrating its on-premises infrastructure to Azure. They plan to set up a multi-tier application architecture that includes a web tier, an application tier, and a database tier. Each tier will reside in its own subnet within a single virtual network. To enhance security and streamline operations, the company wants to delegate subnet management tasks to the respective application teams. You are tasked with configuring subnet delegation for these subnets. What is the most appropriate step to delegate a subnet to a specific service in Azure? ---

A) Use Azure CLI to assign a role to the subnet.

B) Configure Network Security Groups (NSGs) for each subnet.

C) Use Azure Portal to define a custom role for subnet access.

D) Assign a service endpoint to the subnet.

E) Configure subnet delegation by specifying the appropriate service type.

F) Enable private link service on the subnet.

Answer: E

Explanation: Subnet delegation in Azure allows you to delegate subnet management and configuration tasks to specific Azure services by assigning a specific service type to the subnet. This is particularly useful for services like Azure Kubernetes Service (AKS) or Azure SQL managed instances, which may require control over the subnet for operations like configuring network interfaces or setting up particular security rules. By using the Azure portal or Azure CLI, you can configure subnet delegation by specifying the appropriate service type, thereby allowing the service to manage the subnet as required. This does not involve assigning roles or configuring NSGs, which are separate tasks related to access control and security, respectively.

Q482: You are working with a development team that needs to deploy Azure services that require subnet delegation. Which Azure command line interface (CLI) command can be used to list the available delegation service names for a specific Azure region? ---

A) az network vnet subnet list-delegations

B) az network vnet subnet show-service-endpoints

C) az network vnet list-available-delegations

D) az network vnet subnet list-available-delegations

E) az network vnet subnet delegation show

F) az network vnet subnet delegation list

Answer: D

Explanation: The correct Azure CLI command to list the available delegation service names for a specific Azure region is "az network vnet subnet list-available-delegations." This command provides a list of services that can be delegated to a subnet in a particular region. This is critical for understanding what services you can configure for subnet delegation, allowing more precise planning and configuration of network resources. The other options either do not exist or perform different tasks such as listing existing delegations or service endpoints.

Q483: True or False: Subnet delegation automatically enables network security group (NSG) rules and does not require manual configuration of NSGs for the delegated service. ---

A) True

B) False

Answer: B

Explanation: Subnet delegation does not automatically configure network security group (NSG) rules. NSGs are a separate network security feature that controls inbound and outbound traffic to network interfaces, VMs, and subnets. Even when you delegate a subnet to a particular service, you may still need to configure NSGs manually to ensure the desired security posture for your applications and services. Delegation primarily allows the delegated service to manage network configurations, but it does not inherently apply any security rules.

Q484: A company has successfully configured subnet delegation for Azure Kubernetes Service (AKS). However, they are experiencing connectivity issues between pods in the AKS cluster and an Azure SQL database in another subnet. Which of the following actions is most likely to resolve the connectivity issue?

A) Reconfigure the subnet delegation to include Azure SQL service.

B) Enable service endpoints for Azure SQL on the AKS subnet.

C) Increase the subnet CIDR range to accommodate more IP addresses.

D) Configure a route table to direct traffic from the AKS subnet to the Azure SQL subnet.

E) Ensure that both subnets are in the same network security group.

F) Enable network peering between the subnets.

Answer: B

Explanation: The connectivity issue between AKS pods and the Azure SQL database is most commonly resolved by enabling service endpoints for Azure SQL on the AKS subnet. Service endpoints allow you to extend your virtual network's private address space to Azure services over a direct connection, effectively enabling secure and reliable connectivity to the Azure SQL service. While route tables and network peering can facilitate traffic flow, they do not address service-specific connectivity requirements that service endpoints do.

Q485: An organization plans to utilize a subnet for hosting multiple Azure services, each requiring different levels of access and configuration. They aim to maintain a high level of security while optimizing management. What is the best practice for managing these requirements using subnet delegation?

A) Create multiple subnets for each service and apply subnet delegation individually.

B) Use a single subnet with delegation for the most critical service.

C) Apply delegation to the subnet for all services and configure NSGs for access control.

D) Utilize virtual network peering for managing traffic between services.

E) Implement service endpoints instead of subnet delegation for all services.

F) Employ Azure Policy to manage and enforce network configurations.

Answer: A

Explanation: The best practice for managing multiple Azure services that require different levels of access and configuration is to create multiple subnets for each service and apply subnet delegation individually. This approach allows for precise control over the network configuration and security settings for each service, ensuring that each one can be managed according to its specific requirements. By isolating services into separate subnets, you can tailor network security group rules and other settings to the unique needs of each service, enhancing both security and manageability. Using a single subnet with multiple delegations can complicate management and reduce the effectiveness of security measures tailored to individual services.

Q486: A multinational corporation is planning to migrate their existing on-premises data infrastructure to Microsoft Azure. As part of the migration strategy, they wish to bring their own IP address ranges to ensure continuity and compliance with their existing partnerships and regulatory requirements. The IT team is tasked with configuring the Azure environment to accommodate these custom IP addresses. They need to ensure that the IP addresses are correctly registered and available for use in their virtual networks and other Azure resources. Which of the following steps should be taken to successfully implement a custom public IP address prefix in Azure? ---

A) Register the IP address ranges with ARIN before using them in Azure.

B) Use Azure PowerShell to request a public IP prefix and verify ownership.

C) Configure the IP address ranges in Azure using the Azure portal's Import feature.

D) Contact Microsoft Support to manually assign the IP address ranges.

E) Verify the IP address ranges with Azure by creating a support ticket.

F) Use Azure CLI to request a public IP prefix and provide proof of ownership.

Answer: F

Explanation: To bring your own IP address (BYOIP) to Azure, you need to ensure that the IP ranges are registered in the public internet routing tables and that you have the right to use them. Azure requires that the IP ranges be verified and that you can prove your ownership or the right to use these IP addresses. The process involves using the Azure CLI to request a public IP prefix, where you provide proof of ownership or authorization to use the IP addresses. The Azure team then verifies the information and, upon approval, allows you to use these IP ranges within your Azure subscriptions. This process helps maintain the integrity and security of Azure's networking infrastructure and ensures compliance with global networking standards.

Q487: Evaluate the following statement: "When implementing a custom public IP address prefix in Azure, it is mandatory to first create a virtual network before requesting the IP prefix." ---

A) True

B) False

Answer: B

Explanation: It is not mandatory to create a virtual network before requesting a custom public IP address prefix in Azure. The process of bringing your own IP address (BYOIP) involves claiming and verifying the ownership of the IP addresses with Azure, independent of whether a virtual network is already set up. The primary steps involve submitting a request through Azure CLI or PowerShell, providing documentation to prove ownership, and then waiting for Azure to validate the request. Only after Azure approves the public IP prefix can it be associated with Azure resources, including virtual networks if needed. Therefore, the creation of a virtual network is a subsequent step and not a prerequisite for requesting a custom public IP address prefix.

Q488: Which command should you use to initiate the process of bringing your own IP address prefix in Azure using Azure CLI? ---

A) az network public-ip create

B) az network public-ip prefix create

C) az network public-ip update

D) az network public-ip prefix import

E) az network prefix-list create

F) az network public-ip prefix request

Answer: B

Explanation: The command az network public-ip prefix create is used to initiate the process of creating a public IP prefix in Azure. When you are bringing your own IP (BYOIP) to Azure, you start by creating a public IP prefix using the Azure CLI to define the IP ranges you wish to bring. In this command, you specify the prefix length and region, and you provide proof of ownership. This command effectively reserves the IP addresses within your Azure subscription, pending verification and approval by Azure. Once approved, these IP ranges can be utilized within your Azure environment, enabling you to maintain continuity with your existing IP-based resources and services.

Q489: A company has been approved to use their custom public IP address prefix in Azure. They want to ensure that these IP addresses are correctly associated with their applications hosted in Azure App Service. What must be done to associate the custom IP addresses with the application services? ---

A) Use the Azure portal to manually bind the IP prefix to the App Service.

B) Configure the App Service with a custom domain and assign the IP prefix.

C) Update the DNS records to point to the new public IP addresses.

D) Ensure that the custom IP prefix is associated with a public IP address resource and link it to the App Service.

E) Use PowerShell to directly assign the IP prefix to the App Service.

F) Create a new virtual network for the App Service and associate the IP prefix.

Answer: D

Explanation: To associate custom public IP addresses with Azure App Service, the custom IP prefix must first be associated with a public IP address resource. This involves creating a public IP address resource in Azure and linking it with the approved IP prefix. The public IP address resource can then be assigned to the Azure App Service, which allows the application to use these IP addresses. This ensures that any traffic directed to the application will utilize the custom IP addresses, aligning with the company's compliance and continuity requirements. Managing DNS records to reflect these changes is also a necessary step to ensure proper routing of traffic.

Q490: After successfully implementing a custom public IP address prefix in Azure, what is a key consideration for ensuring high availability and fault tolerance for these IP addresses across multiple Azure regions?

A) Implement IP address failover using Azure Load Balancer.

B) Assign the IP addresses to a Traffic Manager profile.

C) Distribute the IP addresses across multiple Azure regions using Azure Front Door.

D) Configure IP address redundancy using Azure Resource Manager templates.

E) Use Azure Peering Service to route traffic across regions.

F) Deploy the IP addresses in a single region with a backup strategy.

Answer: C

Explanation: For high availability and fault tolerance of custom public IP addresses across multiple Azure regions, using Azure Front Door is a preferred solution. Azure Front Door provides global load balancing and helps distribute traffic efficiently across multiple regions. By assigning the custom IP addresses to Azure Front Door, you can ensure that traffic is routed to the nearest and most optimal Azure region, thereby improving performance and providing resilience against regional outages. This setup enhances the availability and reliability of applications and services that rely on these custom IP addresses, ensuring that they remain accessible even during regional failures. Azure Front Door also offers additional benefits like SSL offloading, URL-based routing, and application layer security.

Q491: A large enterprise, Contoso Ltd., is in the process of migrating its on-premises data center to Azure. They have multiple business units, each requiring isolated network environments. The IT team plans to use Azure Virtual Networks to separate these environments. Additionally, they need to ensure that each virtual network can communicate securely with on-premises resources and other virtual networks. Contoso Ltd. wants to implement a high level of security using network segmentation and appropriate address spaces to prevent unauthorized access between business units while maintaining necessary connectivity. What Azure feature should Contoso Ltd. use to achieve this?

A) Azure Virtual Network Peering

B) Azure ExpressRoute

C) Azure VPN Gateway

D) Azure Network Security Groups (NSGs)

E) Azure Bastion

F) Azure Private Link

Answer: A

Explanation: Azure Virtual Network Peering is the best choice for Contoso Ltd. when they require isolated network environments that can communicate securely with each other. Virtual Network Peering enables direct, private IP connectivity between two virtual networks in the same Azure region or across Azure regions. It maintains network isolation while allowing communication between networks, which is crucial for Contoso's need to keep business units isolated yet interconnected. Unlike VPN Gateways, which are used primarily for connecting on-premises networks to Azure, peering avoids the complexity and potential bottlenecks of VPNs and provides low-latency, high-bandwidth connectivity. ExpressRoute could be considered if there was a requirement for dedicated, high-throughput connectivity to on-premises locations, but it doesn't inherently provide network segmentation within Azure. NSGs focus on controlling traffic within a single virtual network, and Azure Bastion is for secure remote access rather than network segmentation. Azure Private Link is for accessing Azure services privately and securely over a virtual network.

Q492: You are tasked with designing the IP address space for an Azure Virtual Network that will host multiple subnets for different departments of your organization. The network design must ensure no overlap with on-premises IP address spaces and allow for future expansion. Which addressing scheme should you implement?

A) Use Azure's default IP address range

B) Utilize a public IP address space

C) Implement a private IP address space using a 10.0.0.0/8 range

D) Choose a 192.168.0.0/16 range for ease of use

E) Assign a 172.16.0.0/12 range for the virtual network

F) Allocate a unique custom address space not overlapping with any existing network

Answer: F

Explanation: When designing an IP address space for an Azure Virtual Network, it is crucial to ensure there is no overlap with existing on-premises IP address spaces to avoid routing conflicts. Therefore, the best choice is to allocate a unique custom address space that does not overlap with any of your existing networks. This allows for seamless connectivity between Azure and on-premises resources. While using private IP address ranges such as 10.0.0.0/8, 172.16.0.0/12, or 192.168.0.0/16 is standard practice, it is essential to ensure these ranges do not conflict with on-premises networks. Azure's default IP range and public IP addresses are not suitable for internal network design due to security and privacy concerns.

Q493: A company needs to enforce strict network segmentation between its development and production environments within Azure. They want to ensure that only specific types of traffic can pass between these environments and that any unauthorized traffic is blocked. Which Azure feature should be implemented to achieve this?

A) Azure Firewall

B) Azure Traffic Manager

C) Azure Load Balancer

D) Azure Application Gateway

E) Azure Security Center

F) Azure DNS

Answer: A

Explanation: Azure Firewall is the optimal solution for enforcing strict network segmentation between different environments in Azure. It is a managed, cloud-based network security service that protects Azure Virtual Network resources. Azure Firewall allows the creation of application and network-level filtering rules, which can specifically allow or deny traffic types and ensure that unauthorized traffic between development and production environments is blocked. While Azure Security Center provides security posture management and threat protection, it does not directly manage network segmentation. Azure Load Balancer and Application Gateway are used primarily for distributing traffic, not for segmentation. Azure Traffic Manager is a DNS-based traffic load balancer, and Azure DNS is for domain hosting within Azure.

Q494: True or False? Azure Virtual Networks automatically provide network segmentation without any additional configuration.

A) True

B) False

Answer: B

Explanation: False. Azure Virtual Networks do not automatically provide network segmentation; additional configuration is required to achieve segmentation. By default, all resources within a single Azure Virtual Network can communicate with each other. To implement network segmentation, you must create separate subnets within the virtual network and apply network security groups (NSGs) or Azure Firewall rules to control traffic flow between these subnets. This additional configuration allows you to isolate different environments or workloads within the same virtual network, ensuring that only authorized traffic is allowed between segments.

Q495: Your organization is planning to connect multiple Azure Virtual Networks across different regions. The design requires low-latency, high-bandwidth connectivity without having to traverse the public internet. Which Azure feature should you choose to meet these requirements?

A) Azure Site-to-Site VPN

B) Azure Virtual Network Peering

C) Azure Application Gateway

D) Azure Front Door

E) Azure Traffic Manager

F) Azure ExpressRoute

Answer: B

Explanation: Azure Virtual Network Peering is the suitable choice for connecting multiple Azure Virtual Networks across different regions while maintaining low-latency, high-bandwidth connectivity. Peering provides direct, private IP connectivity between virtual networks without the need to traverse the public internet, ensuring secure and efficient data transfer. This feature supports both intra-region and cross-region peering, making it ideal for organizations that need to connect resources across different geographical locations. Site-to-Site VPN is used for connecting on-premises networks to Azure, and ExpressRoute provides dedicated, private connections between on-premises and Azure, not for connecting Azure virtual networks to each other. Azure Application Gateway and Front Door are focused on web traffic management, and Traffic Manager is a DNS-based load balancer, neither of which directly address the requirements for virtual network interconnectivity.

Q496: A company named Contoso Ltd. is planning to enhance its network security by restricting external access to its Azure SQL Database. They want to implement private endpoints to ensure that traffic flows through a private IP within the virtual network. The database is currently exposed via a public endpoint and is accessed by on-premises applications as well as Azure virtual machines in different regions. Contoso needs to ensure seamless connectivity from both on-premises and Azure VMs to the database while maintaining the highest security standards. How should Contoso implement private endpoints to secure its database and maintain connectivity?

A) Create a single private endpoint in the virtual network where the Azure SQL Database resides and update the connection strings in applications.

B) Configure multiple private endpoints across different virtual networks for each Azure region the VMs are located in.

C) Use Azure VPN Gateway to establish a site-to-site connection and access the database via a private endpoint.

D) Set up a single private endpoint and configure a DNS zone to resolve the database's private IP for all applications.

E) Implement Azure Front Door in conjunction with private endpoints for enhanced security.

F) Deploy Azure Bastion to manage the secure connection between on-premises and Azure resources.

Answer: D

Explanation: By setting up a single private endpoint for the Azure SQL Database, Contoso can route all traffic through a private IP within their virtual network. However, to ensure that both on-premises applications and Azure VMs in different regions can resolve and connect to this private IP, Contoso should configure a private DNS zone. This DNS zone will allow both on-premises and Azure-based applications to resolve the SQL Database's private endpoint correctly. Creating multiple private endpoints or using Azure Front Door is unnecessary for this scenario, and Azure Bastion and VPN Gateway are not designed for this purpose.

Q497: True or False: A private endpoint in Azure is essentially an IP address within a subnet of a virtual network and can only be used with Azure resources in the same region.

A) True

B) False

Answer: B

Explanation: A private endpoint is indeed an IP address within a subnet of a virtual network, but it is not limited to being used with Azure resources in the same region. Private endpoints enable secure connectivity to Azure services across regions, as long as the DNS configuration allows for resolution of the private endpoint from different locations. This cross-region capability is critical for scenarios where resources need to interact with services hosted in different Azure regions securely.

Q498: When configuring private endpoints for a web application hosted on Azure App Service, which of the following steps is essential to ensure that traffic from on-premises systems can access the application via the private endpoint?

A) Create a private endpoint in the same subnet as the App Service.

B) Implement ExpressRoute with a private peering to connect the on-premises network.

C) Enable service endpoint policies for the subnet where the App Service resides.

D) Configure Azure Traffic Manager to route traffic through the private endpoint.

E) Set up a private DNS zone and link it to the virtual network.

F) Utilize Azure Virtual WAN to manage network traffic between on-premises and Azure.

Answer: E

Explanation: To ensure that on-premises systems can access an Azure App Service via a private endpoint, a private DNS zone must be set up and linked to the virtual network. This configuration allows the on-premises network to resolve the private IP address of the App Service, enabling direct access through the private endpoint. ExpressRoute with private peering is an option for secure connectivity, but without the proper DNS resolution, it won't suffice. Utilizing service endpoint policies, Azure Traffic Manager, or Virtual WAN does not address the DNS resolution requirement directly.

Q499: You are tasked with designing a private endpoint solution for an Azure Blob Storage that needs to be accessed by a distributed application across multiple Azure regions. Which approach will ensure optimized performance and security for the application?

A) Set up a private endpoint in each virtual network where the application is deployed.

B) Use Azure CDN to cache and distribute blob data across regions.

C) Configure a single private endpoint in a central region and use DNS forwarding.

D) Implement Azure Traffic Manager with endpoint monitoring for failover.

E) Establish VNet peering between regions and use a central private endpoint.

F) Enable service endpoints instead of private endpoints for easier configuration.

Answer: A

Explanation: For an application distributed across multiple Azure regions, setting up a private endpoint in each virtual network where the application is deployed ensures optimal performance and security. This approach allows each regional deployment to connect to the Blob Storage using a local private IP, reducing latency and potential bottlenecks associated with a single, centralized endpoint. DNS forwarding or Azure Traffic Manager may help with failover and routing but do not address local performance improvements. VNet peering can facilitate communication but would not optimize for local access, whereas service endpoints do not provide the same security level as private endpoints.

Q500: An organization is planning to migrate its on-premises applications to Azure, requiring secure access to Azure PaaS services. They want to minimize exposure to the public internet and ensure that all PaaS service traffic is routed through private endpoints. Which key consideration should they prioritize when setting up private endpoints for this migration?

A) Ensuring all private endpoints are placed in an isolated subnet for security.

B) Configuring Network Security Groups (NSGs) to block outbound internet traffic.

C) Utilizing Azure Monitor to track private endpoint usage and performance.

D) Setting up Azure Application Gateway with WAF for all private endpoints.

E) Establishing private DNS zones for all PaaS services with linked virtual networks.

F) Deploying Azure Firewall to manage and route traffic through private endpoints.

Answer: E

Explanation: When migrating on-premises applications to Azure and using private endpoints for secure PaaS service access, establishing private DNS zones for all PaaS services with linked virtual networks is crucial. This setup ensures that DNS queries from the migrated applications resolve to the private IP addresses of the PaaS services, maintaining traffic within the Azure network and away from the public internet. While NSGs, Azure Monitor, and Azure Firewall can enhance security and monitoring, they do not address the fundamental requirement of ensuring DNS resolution for private endpoints.

www.ingramcontent.com/pod-product-compliance
Lightning Source LLC
LaVergne TN
LVHW051426050326
832903LV00030BD/2943

* 9 7 9 8 2 8 1 4 8 0 7 0 3 *